Translating Scripture for Sound and Performance

Biblical Performance Criticism

DAVID RHOADS, SERIES EDITOR

The ancient societies of the Bible were overwhelmingly oral. People originally experienced the traditions now in the Bible as oral performances. Focusing on the ancient performance of biblical traditions enables us to shift academic work on the Bible from the mentality of a modern print culture to that of an oral/scribal culture. Conceived broadly, biblical performance criticism embraces many methods as means to reframe the biblical materials in the context of traditional oral cultures, construct scenarios of ancient performances, learn from contemporary performances of these materials, and reinterpret biblical writings accordingly. The result is a foundational paradigm shift that reconfigures traditional disciplines and employs fresh biblical methodologies such as theater studies, speech-act theory, and performance studies. The emerging research of many scholars in this field of study, the development of working groups in scholarly societies, and the appearance of conferences on orality and literacy make it timely to inaugurate this series. For further information on biblical performance criticism, go to www.biblicalperformancecriticism.org.

Books in the Series

Holly E. Hearon and Philip Ruge-Jones, editors
The Bible in Ancient and Modern Media:
Story and Performance

James A. Maxey
From Orality to Orality:
A New Paradigm for Contextual Translation of the Bible

Antoinette Clark Wire
The Case for Mark Composed in Performance

Robert D. Miller
Oral Tradition in Ancient Israel

Pieter J. J. Botha
Orality and Literacy in Early Christianity

James A. Maxey and Ernst R. Wendland, editors
Translating Scripture for Sound and Performance

Forthcoming

Joanna Dewey
Orality, Scribality, and the Gospel of Mark

Translating Scripture for Sound and Performance

New Directions in Biblical Studies

James A. Maxey
and Ernst R. Wendland

CASCADE Books • Eugene, Oregon

TRANSLATING SCRIPTURE FOR SOUND AND PERFORMANCE
New Directions in Biblical Studies

Biblical Performance Criticism 6

Copyright © 2012 James A. Maxey and Ernst R. Wendland. All rights reserved. Except for brief quotations in critical publications or reviews, no part of this book may be reproduced in any manner without prior written permission from the publisher. Write: Permissions, Wipf and Stock Publishers, 199 W. 8th Ave., Suite 3, Eugene, OR 97401.

Cascade Books
An Imprint of Wipf and Stock Publishers
199 W. 8th Ave., Suite 3
Eugene, OR 97401

www.wipfandstock.com

ISBN 13: 978-1-62032-297-0

Cataloguing-in-Publication data:

Translating scripture for sound and performance : new directions in biblical studies / edited by James A. Maxey and Ernst R. Wendland.

xii + 216 pp. ; 23 cm. Includes bibliographical references.

Biblical Performance Criticism 6

ISBN 13: 978-1-62032-297-0

1. Bible—Translating. 2. Storytelling—Religious aspects—Christianity. 3. Translating and interpreting. 4. Oral tradition. I. Maxey, James A. II. Wendland, Ernst R. III. Title. IV. Series.

BS449 T746 2013

Manufactured in the U.S.A.

New Revised Standard Version Bible, copyright 1989, Division of Christian Education of the National Council of the Churches of Christ in the United States of America. Used by permission. All rights reserved.

THE HOLY BIBLE, NEW INTERNATIONAL VERSION®, NIV® Copyright © 1973, 1978, 1984, 2011 by Biblica, Inc.™ Used by permission. All rights reserved worldwide.

Good News Bible © 1994 published by the Bible Societies/HarperCollins Publishers Ltd UK, *Good News Bible* © American Bible Society 1966, 1971, 1976, 1992. Used with permission.

Scripture quotations marked JB are from *The Jerusalem Bible*, copyright © 1966 by Darton, Longman & Todd, Ltd. and Doubleday, a division of Bantam Doubleday Dell Publishing Group, Inc. Reprinted by permission.

The Holy Bible, English Standard Version® (ESV®). Copyright ©2001 by Crossway Bibles, a division of Good News Publishers. Used by permission. All rights reserved.

THE MESSAGE. Copyright © by Eugene H. Peterson 1993, 1994, 1995, 1996, 2000, 2001, 2002. Used by permission of NavPress Publishing Group.

James A. Maxey

There are several roles that David Rhoads has played in relation to me: professor, mentor, colleague, editor, and most important—friend. Having been involved in Bible translation for over a decade in Africa, I arrived at my first class in my doctoral program and experienced for the first time Dave's performance of Luke's passages on poverty. I was hooked. Something very influential happened at that and subsequent performances with Dave.

Ernst R. Wendland

In memory of Dr. Eugene A. Nida
(✞08/25/2011),
who, among the many things he taught me,
clearly highlighted the importance of orality
and the features of sound in Bible translating,
an emphasis found even in his earliest writing
(for example, *Toward a Science of Translating*—p. 246).

Contents

List of Figures / x

Contributors / xi

1. Biblical Performance Criticism and Bible Translation: An Expanding Dialogue—*James A. Maxey* / 1

2. The Art of Translating for Oral Performance —*David Rhoads* / 22

3. Translating the Aural Gospel: The Use of Sound Analysis in Performance-Oriented Translation—*Dan Nässelqvist* / 49

4. Local Oral-Written Interfaces and the Nature, Transmission, Performance, and Translation of Biblical Texts —*Lourens de Vries* / 68

5. Sound and Meaning in the Gbaya Bible: Ideophones, Performance, and Bible Translation—*Philip A. Noss* / 99

6. Translating Habakkuk as a Performance —*Jeanette Mathews* / 119

7. Comparative Rhetorical Poetics, Orality, and Bible Translation: The Case of Jude—*Ernst R. Wendland* / 139

8. Translation and Performance: Interpreter-mediated Scriptures in Manjaku—*Jill Karlik* / 179

Figures

Figure 4.1 Isaiah 52 in the Statenvertaling of 1637, first edition by Van Ravensteyn / 80

Figure 8.1 Diagram showing translation as mediation, after Wilt / 187

Figure 8.2 Llewellyn-Jones's diagram of the Interpreting Process Model / 191

Contributors

JILL KARLIK facilitates Scripture engagement and is a visiting lecturer at the Instituto Bíblico, Ntchumbe, Guinea-Bissau. Her first degree was in Anthropology and Linguistics from SOAS, University of London (1972); she is currently a part-time PhD student at the University of Leeds.

JEANETTE MATHEWS is a lecturer in Old Testament studies at St Mark's National Theological Centre (Canberra). She is the author of *Performing Habakkuk: Faithful Re-enactment in the Midst of Crisis* (Pickwick Publications, 2012) and several articles on biblical performance criticism, lament literature, and the prophetic literature. She is an ordained Baptist minister.

JAMES A. MAXEY is Senior Manager of Translation Training and Course Development at the Nida Institute for Biblical Scholarship at American Bible Society. He is Dean of Faculty for the Nida School of Translation Studies and Managing Editor of the journal, *translation*. His first book, *From Orality to Orality*, is published in the Biblical Performance Criticism series.

DAN NÄSSELQVIST is a PhD student in New Testament Exegesis at Lund University, Sweden. His forthcoming dissertation investigates the performance of John's gospel in early Christian congregations and analyzes the interdependence of compositional features and oral delivery in antiquity.

PHILIP A. NOSS is a consultant for the Nida Institute for Biblical Scholarship at American Bible Society. Formerly, Noss was translation consultant and coordinator for the United Bible Societies and a professor of African languages and literature at the Universities of Wisconsin–Madison and Calabar, Nigeria. He has written extensively on translation and African traditional literature.

DAVID RHOADS is Emeritus Professor of New Testament at the Lutheran School of Theology at Chicago. He is the author of several books, including

Contributors

Mark as Story: An Introduction to the Narrative of a Gospel (3rd edition) with Joanna Dewey and Don Michie (2012), and *The Challenge of Diversity: The Witness of Paul and the Gospels* (1996). He is editor of the Biblical Performance Criticism Series for Cascade Books and a director of the website called biblicalperformancecriticism.org.

LOURENS DE VRIES was appointed Professor of Bible Translation in 1997 at the VU University of Amsterdam, an endowed chair funded by the Netherlands Bible Society. In 2006 he also became Professor of General Linguistics at the same university.

ERNST R. WENDLAND is an instructor at the Lusaka Lutheran Seminary in Zambia. A retired translation consultant for the United Bible Societies, he still serves as visiting professor at the University of Stellenbosch (Ancient Studies and Centre for Bible Interpretation and Translation in Africa). His book, *Orality and Its Implications for the Analysis, Translation, and Transmission of Scripture*, is currently in press.

1

Biblical Performance Criticism and Bible Translation
An Expanding Dialogue

James A. Maxey

NIDA INSTITUTE FOR BIBLICAL SCHOLARSHIP

Introduction: History and Related Disciplines of Biblical Performance Criticism

MY POSITION AT THE Nida Institute currently bears the title, "Translations and Biblical Scholar." It is a curious title in some ways, and I find that I need to negotiate within myself (dialogue about) the relationship between Bible and translation in my research and in my scholarship. Perhaps this is a personal way of saying that the two academic areas must be in dialogue with one another, to the benefit of both. This introductory chapter is divided into three parts. I begin with a brief overview of the history and naming of the various disciplines that have informed and continue to contribute to biblical performance criticism's treatment of translation. I then continue with my own assessment of the productive intersection of biblical studies and translation. The closing section provides highlights and summaries of the articles contained in this collection.[1]

Development of Biblical Performance Criticism and Its Relationship to Bible Translation

I am grateful for this opportunity to reflect upon and assess an emerging approach to biblical studies that for over two decades has informed Bible translation: biblical performance criticism. In New Testament circles this recent conversation has been going on for over twenty-five years. The date that such a method began to gain traction with the distinct name of biblical performance criticism, however, was with the publication in *Biblical Theology Bulletin* by David Rhoads in 2006: "Performance Criticism: An Emerging Methodology in Second Testament Studies."[2] At that time, I was studying with Professor Rhoads, and he soon conceived of a supportive website, www.biblicalperformancecriticism.org, as a means to gather people, bibliographies, calendared events, and pedagogical tools. By 2008, Rhoads had arranged with Wipf and Stock Publishers to support a monograph series in biblical performance criticism that currently has five volumes published and at least seven more titles at various stages of writing and editing.[3] As an indication of the growth of interest in this methodology, the annual meeting of the Society of Biblical Literature has demonstrated an exponential increase in the number of sessions being held that focus on biblical performance criticism, as well as the innumerable papers that make reference to it in other sessions. *All this to say that biblical performance criticism as a distinct approach is very new and continues to be shaped by numerous people and research projects.*

What is biblical performance criticism? Rhoads defines it this way: "Biblical performance criticism seeks to re-imagine ancient Israel and the

---

1. Parts of this chapter were first presented in a paper titled, "Beyond the Written Word: Orality-Performance Studies and Religious Discourse" at a conference sponsored by *Centro Internazionale di Studi Interculturali di Semiotica e Morfologia* with the theme of "Translation: Towards a Semiotics of Cultures" in Urbino, Italy, September 2010, and at an intersemiotic translation seminar sponsored by the Nida Institute for Biblical Scholarship at its campus with the San Pellegrino University Foundation in Misano Adriatico, Italy, in March 2011.

2. Rhoads, "Performance Criticism: An Emerging Methodology in Second Testament Studies."

3. See list in the front matter of this book.

early church as predominantly oral cultures, to construct scenarios of ancient performances as means to interpret anew the traditions of the Bible, and to reconsider the disciplines we use to study the Bible so as to take account of oral modes of analysis."[4] By definition, biblical performance criticism is eclectic and acknowledges the tremendous contributions of other, very established biblical methodologies. From its website, these include the following critical approaches: historical, narrative, form and genre, reader-response, rhetorical, textual, orality, speech-act theory, social-science, linguistic, ideological, theater studies, and oral interpretation studies. Also included in this list is "the art of translation," and this is the direction I will be taking in this chapter.

Here are two comments about the name of this methodology: First, we recognize that performance criticism is an established discipline within theater studies. The decision was made to distinguish this approach by stating the object of study: biblical texts. Second, there is controversy about its mode, performance. I remember when an early version of Professor Rhoads's paper was presented in Chicago at a gathering of New Testament scholars. At that time the biblical scholars' voices were unanimous: change the word! Fast-forward to November 2010 at SBL in Atlanta in a section on biblical performance criticism sponsored by the United Bible Societies. The message was similar: perhaps something like "proclamation" or "public reading" would be more appropriate and less troublesome. But the word "performance" has remained. Rhoads defends the term in this way.

> We have chosen this word because it covers the presentation both of stories and other kinds of writings in the Bible, such as letters, wisdom, and prophets. We have chosen it because we now know that ancient performances were more than "presentations" or "recitations"; they were dramatic and artful, engaging and emotional, powerful and life-transforming, done usually by people with training or by people who had a natural knack for engaging people. Also, ancient performances involved active audience participation. Furthermore, there is a positive use of performance in our culture when we talk about a theater performance or a musical performance, say by an orchestra.[5]

A description of biblical performance criticism's commitment "to re-imagine ancient Israel and the early church as predominantly oral cultures,

---

4. Rhoads, "Biblical Performance Criticism: What It Is and How It Works," 1.
5. Ibid., 3.

to construct scenarios of ancient performances" indicates an interest in antiquity that informs our understanding for today's world. This is important for translation as we consider translations *of* performance (antiquity) and translations *for* performance (today). The ephemeral nature of performance along with technological limitations make the historical study *of* translation of performance a challenge. We are left with fossil remnants whether intentionally left or not. Most scholarly activity therefore involves examining the clues that remain whether through cultural artifacts of rhetorical handbooks or a close examination of the primary sources. Another approach is to accept the biblical material as performative and then turn to the task of how to transmit its nature in contemporary languages and media.

Early Interactions between Bible Translation and "Performance"

As with biblical studies, the early interest of translation studies with relation to biblical performance criticism was the phenomenon of sound. With regard to plays on sound that seem intentional in the early compositions, these are a challenge to translate. Equally challenging is translating the absence of sound, namely, *silence* whether this is meant to mark a transition or border in the performance or to add to the dramatic nature of a performance. Just as orality studies in general have become linked to performance studies in particular, so translation studies has moved beyond sound to performance features such as kinetics, gestures, and proxemics. That is, the challenge is significant enough when presented as sound vs. silence. It becomes significantly more of a challenge when the movement and physical expression are considered in a performance event. With regard to translation, the consideration of orality is a dramatic shift and challenge. This challenge is augmented by the canonical nature of the Bible not only of its contents, but the canonical nature of the medium of print that has developed in recent centuries. Modern translation methods and theories of the Bible are significantly underdeveloped to address such challenges.

Fortunately, there are some forerunners to guide us along. The multimedia project at the American Bible Society during the 1990s resulted in two collections of articles as well as several products of the researchers' practical applications.[6] This important work has suggested *semiotics* as a

---

6. Hodgson and Soukup, *From One Medium to Another*; Soukup and Hodgson, *Fidelity and Translation*.

significant theoretical framework for exploring translation from one medium to another. Semiotics asserts the principle that "we always interpret and translate signs in terms of other signs, sometimes mixing and matching classes of signs."[7] It is one of the lasting achievements of modern semiotics to show that all human communication and cultural construction, perhaps even communication and cultural construction between *all* forms of life, share in *semiosis*, that is, in the making of meaning using signs of one form or another. For the breed of intercultural communicators known as translators, the relevant and often the only sign systems involve lexical choices—words and narratives found in written or printed texts. However, this narrow view of translation impoverishes a form of human thinking and behavior by reducing it to literary production and by ignoring the many other ways in which humans communicate across languages, cultures, and media—that is, the ways humans translate and interpret in non-print forms.

Perhaps the most persistent question regarding translation, within the medium of print but even more acutely beyond print, is that of fidelity. American Bible Society research explored this important theme in much of its audiovisual translation of biblical narratives. United Bible Societies' translation services have been supportive in exploring the intersection of orality and translation in the first decade of the twenty-first century by publishing a volume on this subject in their monograph series.[8] United Bible Societies also participated in a three-year section of *Studiorum Novi Testamenti Societas* on orality that resulted in several papers and the documentary film *Orality, Print Culture, and Biblical Interpretation*.[9]

The evangelical movement has been energized by discussions of orality (and translation). Whole strategies and departments have been created: International Orality Network, Oral Strategies, Chronological Bible Storying, and Jesus Film Project. Within specific Bible translation agencies, departments have been created to promote orality: the Oral Strategies department of The Seed Company, and the World Arts Program of the Graduate Institute for Applied Linguistics, to name two. These initiatives primarily focus on applying orality strategies in translation for evangelical purposes. My observation is that whereas biblical scholars involved in orality studies are concerned primarily with developing an academic approach to the Bible, many of the orality movements and departments related to

---

7. Hodgson and Soukup, *From One Medium to Another*, 15.
8. Thomas and Thomas, *Structure and Orality in 1 Peter*.
9. Botha, *Orality, Print Culture, and Biblical Interpretation*.

translation are interested in applying strategies to field cases. Although this seems complementary, I am not convinced that there is presently an adequate dialogue between Bible scholars and translators. The challenge is that those who implement strategies in the field tend to become impatient with the development of careful scholarly research, while biblical scholars tend to think that their work is co-opted for applications not intended or desired. As with all responsible scholarship, orality studies involves ethics. This is especially the case in what I would call applied orality studies involving translation. Bible translation agencies and those involved in such activities are just beginning to articulate the ethical questions. It is important that orality studies and performance studies in the Bible consider these issues as well.

Related Disciplines

While biblical performance criticism was forming its assertions within biblical studies, several other disciplines have been exploring translation, orality, and performance. The early twentieth-century research on Homeric epics led to modern-day explorations of orality that is in many ways an extension of folklore studies as it has developed into "ethnopoetics" as a specific approach to oral traditions.[10] In the recent past, the focus of such research has been American Indian folklore, with Dennis Tedlock and Richard Bauman providing ample field data and theoretical research. However, beyond this regional focus, we find the extensive contributions of John Miles Foley. Foley's work has slowly become known to those biblical scholars interested in a multidisciplined approach to orality and performance studies.[11] However, there remains a tension within biblical studies about the appropriateness of dialoguing with folklore and other anthropological studies of modern oral traditions. The concern seems to be with a desire not to project upon antiquity assertions where historical research does not find such evidence in antiquity. By contrast, those involved in translation

---

10. Lord, *The Singer of Tales*; Foley, *The Theory of Oral Composition*; Tedlock (trans.), *Finding the Center*; Tedlock, *The Spoken Word and the Work of Interpretation*; Bauman, *Verbal Art as Performance*; Bauman, *Story, Performance, and Event*; Bauman, "Performance."

11. Foley, *Immanent Art*; Foley, *The Singer of Tales in Performance*; Foley, *How to Read an Oral Poem*.

studies are quite fluent in cultural studies of today, and therefore this tension is not felt as acutely.

Translation studies as a distinct academic discipline offers important contributions to this subject by means of screen translations, adaptation studies, and interpretive studies.[12] Whereas there remains in translation studies generally a bias towards the print medium, globalization and marketing strategies have provided motivation for this discipline to expand beyond print both in theory and in practice. Translation studies is only now in the early stages of dialogue with certain sectors of Bible translation. The most direct interaction has been through those translation studies scholars who are involved in semiotics or theater and performance studies. The points of contact involve viewing biblical performance criticism as one expression of intersemiotic translation. It was the renowned Russian linguist Roman Jakobson who best made a case for thinking about translation in this broader sense.[13] For Jakobson, interpretive processes and phenomena fell into three categories: interlinguistic, intralinguistic, and intersemiotic. Intersemiotics incorporates numerous sign systems of communication, including the promising areas of film adaptation and sign language for deaf communities. As for theater and performance studies, the most promising established discipline for biblical performance criticism seems to be dramaturgy, which often combines the translation of a script with preparation for its dramatization on the stage.[14]

Biblical Performance Criticism and Its Intersection with Bible Translation

Biblical performance criticism proposes a paradigmatic shift rather than an incremental adjustment to biblical studies. As I claim elsewhere, "performance challenges earlier models of communication and requires new methods for appreciating the epistemological shift involved in this mode of communication."[15] Several biblical scholars have sought to demonstrate

---

12. Gambier, "Screen Translation."
13. Jakobson, "On Linguistic Aspects of Translation."
14. Although promising, little interaction between the two has taken place. I gave a paper on "The Bible as Performance Literature: The Emerging Discipline of Biblical Performance Criticism" at a conference at Queen's University Belfast with the theme "Invisible Presences: Translation, Dramaturgy and Performance" in April 2011.
15. Maxey, *From Orality to Orality*, 132.

this shift in their research and publications. These scholars have exhibited a broad spectrum of interests in such research, but few have intentionally looked at this shift as it affects translation. This lacuna is our motivation for this current volume.

My own approach to biblical performance criticism as a translation scholar focuses on translation of biblical texts for today. Whereas it is true that we want to learn from performances in antiquity, my goal in translation is not to promote ancient performances. However, I find biblical performance criticism especially helpful in promoting contemporary performances that remain linked (in some way) to these ancient performances. *Of course, the discussion of what "in some way" means continues.*

It is important in discussing biblical performance criticism and translation to state some of my assumptions. To state these assumptions is my attempt at transparency as I am conscious of the ideologies that I bring to this discussion. First, everyone involved in biblical performance criticism is doing translation. Therefore, translation is critical to the discussion of biblical performance criticism. Secondly, Bible Translation has always been intersemiotic from artwork to architecture; from music to dance; from the page to the stage; from analog to digital. All of this is intersemiotic. What remains a debate for some is how we understand these media in terms of validity and primacy. The assertion has been made that the written form is primary; it is the most authoritative. Biblical Performance Criticism challenges this assertion. But there remains both within and outside of Bible discussions the assumption of the primacy of the printed page. Such a view is ideologically driven and has political and economic backing, which makes it very difficult to challenge and to convince people otherwise. Although not its primary battle, biblical performance criticism is involved in a campaign of media democracy.

Biblical performance criticism asserts a fluidity of the text. David Carr's work along with many others has challenged biblical scholars' assumptions of a fixed biblical text whether written or spoken.[16] Words, phrases, and discourse structures were changed, and these changes were not alarming to the ancients. There were parameters. This modern fixation on the fixed text is not evident in antiquity and biblical performance criticism leverages this reality. I find that the objections to this fluidity can be motivated for reasons of theology, communication assumptions, and historical reasons. Theologically, many have a fundamentalist idea of what is the Word of God,

---

16. Carr, *Writing on the Tablet of the Heart*.

and such fluidity disturbs a view of an unchangeable nature of God. Communication theories have evolved beyond a conduit model where one can locate entirely "the meaning" in a written word. Historical events such as the printing press have shaped how we understand words. Walter Ong and others treated such biases decades ago.[17] Nevertheless, the commitment to fixity persists.

Biblical performance criticism places great value on memory. Several people have recognized that all five of Aristotle's elements of rhetoric—invention, arrangement, style, memory, and delivery—are seldom treated in biblical studies. Biblical performance criticism does presuppose some form of memorization (memory) of texts. However, one should not assume that this means only rote memorization. Frances Yates's *Art of Memory* is a wonderful look at medieval approaches to memory. Perhaps most evocatively Yates treats the "memory palaces," mnemonic devices whereby memorization strategies leveraged attaching parts of memory to physical locales.[18] Biblical performance criticism invites people to connect space to memory both for performers and audiences. Biblical performance criticism values memory also as social or collective memory. And perhaps this is connected most intimately with ritual and narrative. The explosion of studies on social memory by such people as Jan Assmann and Barry Schwartz has been accessed by biblical scholars who are gaining insights into identity formation and community maintenance.[19]

Biblical performance criticism connects memory through story, and here I think of Ricoeur and narrative.[20] Biblical performance criticism does not simply involve storytelling; it involves story creation through the performance event. Audiences do not simply hear a story; they experience an event. And biblical performance criticism intentionally fronts the performance event with an understanding that through such experiences there are connections with the audience and their own stories. John Foley describes this phenomenon in *Immanent Art* as metonymy, where a part stands for a whole.[21] This idea of social memory brings us to another presupposition.

---

17. Ong, *Orality and Literacy*.

18. Yates, *The Art of Memory*; Carruthers, *The Book of Memory*.

19. Assmann, "Form as a Mnemonic Device"; Schwartz, "What Difference Does the Medium Make?"

20. Ricoeur, *Time and Narrative*.

21. Foley, *Immanent Art*, 7.

Translating Scripture for Sound and Performance

Biblical performance criticism presupposes a community. Biblical performance criticism is more than a performer; it demands an audience. This audience is not passive, but active. There are tremendous cultural differences in audience involvement. My Norwegian ancestors with their restricted sense of showing emotion differ markedly from my dear friends in Cameroon, who as audiences are constantly interacting openly through laughter, questions, applause, dancing, and the like. However, in addition to these outward activities, let me return to Foley's assertion of *Immanent Art*. Performances call up to us our common stories, and our experiences. At times the audience needs to provide missing pieces to the performance as asserted by Relevance Theory so that there is a deep sense of satisfaction when the audience places the puzzle piece in the gap.[22]

I have struggled with the distinction between live performance and recorded performance. There are differences. However, on further reflection, difference is of degree rather than type. Audiences influence performers. The reaction of an audience to a performer can encourage or deflate a performer. The mood of the audience can affect the performer. But how does this happen in a recorded performance, for example, with a DVD? A recorded performance anticipates the type of audience or learns from past reactions of audiences, and all of this influences the performer in the recording. Ultimately, though, it is by experience that I cannot subordinate recorded performances to live ones. I have walked away from too many films a changed person; I have listened to recorded music and know that I have experienced something of significance. Nevertheless, the assertion of biblical performance criticism remains: it presupposes an audience; it assumes a community.

Biblical performance criticism shares with others certain views about translation. Translation always without exception involves interpretation. An argument that biblical performance criticism is simply interpretation is accurate as long as one understands that all forms of translation are interpretive. Biblical performance criticism does not reluctantly acknowledge this; it celebrates it! This seems a very mundane statement in translation studies and semiotics, but within the world of biblical studies and philological approaches to biblical texts, this assertion remains debated. Biblical performance criticism cannot support a position of objectivity or neutrality on the part of anyone involved in translation, a performance, or its evaluation. In performance, the performer is the medium. And people are

---

22. Gutt, *Translation and Relevance*.

not neutral. This is an important area where translation studies can guide Bible translation. Translation studies has gone through a series of turns, starting with the linguistic, moving to the cultural, on to the power, and beyond.[23] These turns address issues of ideology and ethics, subjects still seeking full recognition in Bible translation.[24] With regard to interpretation and translation, a claim to neutrality is a power move that sets an individual's interpretation on an elevated plane. Biblical performance criticism dismantles this hierarchy on several fronts. A performer admits that she has limited understanding of earlier performances of the Bible. Authorial intent is researched, but there remains a healthy level of doubt with the use of a definite article, *the* authorial intent. The performer herself adds to the communication with both conscious and unconscious aspects of her social location. Turning to the performance event, so much informs this communicative situation— from the physical surroundings to the composition of the audience. As indicated earlier, the audience itself brings much to the performance. *All this to say that biblical performance criticism understands that not only is meaning interpreted, but it is negotiated in the very performance itself.* Here biblical performance criticism finds similarities with a moderated version of reader-response criticism and receptionalism. In relation to other response criticisms, it would be more appropriate to call biblical performance criticism audience-response criticism.[25] One can immediately recognize that this method differentiates itself significantly from what has been promoted as the dynamic/functional equivalence approach in translation. Although historical research seeks to find components of original meaning, any confidence in dislocating form from original meaning has been shaken. We understand that form holds meaning.

Related to this discussion of location of meaning is location of authority. I have attempted elsewhere to discuss this in terms of the phrase "biblical authority."[26] In short, biblical performance criticism is not asserting anything new when it assumes that authority resides in the community. By community, I do not suggest that this is limited to the immediate community, the contemporary audience, but in a larger temporal and geographic

---

23. Gentzler. *Contemporary Translation Theories*; Gentzler, *Translation and Identity in the Americas.*

24. Voth, "Towards an Ethic of Liberation for Bible Translation"; Harmelink, "Ethical Dimensions of Bible Translation Strategies"; van der Jagt, "Ethical Concerns and Worldview Perspectives in Bible Translation."

25. For a focus on audience, see Soukup, "Understanding Audience Understanding."

26. Maxey, "Fidelity and Authority."

sense to community as passed down through the ages; in other words, tradition. This assertion is in direct contrast with an idea of authority being located solely in a written text.

Biblical performance criticism does not set itself in opposition to the historical-critical method. It benefits greatly from historical-critical methods. Biblical performance criticism's efforts include researching how communication in antiquity took place. Archeology as well as studies of extrabiblical documents contribute to formulating hypotheses. At the end of the day, however, we admit that much is unknown. In my own research, I adopt a posture similar to those who do narrative criticism. So first I accept a reconstructed canonical text as the point of departure.[27] Such an approach has many shortcomings, and I recognize how textual critics continue to contribute to our understanding of this text. But I start with this text recognized by biblical scholars worldwide. Second, and in relation to this choice, my research is not limited to how performances took place in antiquity. My goal is not to recover lost performances. I recognize that the documents that remain are skeletal to the vibrant performances that they reflect. Another way of saying this is that biblical performance criticism is not simply the result of historical-critical methods. Biblical performance criticism is a methodology of exegesis in and of itself. The question posed in a very practical sense is, what insights can biblical performance criticism provide that cannot be found through other established biblical criticisms? A form of this question can be posed in relation to our discussion of Bible translation today.

Biblical Performance Criticism's Eclectic Nature Contributes to Bible Translation

In biblical performance criticism the performance event is central. This is a shift from related approaches such as orality criticism. Narrowly defined, orality studies was interested in the sound of a text. This important area of research was in response to the lacuna in biblical studies that assumed silence. Orality studies in biblical research has given voice to the silent text. Texts were composed to be heard. There are intentional word and sound plays that cannot be appreciated with a silent reading. The work of people such as Brandon Scott and Margaret Lee is a rigorous approach to "sound

---

27. Trobisch labels this "published literature" in "Performance Criticism as an Exegetical Method," 197.

mapping" of biblical texts.[28] This oral/aural nature of the Bible was the first adjustment that needed to be made from print-biased assumptions. People such as Ernst Wendland have played a critical role for Bible Translation in creating methodologies to discover and translate the oral features of biblical texts.[29] Although significant attention has been paid to sound, it would be incorrect to assess biblical performance criticism scholars as setting up a "Great Divide" between the oral and the written.

However, biblical performance criticism goes beyond orality. And this is something, I think, that has been underdiscussed. Biblical performance criticism is inherently multimedia. Performance is more than sound; it is visual. A performer is seen. The audience sees her gestures, posture, facial expressions, proximity in relation to the audience. If there are props, these are seen. Clothing, hair, the body—all of this informs the performance and shapes the experience of the audience. As a result of these multimedia, biblical performance criticism has had to look beyond the traditional disciplines of biblical studies for resources both theoretically and methodologically. Theater studies, speech-act theory, dramaturgy, and semiotics become important disciplines for biblical performance criticism. I have attempted to bring into the discussion folklore studies and, more specifically, ethnopoetics.[30] Ethnopoetics as practiced by Richard Bauman and Dennis Tedlock offer many insights for Bible translators. Folklore studies with regard to performance branches into situations: recording live performances or researching the transcripts of past performances. Both folklore studies and ethnopoetics can contribute to biblical performance criticism.

However, the question immediately arises about genre. Can one compare a folk-story tradition to the canon of Scripture? The assertion of the Nida School of Translation Studies is that Bible translation as an activity has similarities with other types of translation and therefore is a part of translation studies.[31] It also asserts similarities between the Christian Bible translation and the translation of other religious canons, such as Buddhist Sutras, texts from African Traditional Religion, the Koran, the Hebrew Bible, and so on. It is important that we differentiate the genre of texts as we look to borrowing methodologies for biblical performance criticism. *The point that I would make, however, is that biblical performance criticism*

---

28. Lee and Scott, *Sound Mapping the New Testament*.
29. Wendland, *Translating the Literature of Scripture*.
30. Maxey, *From Orality to Orality*, 86–91.
31. Online: http://nsts.fusp.it/.

remains eclectic—not only in relation to other biblical criticisms but also with other disciplines that treat performance and canon.

The strongest link between biblical performance criticism and intersemiotic translation is this: biblical performance criticism does not simply involve textual translation from one language to another. Biblical performance criticism understands that performance itself *is* translation. And the theoretical support for such an assertion resides with semiotics. Therefore, when Bible translation is discussed in a biblical performance criticism framework, it is important not to fall into the trap of thinking that the translation aspect only involves an exercise from biblical languages to some other language. Translation takes place in the performance, through sound, silence, gestures, and interactions with the audience. *The challenge presented from this perspective is to create a series of questions not limited by the media bias of Bible translation being primarily interlingual from one written form to another.* If the ABCs of Bible Translation have been accuracy, beauty, and clarity, how are these to be understood when the context is performance? Great strides have been taken in the past by revisiting the issue of fidelity and translation. What other assumptions of Bible Translation need to be revisited?

As much as I think biblical performance criticism has to offer Bible translation, I do not want to overstate its value. Within a *skopostheorie* approach (where the commissioned purpose of a translation determines what type of translation that is done), there are times that performance translation is not appropriate.[32] There are contexts where print media are ideal. Permitting a variety of media with Bible translation, therefore, promotes contextualization. For me, contextualization is an overarching theme in translation. The texts we translate are contextual. The languages in which these texts are translated contextualize the texts. The media used for translation contextualizes them.

There remain lingering questions of what exactly we have with biblical performance criticism. Is the performance an interpretation? As with all translation, yes, it is interpretive. Is it a commentary? Behind such a question is the notion of extrabiblical (as opposed to "purely" biblical). Is a performance extrabiblical? Yes, as with all communication, newness enters through the performance event by means of the performance, performer, and audience. But the critical question remains: Are these performances the Bible? Such a question asserts that the Bible is distinct. Its distinctiveness is

---

32. Nord, *Translating as a Purposeful Activity.*

that it is written. If we define the Bible only as what is written, then, no, the performance is not the Bible. But if we understand the Bible as communication for numerous communities and their traditions, then we might be able to understand these performances as the Bible.

Questions must continue in terms of authenticity, and this is where other disciplines can help—especially recent discussions about contextual theologies. Since the 1960s there has been a growing challenge against the idea of one universal theology. All theologies, it is asserted, are contextual. It is from this understanding that I assert that Bible translation is an activity of doing contextual theology. I recognize the desire to distinguish biblical studies from theology, but it appears to me that one of the strongest examples of contextual theology is Bible translation. Worldviews that were never a part of the original composers are introduced when translation occurs. Rather than shy away from such a reality, it appears to me that this is a major contribution to both translation studies as well as biblical and theological studies.

I imagine that the preceding paragraphs have raised many questions for readers. These questions are welcome. The discipline of biblical performance criticism and its intersection with Bible translation is very new. There are many issues to explore and it would not be productive to establish parameters to indicate what is off limits. I anticipate that these coming years will bring together theorists and practitioners who will enrich the conversation.

Article Summaries

The articles in this collection do not seek to respond to all these questions or employ all these disciplines. However, the research here does underscore the foundational matter of translation in biblical studies as understood by biblical performance criticism. If the assumption for the biblical messages being received is not individual, silent reading, then the question becomes, how does this communication shift affect the translation of this biblical material? Rather than respond to this in general theoretical terms, many in this collection of articles offer specific applications to particular Hebrew and Greek biblical passages. Many authors of articles in this collection have firsthand experience with translation of biblical materials into non-European languages in communities that maintain a vibrant oral tradition.

The name most directly attached to biblical performance criticism is Emeritus Professor of New Testament, David Rhoads. To his credit, he has ventured into the domain of translation to contribute an article that underscores the artistry of translation for oral performance. Rhoads's claim is that the New Testament is performance literature. Therefore, any translation of the New Testament involves translating the "script" that contains traces of performance in antiquity. Rhoads underscores that such a translation for performance goes beyond the auditory senses to the visual. However, he remains fascinated by sound and the various ways of exploring it in contemporary translation, including by ideophones, a phenomenon discussed in greater depth in the article by Philip Noss. The traditional approach to Bible translation is to begin with exegesis that informs a translation. Rhoads insists that one of the fundamental shifts in biblical performance criticism is that performance itself is one methodology of exegesis. Therefore the borders of exegesis, translation, and performance become blurred. Insights into exegesis can be found in the act of performing. When presented with two viable exegetical choices from a text, the act of performance can indicate which selection is more likely. In this way, choices of performance and exegesis inform a translation.

In 2009, a very helpful book was published that discussed methodologically how to do "Sound Mapping of the New Testament."[33] In our own collection, Dan Nässelqvist takes this methodology and applies it to translation. One of the gaps in Bible translation has been the consideration of the sound plays of texts in biblical languages. This oral/aural factor is central to Nässelqvist's research as he explores John's prologue. His experimentation combines both an historical method of translation of performances from antiquity but also the contemporary challenge of translation for performance. His approach underscores the importance of form as it informs meaning, thus refuting a simple dichotomy. Following Lee and Scott's methodology of presenting the text in a colometric format, Nässelqvist attempts to maintain the semantic, lexical similarities of the source in his English translations. Although these efforts are tentative and experimental, he shows us how to employ sound-mapping with translation as its focus.

Lourens de Vries's experience in the South Pacific and professorship of two chairs at the Vrije Universiteit in Amsterdam in linguistics and Bible translation locate him as an important voice in this discussion of orality, performance, and Bible translation. De Vries is critical of a universalistic

---

33. Lee and Scott, *Sound Mapping the New Testament*.

approach to "oral cultures" and demonstrates by his research that it is important to shift from a prescriptive to a descriptive approach in orality studies. De Vries leverages the research of David Carr in discussing the interface of writing and orality in relation to biblical material. He focuses on "long-duration texts," which include biblical as well as other culturally significant and diverse traditions.[34] De Vries's assertion about oral features in written texts challenges the notion that these are remnants. Rather, these are literary features that serve as reminders of a complex interplay of oral and literary strategies of communication. He looks at several Bible translations ranging from seventeenth-century Dutch to twentieth-century translations for communities in New Guinea to the German translation of the Hebrew Bible by Buber and Rosenzweig. A common theme of the article is a critique of the romantic pursuit of an exclusive oral context that does not consider the interface of media or the evolution of textual genres.

As a linguist with extensive personal and scholarly experience in Africa, Phil Noss introduces us to ideophones. He unfolds for readers a compelling articulation of the elocutionary value of this linguistic phenomenon in the Gbaya community of central Africa. Beyond his linguistic expertise, Noss has played a strategic role in the world of Bible translation for several decades, most recently as the scholarly editor for a monograph series on the history of Bible translation.[35] These interests and experiences permit Noss to present a nuanced understanding of the role of orality and performance in Bible translation, with Gbaya examples that illustrate the diverse functions of ideophones. Through historical research, he describes how Bible publications wrestled with sound plays both in the biblical languages as well as in several important translations. Noss explores how a Bible-translation model that goes beyond communication to engagement is served by considering performance.

Jeanette Mathews provides a contribution from the Hebrew Bible on performance in Habakkuk. Working from the Masoretic Text, Matthews presents indications of how the text can be translated for performance. Her first step is to start with a "literal translation" with regard to verbal constructions, definite articles, and particles. A literal translation aims at lexical consistency to maintain the clichés in the text that function as markers for the audience who understands the depth of these expressions from a shared cultural background. Beyond grammar, Mathews describes

34. Carr, *Writing on the Tablet of the Heart*.
35. Noss, *A History of Bible Translation*.

the performance themes in Habakkuk: embodiment, process, and reenactment. Mathews's final sections provoke us to consider the creative aspect of translation. She claims that Habakkuk itself demonstrates improvisation and challenges the translator's task of simply relaying a set script. Her assertions and questions lead the reader to consider the broader concerns of interpretation and authority as related to translating a biblical text.

Anyone familiar with the scholarship of Ernst Wendland over the past forty years will not be surprised by the thorough treatment given in his article to the subject under consideration. The letter of Jude is the focus of Wendland's comparative approach in which he explores a Greco-Roman rhetorical methodology while at the same time suggesting that a literary-structural methodology offers significant insights. These methods are subsumed in a discourse-linguistic approach to Jude that is careful to measure lexical and structural choices beyond the sentence level. Wendland's complex network of approaches is complemented in this paper by suggesting several examples of the oral/aural contribution to the letter's rhetorical strategy. These methods are then turned into evaluative tools used to assess several English translations of Jude. Claiming a careful literary construction intended for aural reception, Wendland admits that a translation negotiates formal literary strategies with communicative strategies. Furthermore, he is quick to affirm that the purpose and audience for a given strategy are integral in determining the strategies used in a translation.

In a contribution significantly different than the other papers, and yet certainly complementing them, Jill Karlik demonstrates the creative trajectory of biblical performance criticism by looking at the activity of interpreters of sermons in West African contexts. Linked closely with translation studies is interpretive studies, and Karlik demonstrates her expertise in this academic field along with her extensive research in Africa by a case study of interpreter-mediation of Scripture in the Guinea-Bissau language of Manjaku. Confronted by a lack of translated Scriptures in print, Karlik understood that the primary way people were gaining access to Scripture was by experiencing it through an oral interpreter, by an oral performance of the text. Although there are numerous interpretive studies, ranging from the United Nations and European Union, seldom have the interpretation of biblical texts in sermons and especially in Africa been a focus of academic research. The result of this ongoing research is that we glimpse a systematic approach to the fluid activity of oral interpretation of biblical material.

Conclusion

This volume is an invitation to others to join us in researching more intensely this intersection of sound, performance, and Bible translation. Beyond general theorizing, many of the contributions in this volume take specific biblical passages and delve into the questions of translation when the premise is that the biblical material was composed for performance and is being prepared again for audiences who will receive the material in community by means other than the printed word.

Bibliography

Assmann, Jan. "Form as a Mnemonic Device." In *Performing the Gospel: Orality, Memory and Mark*, edited by Richard A. Horsley et al., 67–82. Minneapolis: Fortress, 2006.

Bauman, Richard. *Verbal Art as Performance*. Prospect Heights, IL: Waveland, 1984 [1977].

———. *Story, Performance, and Event: Contextual Studies of Oral Narrative*. Cambridge Studies in Oral and Literate Culture 10. Cambridge: Cambridge University Press, 1986.

———. "Performance." In *Folklore, Cultural Performances, and Popular Entertainments: A Communications-centered Handbook*, edited by Richard Bauman, 41–49. New York: Oxford University Press, 1992.

Botha, Eugene, director. *Orality, Print Culture, and Biblical Interpretation*. Produced by It's a Wrap Productions (2009).

Carr, David M. *Writing on the Tablet of the Heart: Origins of Scripture and Literature*. Oxford: Oxford University Press, 2005.

Carruthers, Mary. *The Book of Memory: A Study of Memory in Medieval Culture*. Cambridge Studies in Medieval Culture 10. Cambridge: Cambridge University Press, 1990.

Foley, John Miles. *The Theory of Oral Composition: History and Methodology*. Folkloristics. Bloomington: Indiana University Press, 1988.

———. *Immanent Art: From Structure to Meaning in Traditional Oral Epic*. Bloomington: Indiana University Press, 1991.

———. *The Singer of Tales in Performance*. Voices in Performance and Text. Bloomington: Indiana University Press, 1995.

———. *How to Read an Oral Poem*. Urbana: University of Illinois Press, 2002.

Gambier, Yves, editor. *Screen Translation*. The Translator: Studies in Intercultural Communication 9/2. Manchester: St. Jerome, 2003.

Gentzler, Edwin. *Contemporary Translation Theories*. 2nd rev. ed. Topics in Translation 21. Clevedon, UK: Multilingual Matters, 2001.

———. *Translation and Identity in the Americas: New Directions in Translation Theory*. London: Routledge, 2008.

Gutt, Ernst-August. *Translation and Relevance: Cognition and Context*. 2nd ed. Manchester, UK: St. Jerome, 2000.

Translating Scripture for Sound and Performance

Harmelink, Bryan, "Ethical Dimensions of Bible Translation Strategies." Paper presented at the annual meeting of the Society of Biblical Literature, November 2010.

Hodgson, Robert, and Paul Soukup, editors. *From One Medium to Another: Basic Issues for Communicating the Scriptures in New Media*. Kansas City: Sheed & Ward, 1997.

Jagt, Krijn Adriaan van der. "Ethical Concerns and Worldview Perspectives in Bible Translation: An Inquiry into the Ethics of Bible Translation." *Bible Translator* 61/3 (2010) 101–22.

Jakobson, Roman. "On Linguistic Aspects of Translation." In *On Translation*, edited by R. A. Brower, 232–39. Harvard Studies in Comparative Literature 23. Cambridge: Harvard University Press, 1959.

Lee, Margaret Ellen, and Bernard Brandon Scott. *Sound Mapping the New Testament*. Salem, OR: Polebridge, 2009.

Lord, Albert Bates. *The Singer of Tales*. Edited by Stephen Mitchell and Gregory Nagy. 2nd ed. Cambridge: Harvard University Press, 2000.

Maxey, James. *From Orality to Orality: A New Paradigm for Contextual Translation of the Bible*. Biblical Performance Criticism Series 2. Eugene, OR: Cascade Books, 2009.

———. "Fidelity and Authority: Perspectives from Translation Studies and Biblical Performance Criticism." Paper presented at Society of Biblical Literature in Atlanta in the section "Ideology, Culture, and Translation", November 2009.

———. "Beyond the Written Word: Orality-Performance Studies and Religious Discourse." Paper presented at a conference sponsored by Centro Internazionale di Studi Interculturali di Semiotica e Morfologia, with the theme of "Translation: Towards a semiotics of cultures" in Urbino, Italy, September 2010.

———. "The Bible as Performance Literature: The Emerging Discipline of Biblical Performance Criticism" Paper presented at a conference at Queen's University Belfast with the theme "Invisible Presences: Translation, Dramaturgy and Performance", April 2011.

Nord, Christiane. *Translating as a Purposeful Activity: Functionalist Approaches Explained*. Manchester, UK: St. Jerome. 1997.

Noss, Philip A., editor. *A History of Bible Translation*. Corrected ed. Manchester, UK: St. Jerome, 2011.

Ong, Walter J. *Orality and Literacy: The Technologizing of the Word*. New Accents. London: Routledge, 1982.

Rhoads, David. "Performance Criticism: An Emerging Methodology in Second Testament Studies—Part I." *Biblical Theology Bulletin* 36/3 (2006) 1–16.

———. "Performance Criticism: An Emerging Methodology in Second Testament Studies—Part II." *Biblical Theology Bulletin* 36/4 (2006) 164–84.

———. "Biblical Performance Criticism: What It Is and How It Works." Paper presented at the Network of Biblical Storytellers annual meeting, August 2010.

Ricoeur, Paul. *Time and Narrative*. 3 vols. Chicago: University of Chicago Press, 1990

Schwartz, Barry. "What Difference Does the Medium Make?" In *The Fourth Gospel in First-Century Media Culture*, edited by Anthony Le Donne and Tom Thatcher, 225–38. Library of New Testament Studies 426. European Studies on Christian Origins. London: T. & T. Clark, 2011.

Soukup, Paul A., S J, and Robert Hodgson, editors. *Fidelity and Translation: Communicating the Bible in the New Media*. Franklin, WI: Sheed & Ward.

———. "Understanding Audience Understanding." In *From One Medium to Another: Basic Issues for Communicating the Scriptures in New Media,* edited by Robert Hodgson and Paul Soukup. Kansas City: Sheed & Ward, 1997.

Tedlock, Dennis. *The Spoken Word and the Work of Interpretation.* University of Pennsylvania Publications in Conduct and Communication. Philadelphia: University of Pennsylvania Press, 1983.

———, translator. *Finding the Center: The Art of the Zuni Storyteller.* 2nd ed. Lincoln: University of Nebraska Press, 1999.

Thomas, Kenneth J., and Margaret Orr Thomas. *Structure and Orality in 1 Peter: A Guide for Translators.* New York: United Bible Societies, 2006.

Trobisch, David. "Performance Criticism as an Exegetical Method: A Story, Three Insights, and Two Jokes." In *The Interface of Orality and Writing: Speaking, Seeing, Writing in the Shaping of New Genres,* edited by Annette Weissenrieder and Robert B. Coote, 194–201. WUNT 260. Tübingen: Mohr/Siebeck, 2010.

Voth, Steven. "Towards an Ethic of Liberation for Bible Translation; Part 1: Ideology." SBL Forum. Online: http://sbl-site.org/Article.aspx?ArticleID=754.

———. "Towards an Ethic of Liberation for Bible Translation: Marketing." SBL Forum. Online: http://www.sbl-site.org/publications/article.aspx?articleId=774

Wendland, Ernst. *Translating the Literature of Scripture: A Literary-Rhetorical Approach to Bible Translation.* Publications in Translation and Textlinguistics 1. Dallas: SIL Inter-national, 2004.

Yates, Frances. *The Art of Memory.* Chicago: University of Chicago Press, 1966.

2

The Art of Translating for Oral Performance

David Rhoads

EMERITUS PROFESSOR OF NEW TESTAMENT
LUTHERAN SCHOOL OF THEOLOGY AT CHICAGO

Introduction

TRANSLATION IS AN ART, because the act of rendering biblical works into contemporary languages is more than a purely technical process. It is an artistic achievement. Translation involves, first, understanding the profound content, the significant artistry, and the powerful impact of the original languages of the writings in the Bible in their context. Second, translation involves finding contemporary ways to express the meanings, the power, the vibrancy, the passion, and the potential impacts of the original compositions in modern tongues. In these efforts, theorists of translation have sought to address the following functions of communication: expressive, cognitive, interpersonal, informative, imperative, performative, emotive, and aesthetic.[1] The art of translation requires that those who do translation bridge the world of biblical scholarship and the needs of the contemporary church.

1. Listed in Noss, "A Translator's Trail," 25–31.

Now we are entering a new development that makes translating even more challenging, because it places both biblical discourse and contemporary translation squarely in the context of the *art of oral performance*. My own limited forays into translation have been in preparation for oral performances of biblical compositions. Over the last three decades, as part of my vocation as a New Testament scholar, I have offered memorized performances of several New Testament writings in dramatic form before gathered audiences of students, church communities, and academic societies: the Gospel of Mark, the Sermon on the Mount, Selections from Luke, Scenes from John, Galatians, Philemon, James, 1 Peter, and the book of Revelation.[2] In some of these performances, I have adapted the translations of others. In most instances, however, I have developed my own translations.

In these efforts, I have come to appreciate as a scholar the *orality* of the original compositions and the challenge of translating them for *performance* in contemporary contexts. Many New Testament scholars have begun to study various aspects of the orality of early Christianity and the oral dynamics of biblical compositions.[3] In recent years, I have sought to articulate a framework of "biblical-performance criticism" for our common study of the orality of the New Testament writings.[4] Similarly, there is also now emerging a movement on the part of professional biblical translators to translate for orality. Although this movement relates to the entire Bible, my focus here is on the New Testament.

Common Approaches to Translation for Print

Most of us are aware of the common distinction between a literal, word-for-word approach to translation and a freer dynamic-equivalence approach that seeks to replicate or reproduce meaning more freely in ways appropriate to particular contemporary cultures of reception. We may also be aware that the most widely used Translations are prepared mainly for public reading of selected passages in the context of worship and education or for private devotional reading. These translations are done almost

---

2. For reflections on my performances of several New Testament compositions and for information on current developments in this field along with an extensive bibliography, see the website http://www.biblicalperformancecriticism.org.

3. See also the other volumes in the Cascade Books series on Biblical Performance Criticism.

4. See Rhoads, "Performance Criticism: Part I," and "Performance Criticism: Part II."

exclusively out of a print mentality—translating from ancient written texts in order to produce printed texts in a contemporary language. Even when the translation is intended for one of the considerable number of oral cultures that remain in the world, the goal is a written text—for use not only in Bible reading but also as an opportunity to teach literacy to people who are nonliterate.

With a print mentality, the focus is on a text rather than on an oral performance. Therefore, the emphasis falls more on a single meaning of a text than on the "meaning potential"[5] that might be brought out in different ways in performance; more on faithfulness to the original than on creativity in the oral register of the receptor language; more on the intention of the author or text than on the potential impacts upon an audience; more on the effect on an individual reader than on the collective experience of a gathered community; more on the cognitive sense made by a reader than on the emotional experience of the listeners. This model rooted in a print mentality has been critiqued in recent years by postmodernists, who argue that meaning does not inhere in a text but is multivalent—negotiated and renegotiated between text, reader (audience), and context.[6] It has also been critiqued by postcolonial scholars, who point to the power dynamics in the presumed assumption of the superiority of a printed text and of literacy itself over orality.[7]

Significant efforts have been made in recent years to expand and reorient traditional models of translation. Advances include a move from dynamic equivalence to a more encompassing functional equivalence, which goes beyond a focus on meaning to include significant analysis also of the form of the passage to be translated, such as its genre as well as its patterns of discourse; and a consequent effort to find comparable patterns of discourse in the receptor language.[8] The most significant endeavors in this regard go beyond a *communication model,* which focuses on finding

5. See Cosgrove, *Meanings.*
6. For a review of these issues, see Rhoads, *From Every People,* 4–18.
7. Discussed by Porter, "Assessing." See also Porter's earlier essay, "Some Issues."
8. Noss, "A Translator's Trail," 353–54. On the important field of biblical discourse analysis, see Porter and Carson, *Discourse Analysis*; Reed, "Discourse Analysis"; Porter and Reed, *Discourse Analysis*; Westfall, *Discourse Analysis,* 22–87. For an excellent workbook on the smaller units of discourse analysis, see Levinsohn, *Discourse Features.* Other sources listed above seek to give detailed analyses of entire literary pieces as integrated units of discourse. The many insights from discourse analysis can be reoriented and reconceived in terms of their function as "oral arts."

the (single?) meaning/form in the language of the originating text and then attempts to replicate that meaning/form in the receptor language. In the new efforts, the movement is toward an *engagement model,* which takes more seriously the potential *impacts* of translation on audiences. This shift of emphasis from original text to audience engagement involves a somewhat freer rendering in the idiom and culture of reception so as to create a more powerful experience and a more emotional encounter with the Bible on the part of cultures of reception.[9] In addition, another movement urges that translations include relevant information regarding local customs and culture-specific worldviews—of ancient texts and modern contexts—so as to make the translations more understandable and relevant in the receptor language.[10] Finally some experiments translate biblical texts into new media, such as video renditions of biblical stories and the format of graphic novels and comic books.

Now we are on the threshold of another new dynamic in translation theory and practice, namely, immersing the whole process in the medium of orality.[11] Because it is a change in medium, and because it is relevant to the full spectrum of discourse levels and functions, orality is not added on as though it were just another factor to be considered. Rather, the shift from translating for print to translating for oral performance represents a fundamental paradigm shift.[12] It involves analyzing the original text as a witness to oral performances in the ancient world. And it involves several other new factors: seeing translation as an embodiment, attending to the oral

9. Noss, "A Translator's Trail," 354–56. A recent essay by Scott Elliott of the Nida Institute for Biblical Scholarship emphasizes open creativity in the shift to address receptor audiences. He writes: "No longer concerned primarily with equivalence or fidelity, modern Translation Studies now attends to frames of reference, ethics, ideology, identity, and so forth" (Elliott, "Translation").

10. Porter, "Assessing," 17–21. Such relevant information may be supplied in explanatory footnotes, for example. For further discussion of relevance theory along with bibliography, see Maxey, "Performance Criticism." The danger of making the source language relevant in the receptor language is that we so domesticate it in the new context as to lose the cultural meaning and impact of the original. On this point, see Rohrbaugh, "Foreignizing."

11. On the issue of *media* shifts in relation to translation (including electronic media), see Boomershine, "Bible Translation"; Boomershine, "Transmediation Theory"; Loubser, "How Do You Report?"; Loubser, *Oral and Manuscript Culture.*

12. On paradigm shifts, see Kuhn, *Structure.* For a very helpful brief example of the shift to orality, see Rebera, "Translating." On the paradigmatic nature of the shift in biblical studies represented by orality studies, see *Orality, Print Culture, and Biblical Interpretation,* a documentary film by Eugene Botha (www.eugenebotha.co.za/).

arts, discerning the potential meanings of a composition in performance, assessing the rhetorical impacts on gathered audiences, appreciating the emotional experiences of an audience, and allowing for the possibility of spontaneous creativity between performer and audience in the course of a performance. Fresh efforts are being made by biblical scholars and translators alike to explore these dynamics of oral translation.

The oral approach to translation is driven in part as a response to the need for new approaches to translations in oral cultures or predominantly oral cultures still existing throughout the world. And it is in response to a growing interest in performing biblical texts in predominantly literate, electronic cultures.[13] However, as I have suggested, it is also driven by new developments in biblical scholarship involving both the study of the biblical world as a predominantly oral culture and the rise of biblical-performance criticism. What follows is an effort to unpack some of the work emerging in biblical studies and to point to some cutting-edge work in oral translation.

The New Testament as Performance Literature

Biblical-performance criticism is an effort to recover the oral performative nature of biblical materials at their origins—through an understanding of the oral cultures of antiquity, the mechanics of writing, reading, and memory work, and the dynamics of performance scenarios, as well as through an appreciation for the difference that performance can make in our interpretation and understanding of biblical writings.[14] The New Testament is a collection of Christian narratives and letters that were originally composed in the genre of stories and letters (not originally composed *as* Scripture) that were primarily presented and received as oral performances, each probably presented in its entirety in a performance event. I understand "performance event" as an expressive presentation of a gospel or letter or the book of Revelation by a storyteller composing or recomposing from

---

13. There is an extensive Network of Biblical Storytellers fostering performance in many venues (http://www.nbsint.org and www.gotell.org). See also the website on Biblical Performance Criticism for a variety of performers (http://www.biblicalperformancecriticism.org).

14. A movement to understand anew the orality of early Christianity began with the publication of Kelber, *The Oral and the Written Gospel,* and the work of the Society of Biblical Literature (SBL) Seminar, "The Bible in Ancient and Modern Media," under the leadership of Thomas Boomershine.

memory in performance, or by a lector performing from a scroll to a gathered audience in a particular time and place.

In the first century, virtually everyone would have experienced these compositions now in the New Testament as expressive readings or performances to gathered communities. It is considered likely that more than 90 to 95 percent of the people in the Mediterranean world, including Israel in Palestine, were nonliterate.[15] Even the 2 or 3 percent who were fully able to write and read were also steeped in orality. Some scholars are now considering whether some of the gospel materials, particularly the Gospel of Mark and the reconstructed Q, may well have originally been composed mentally and orally. Compositions such as we see with the letters of Paul were composed mentally and orally and then dictated to a scribe. Many if not most performances were done without a script.[16] Virtually all reading was aloud at a public or private gathering. Everything we know about storytellers and orators in the ancient world suggests that storytelling and public reading alike would have been animated, emotional, and engaging.

The handwritten scrolls that retain transcriptions of these oral presentations were nothing like our printed Bibles. These handwritten scrolls with continuous script—one uppercase letter after another without spaces between words, with no sentence or paragraph markers, and having no punctuation or accents—were fundamentally phonetic storehouses of sounds-in-syllables waiting to be put back into orality, like scores of music. It is unlikely that an author would have composed in the act of scribing such a manuscript. Like musical composers, originators of stories and speeches probably would have composed in their imagination or sounded out what they were composing—and later transcribed it. In fact, they likely visualized their whole embodied performance—gestures, movements, and facial expressions—as they composed ahead of actually performing.[17] The scrolls served mainly to assist a performer's memory and, particularly in relation to the letters, to enable performances to be repeated on new occasions and in other locations, even though it is likely that compositions would also have passed in memory from oral performance to oral performance without the aid of a manuscript. Obviously, we are extremely fortunate to have

---

15. For a summary of these assessments of literacy and their implications, with relevant bibliography, see Botha, "Greco-Roman Literacy."

16. The study of memory in the ancient world is as important as the analysis of orality and literacy. See Small, *Wax Tablets*.

17. See similar comments on a performer's visualization in Shiell, *Reading Acts*, 100.

these writings preserved for us. They are virtually the only sources we have as witnesses to the life of Jesus and the life of the early church. Nevertheless, these scrolls originally functioned in a predominantly oral culture in ways that are unfamiliar to us today. Therefore they are also virtually the only sources we have as witnesses for oral performances.

The writings preserved for us in the New Testament are like fossil remains of living oral performances.[18] Walter Ong has said that the New Testament writings contain a high degree of "residual orality"—traces of oral features of language embedded in written texts. He was referring to oral arts cultivated in oral cultures as means to communicate in memorable and persuasive ways.[19] Now that we are taking seriously the biblical world as oral culture, we are able to see the extent of the presence of oral arts in the New Testament writings. Consider, for example, the number of oral poetic features in the Gospel of Mark that have been identified in the work of Joanna Dewey and Whitney Shiner: interconnections, patterns of repetition, type scenes, forecasts and echoes, hook words, inclusios, intercalations, frames, parallelism, chiastic patterns, ring compositions, series of three, a paratactic style, nonlinear plot developments, among other features.[20] John Harvey and Casey Davis have done a similar analysis of the oral features of letters of Paul, finding formulaic language, topical introductions, quotations, antithesis, synonymy, vagueness, metaphor, compactness, wordplay, many forms of repetition, rare words chosen to have an impact, mnemonic devices, bridge words, run-on sentences, resonance, chiastic patterns, and various forms of parallelism.[21] Learning to listen to the Greek will assist us in appreciating these oral arts and in being able to discern them in sound.[22]

Translations for performance will differ in many ways from translations for reading. For example, a translation for performance can include

---

18. I attribute this insightful analogy to Dennis Dewey.

19. Ong, *Orality and Literacy*, 30–77. One of the challenges of performance criticism is to distinguish oral arts from literary arts, if such a distinction can be made. Since we know that the early Christian writings were indeed performed orally by memory or by reading, we can assume that the structural features and sounds of the text did indeed function as oral art, whatever their origin. So we need to ask how indeed they worked as oral art.

20. Dewey, "Mark as Oral Narrative"; Dewey, "The Gospel of Mark"; Dewey, "Oral Methods"; Dewey, "Mark as Interwoven Tapestry"; and Shiner, *Proclaiming*.

21. Davis, *Oral Biblical Criticism*; and Harvey, *Listening*.

22. See (or hear!) Simon, *Greek-Latin New Testament*; and Phemister, *Audio Greek New Testament*.

the use of the "historical present." One can shift back and forth with facility from past to present tense in oral performance in a way that seems very awkward in writing. Furthermore, one can preserve word order in oral narration that does not make sense or is misleading in a text for reading. Such word order in the translation can bring out the suspense and the emphases of the original. Seeking to replicate onomatopoeic words and the sounds of the Greek sentences as they relate to the content being presented is helpful in translations for performance. The lengths of sentences, clues to punctuation, places for pauses and stops, along with contractions and elision are features that are crucial for performance. In the translation of a given text, the choice to use the same word or cognate in the receptor language as means to translate repeated occurrences of the same Greek word (even when they have somewhat different nuances of meaning) becomes important for performance. Such verbal repetitions serve to forecast and to echo events and motifs. Parallelism and chiastic patterns become significant dimensions of translation, because they contribute to rhythm and pace.

In addition, however, the writings contain not only residual traces of oral arts of sound, they also contain residual traces of the *arts of performance*. The text is a record of a performance which, by its very nature, could also serve as a script for subsequent performances. As such, the writings contain "stage directions" for voice inflection and volume, gestures, movement, body language, and emotions. As the story is told, directions for performing the story are also suggested. These suggestions occur in virtually every episode of the gospel stories and are present throughout the letters and the book of Revelation: "He cried in a loud cry . . ." (voice volume of what follows); "They were astonished . . ." (tone, facial expression); "He sighed deeply in his spirit . . ." (sound, body posture); "He stretched out his hand and touched him . . ." (gesture, pace); "He looked up to heaven . . ." (head gesture, facial expression); ". . . gave to me and to Barnabas the right hand of partnership" (hand gesture); "The sixth angel poured his bowl over . . ." (gesture, tone of suspense); ". . . and in his mouth it tasted bitter" (facial expression). And the composition implies other performance features by virtue of grammar, syntax, word order, position of subordinate clauses, various forms of parallelism, length of sentences, choice of words, and devices of discourse, such as irony and innuendo, questions, depictions of characters by word and action, descriptions of movement, and so on.

Note that intonation, gestures, nonverbal sounds, and facial expressions are not just illustrative of meaning. They do not simply accompany words. Rather, they are features that can also *determine* meaning. In an oral performance, the meaning of a line is conveyed not only by *what* one says but also by *how* one says it. In performance studies, the implicit message on how a line is delivered is called the "subtext." In performance, all lines have a subtext as well as a text. Most lines can be inflected with different subtexts, which reflect different meanings and connotations and which generate different impacts. Of course, in performance, *how* a line is delivered includes the expression of the whole person. Facial expressions and gestures are not add-ons; they are part of one integrated act of delivery. Facial expressions of a smile or a frown or a grimace or a raised eyebrow can bring out different meanings of a line or intensify its emotional effects. A gesture alone can "be worth a thousand words." Recent studies show that gestures were very important to the ancients in communication. Attention to these features in the New Testament writings reveals hundreds of gestures depicted or implied for performance.[23]

Furthermore, a study of the writings as witnesses to oral performance leads to reflection on the whole performance-event as integral to the determination of meaning and impact: the physical location, the cultural context, the situation of the audience, the social location of the audience, the possible impact of the performance upon the audience, the reaction of the audience, and the part that an audience takes in shaping the performance in progress.[24] When we think of orality, we are dealing with a performer who is composing and recomposing in the act of performance in light of the circumstances and in interaction with the audience. The "embodied composition" is not fixed. Rather, to a greater or lesser degree, it is fluid. Also, we cannot ignore the fact that a performance was meant to transform an audience, to generate action and commitment, to create a certain kind of community of the audience. From what we know of ancient audiences, they were very involved, responding verbally and emotionally throughout a performance. How can we as biblical scholars faithfully imagine how a performance may have affected its ancient audiences?

---

23. See Shiner, *Proclaiming*, 127–42; and Elliott, "A Dog." Both of these resources have an extensive bibliography.

24. For examples of the dramatic ways that audiences shape, indeed may take over, performances in oral cultures, see Tymoczko, "Translation."

Moving Toward Oral Translation

All of this analysis suggests that the writings now in the New Testament are the "written remains" of what were originally oral compositions in performance to gathered communities. Regarding translation for performance, some of the questions we may be led to ask are: When we translate, do we take seriously the fact that the writings reflect features of the sounds and actions of performance? Are we translating the written text taking into account all the oral arts and performative dynamics to which the written text gives witness? And what are we translating? Are we translating the text alone? Could we go even further and consider the possibility of translating an imagined oral performance upon which the written text was originally based? And could we orient the translation to the implied rhetorical impact such a performance may have had upon an ancient audience? Then these questions arise: How could we think about translating something that was once oral into a contemporary culture of reception? How would it "transfer"? What would such a translation be like? What process of translation might take place to keep it within the parameters of orality and at the same time honor fidelity to the original meaning potential?

In two interesting articles on ideophones, Philip Noss points us in some intriguing directions.[25] An ideophone is a word that "expresses what is perceived by the five senses, sound, sight, smell, taste, and feeling, both physical and emotional."[26] Such sounds punctuate the common conversation and performance dynamics of many cultures, particularly in Africa. In a Gbaya-French dictionary, almost one-fourth of the words are ideophones.[27] Ideophones (idea+sound+emotion/attitude) encompass a range of words. Some are simple sound representations that might stand alone, such as *whoosh* or *snap*. Others are onomatopoeic words used in sentences, such as "the man *ripped* his clothes" or "she *whacked* him over the head," both of which have connotations as well as denotations.

However, ideophones in African languages are more profound and complex. They convey an experience and have complex cultural associations. These are not easy to grasp. A possible example in English might be the word *sizzle*, which depicts the hissing sound (and maybe the sight) of something cooking or burning up on high heat. It can also be used

---

25. Noss, "A Translator's Trail"; and Noss, "The Ideophone."
26. Noss, "A Translator's Trail," 362. See also chapter 5 in this volume.
27. Noss, "The Ideophone," 423.

metaphorically of someone sizzling with anger, or it can refer to a hot entertainer as one who is sizzling. Noss gives some examples in Gbaya: *hafafa* ("a swallow's flight over the surface of the water as it catches insects"); *hufuk* ("the action of tossing one's opponent to the ground in a wrestling match"); *bereng* ("reddish bright color of the evening sky"); *gete-gete* ("the action of breaking apart into small pieces"); and *lek-lek* ("the consuming action of flames as they burn and devour").[28] These sound-words can function as adverbs, adjectives, nouns, or verbs, or they can stand alone; and they can be used literally and metaphorically. Again, they may compose a large part of the vocabulary, and convey whole actions as well as experiences and emotions related to sensation expressed in sound. In Noss's view, they should be used with caution since they can be overdone.[29] Nevertheless, a performance peppered with such words can sizzle—can stimulate the imagination, generate empathy, and provoke engagement on the part of an audience.

The question Noss raises is this: If Hebrew and Greek have only a few ideophones, what license do translators have to use them generously in a receptor language? Using the *engagement model* of translation (noted above), Noss answers that we should use them carefully but generously in the receptor language when ideographs are native to that language because they increase the power of the biblical message and its potential impact upon the culture of reception.[30] The point is that translation can creatively draw upon the *oral* features of the language of reception. I believe that this step opens the door in translation to include many aspects of orality—as well as dynamics of performance—distinctive to each culture of reception.

But Noss takes a second and more significant step. He suggests that transposition to a *new medium* may allow for an even greater freedom of translation in relation to ideophones. He refers, for example, to the United Bible Societies' transposition from print to video, a medium in which sounds are integral to the presentation. He also names the comic book genre and illustrated novels.[31] In these media, words like *bonk!* and *thunk!* are common. These are stand-alone ideophones that can enhance or determine meaning. And while they add words to the text being translated, they

---

28. Ibid., passim.
29. Ibid., 429.
30. Noss, "A Translator's Trail," 369–70.
31. Ibid., 371–73.

may be so characteristic of the genre in the receptor language that their absence would actually result in a translation that seemed unnatural.

What if we extended the points Noss is making about the *sound* of ideophones to the *physicality* of performance? To start with, we would be preparing a printed translation for contemporary performances making liberal use of the oral arts of the receptor culture.[32] But what if we made use not only of the oral arts but also the performative arts? Here we could even take the bold step of going to a wholly new medium—embodiment in a performance? What if the translation was actually a live performance.[33] I do not just mean that there would be a printed translation designed *for* performances (presumably by professional or cultural storytellers), although these are desirable and significant. Nor do I mean an audio or a video rendering. Rather, I mean that live performances would *be* the translations in a new medium. Here we would be dealing not just with ideophones but also with noises, gestures, movement, facial expressions, volume and inflection, pace, and so on. Performers would work to bring to expression the explicit and implicit suggestions for performance in the original text. And we would be working with the new cultural context to explore for translation not only the oral arts but also the performance arts common to that culture as a basis for bringing out the full potential of the original—in performance.

In a sense, oral performance would not actually be a new medium, because it would correlate with the original oral performance medium of the biblical writings themselves. However, obstacles abound. For example, although we have the written text in the original language, we have quite limited ideas about the actual inflections or facial expressions or gestures from ancient performances. However, even though we cannot recover the actual performance techniques, we do have evidence that ancient performances were very expressive and emotional. Efforts are now being made by means of a study of ancient rhetorical handbooks, descriptions of performances, and artistic depictions to discern what specific ancient gestures might have accompanied and expressed such actions as a curse or a blessing or an act of mourning, and so on.[34] Although we have no way of

---

32. This is the focus of the work of Ernst Wendland and the Thomases (see below).

33. This is what James Maxey is also proposing and exploring (see below).

34. On gestures, see Shiner, *Proclaiming*, 127–42; Elliott, "A Dog"; Botha, "Pragmatic Models"; and Sheill, *Reading Acts*, 34–101. The ancient handbooks describing rhetorical gestures were written for the upper classes. However, the gestures would likely have been universally understood. What additional gestures the popular storytellers may have used are obviously difficult to recover.

knowing precisely what an ancient performer may have done with these stage directions, we do have good reason to think *something* is being called for on the part of the performer—a gesture, a raised voice, a bodily show of an emotion. Although we may not know precisely what physical expression we are translating, we could nevertheless be fairly confident that there was *something* there as part of an ancient performance *to be translated* into a contemporary performance.

The most appropriate approach may be to extend and extrapolate on what Noss suggests: supply culture-specific expressions of performance arts in the culture of reception, even when they are not explicit in the original. For example, an ancient storyteller may have originally performed of the Gospel of Mark in a popular style that today's audiences might consider to be overly dramatic and therefore somewhat distracting.[35]

Oral Approaches to Translation

In the last decade or so, articles and books on translation have been moving in the direction of incorporating issues of orality into translation.[36] Now there are two full-length monographs that have placed translation squarely within the theory and the practice of oral performance in ancient and modern contexts.

An Oratorical-Performative Approach to Translation

The first volume is titled *Finding and Translating the Oral-Aural Elements in Written Language: The Case of the New Testament Epistles* by Ernst Wendland. Wendland applies performance criticism to the biblical materials as a foundation for developing what he calls an *oratorical-performative* approach to translation.[37] He begins with the assumption that the original contexts for the writings now in the New Testament were oral performances. He seeks to understand these performance events and the traces of oral

---

35. See Shiner, *Proclaiming*, 5, where he describes ancient storytelling as "bombastic."

36. See, for example, Bartsch, "Oral Style"; E. Botha, "Pragmatic Models"; de Vries, "Bible Translation"; Fry, "An Oral Approach"; Noss, "The Oral Story"; Noss, "The Ideophone"; Van Niekerk and Pauw, "Understanding"; and Scott, "A New Voice." The first monograph devoted to the orality of a New Testament writing for translators was Thomas and Thomas, *Structure*.

37. Wendland, *Finding and Translating*, 275.

arts embedded in the writings. And he is eager to provide translations that facilitate oral reading/oral performance events in contemporary cultures. Therefore, he brings the dynamics of ancient oral performance into the translation *process* as well as the translation *text*.

Wendland's oratorical-performative approach addresses translation in three areas.[38] The *oral-meaning dynamic* follows the traditional semantic approach placed now in the context of orality. Taking seriously performative features of the text, Wendland considers that meaning can also include the "paralinguistic" features implied by the text (tone, pace, rhythm, inflection) as well as the "extralinguistic" (non-verbal) features suggested by the text (gestures, posture, movement). Then there is the *oral-stylistic dynamic* that involves all of the ancient oral arts embedded in the texts—an effort to find comparable or at least compatible oral arts—in the culture for which the translation is intended. Finally, there is the *oral-impact dynamic* that seeks to discern the rhetorical effects that the oration (in part and as a whole) may have had on an ancient listening audience, in an effort to replicate a similar impact upon a listening audience in a particular modern culture. Wendland focuses primarily on the oral arts of the original as a means to prepare printed translations for public oral performance in a new cultural context.

I highlight briefly four aspects of Wendland's work: oral arts, sound, memory, and context. First, Wendland pays particular attention to the oral arts, drawing upon many different ways to assess the features of language in an oral culture.[39] Ken and Margaret Thomas also display these features in their analysis and translation of 1 Peter.[40] Second, Wendland includes acoustic dynamics such as onomatopoeic words, sound repetition, wordplay, and sound structuring. Here the work of Wendland is considerably amplified by the studies of Lee and Scott[41] and Shiner,[42] who focus on the impact of the "sound" of the original language. Third, Wendland believes that features of ancient oral art that facilitated memory—mnemonic techniques—were also embedded in the biblical writings. These were designed

---

38. Ibid.

39. For a comprehensive list of oral features, see ibid., 24–31. Wendland draws substantially upon the work of Walter Ong, who discusses the following traits of language in an oral culture: formulas, repetition, contrasts, traditional, experiential, colorful, hyperbolic, emotionally charged, and acoustically oriented, in *Orality and Literacy*, 37–57.

40. Thomas and Thomas, *Structure*.

41 Scott, "A New Voice." See also Lee and Scott, *Sound Mapping*.

42. Shiner, *Proclaiming*, 162–65.

both to assist the performer in remembering and to aid the audience in recalling.[43] For further exploration of memory arts, consult Shiner's very helpful chapter explaining ancient memory techniques.[44] Finally, in Wendland's view, a translation may need to bear some minimal situational and cultural knowledge from the contemporary context in order for an audience to understand the meaning and to experience the impact in a way faithful to the original.

Wendland offers examples of translations of selections from four New Testament letters: James, Philemon, 1 John, and 1 Peter.[45] In his treatment of each letter, he provides a fairly comprehensive study of the oral arts of the Greek. He also sets out the Greek and English in schemata that feature what he sees to be their oral patterns and structures. Then he gives excerpts from a number of contemporary English translations as well as translations into Chewa, a Bantu language widely spoken in south-central Africa. And he gives "back-translations" from Chewa into English to illustrate how translation can feature oral arts from a predominantly oral culture in the contemporary world. It poses a significant challenge to biblical scholars and to translators to incorporate the plenum of oral features in the biblical writings into the translation process in another culture.[46] To assist with this, Wendland offers a brief step-by-step procedure to do an oral-rhetorical analysis of a biblical writing and to prepare an oratorical-performative translation.[47]

A Translation-as-Performance Approach

My second example is a volume called *From Orality to Orality: A New Paradigm for Contextual Translation of the Bible* by James Maxey. Maxey aims for "translations for performance."[48] This approach involves the radical step of making performance itself part of the translation process and the goal of the endeavor. Maxey seeks to understand and analyze the biblical

43. Wendland, *Finding and Translating*, 18–22.
44. Shiner, *Proclaiming*, 103–26. See also Kelber, "The Oral."
45. Wendland, *Finding and Translating*, chapters 2 through 6.
46. This is especially challenging when there is no comparable parallel in the culture of reception, as, for example, there might not be with regard to genre such as an apocalypse.
47. Wendland, *Finding*, 367–82 and 383–84.
48. See also Maxey, "Performance Criticism."

materials in the imagined context of *performance events* of the early church, with a full understanding of the performative arts, the audience participation, and the rhetorical impact this might involve.[49] At the same time, he is seeking to place the translation in the context of performance events of a contemporary oral culture. He describes his experiences working with the Vuté people of Cameroon.[50] This is a predominantly oral culture that now, thanks to Maxey's earlier work with them, has attained literacy and a printed Bible translation. Recently, Maxey facilitated an opportunity for storytellers from among the Vuté people to develop translations-in-performance of five stories from the Gospel of Mark. The performers made their own translations-in-performance for the Vuté community.

In his experience of their work, Maxey learned much about performance in an oral culture. He details some of the features of their translations-in-performance: the occasional addition of information about the first century to clarify a storytelling point; selection of vocabulary that *evokes* emotion rather than just *describing* it; a preference for direct speech; a preference for short, less complex sentences with briefer clauses; the use of ideophones; the incorporation of meaning-making gestures that are culture-specific to the Vuté community; questions directed to the audience to engage them; interactions with audience responses; interjections emphasizing local Vuté values, such as gratitude and humor; effective use of pace and silence; pointing to imagined props and characters in the story; and the use of costumes, actual props, and staging.[51] When we consider that the performance *is* the translation in voice and action, this list represents a fascinating array of oral-effective features.

In this context, translation is fluid and somewhat open ended, probably much like the performances in the oral cultures of the early church. The end product is not necessarily a printed Bible to be reproduced and distributed, unless it is a working text or one that changes over time from performance to performance. Rather, the goal is to create fleeting, ephemeral moments of performance—events that occur and are gone. The translation happens *as* the performance, not just in preparation for it. The translation is the performance unfolding in real time. There would be as many translations as there are performances. If there is a text, it would include

---

49. Maxey, *From Orality*, 134–38. For Maxey's reflections on his own experience of memorizing and performing Paul's *Letter to Philemon*, see ibid., 147.

50. Maxey, *From Orality*, 1–14, 167–92.

51. Ibid., 218–23.

references to the paralinguistic and extralinguistic aspects of the stories as they are displayed in performance (see below). Or there might be a video tape, with regard to which, Maxey laments, much is lost in comparison to a live performance event. Yet, for Maxey, the goal of the biblical story is "transformation"—such that the stories live on in the telling and retelling in homes and village events (in story and song) in the lives of those who have told and heard them. Through this process, the stories have entered their collective life and memory and now belong to the people.[52] The Scriptures are embodied in the people as well as in a book. The stories have gone from the orality implied in the biblical materials to the orality of the Vuté people.

Three Key Issues

Here let me highlight three key issues that relate to this overall paradigm shift from a print orientation to orality: the desire to capture the artistry and even the beauty of the original language in translation; the innovative efforts to "format" translations for performance; and the dynamics of power in the translation process.

Artistry and Beauty

The ancient world valued the *artistry* of speaking, not just in terms of delivery but also in regard to all the verbal arts in a wide range of performances: epic recitation, storytelling, rhetorical speeches, orations of letters, and so on. Rhetorical handbooks and other writings touted the engaging beauty and power of the euphony, the flow, the imagery, the stories, and even the argumentation of speeches. The choice of words, the arrangement, the patterns of repetition with variation, the pleasantness of sound to the ear, the memorable nature of sayings and images, and the developing power of the persuasion—all these worked together to produce riveting experiences for ancient audiences. Outstanding orators and engaging orations were highly valued as central to public and private life both for elites and for the populace. We are fortunate to have extant in writing some of the handbooks on the art of persuasion as well as some Greco-Roman orations. These sources provide the context for our study of the oral traditions that have survived in written form in the New Testament. Although the rhetorical handbooks

---

52. Ibid., 232.

are products of elites, there is good reason to believe that native storytellers, likely not literate, were quite skilled in the dynamics of telling engaging stories.[53] Those of us who engage in translation in New Testament studies have much to learn from our colleagues in classical studies who are engaged in the translation of epic stories and rhetorical orations.[54]

Appreciation for the beauty of oral traditions is also expressed by those who explore the oral roots of the New Testament writings. Ernst Wendland wants to reproduce

> at least part of the artistic *beauty* and rhetorical *power* that are present in the original text . . . the energy and vibrancy of the language as a whole, including in particular the entire *phonological* dimension of a biblical discourse in translation—the varied rhythms and euphony of speech as this is orally communicated to a *listening* audience.[55]

Ken and Margaret Thomas devote a chapter to the "beauty and meaning of the language" of 1 Peter.[56] Not only do they explore the "phonological resonances"[57] or the sound repetitions. They also explore the beauty and persuasiveness of various figures of speech, such as metaphors, similes, and substitution, because, they argue, "figurative speech can draw upon the hearer's imagination, excite attention, and expand meaning."[58] The goal of translation is to capture not just the signification of this imagery but also the beauty of it and its capacity to provoke vivid imaging in an audience. Just as translation committees have often included poets and prose writers on their teams, we might now also consider the inclusion of people gifted in oratory and storytelling in the work of translation, as Maxey has done, for example, with the Vuté people.[59]

---

53. The same is true in some areas of Africa even today; the renowned, oratorically skilled storytellers or poets may not even be literate at all.
54. See for example, Edwards, *Sound*; and Foley, *The Singer*.
55. Wendland, *Finding*, v, 146.
56. Thomas and Thomas, *Structure*, 37–54.
57. Ibid., 3. This is a term they have drawn from Ernst Wendland.
58. Ibid., 37.
59. Maxey, *From Orality*, 167–91.

Translating Scripture for Sound and Performance

Formatting

Traditional formatting—chapters, verses, brief paragraphs, headings—may not be adequate when considering translations for an oral performance or for a performative reading. Formatting itself is not neutral, and new features may need to be brought into play as means to reflect performance in print.

Folklorists have developed schemata to record an oral performance in print in such a way as to preserve some of the oral artistry involved in the performance.[60] The efforts involve notations and annotations about the use of the voice and the physical gestures and the movement of the performers. Translators are "reversing" the transcription process so that the notations not only may record a performance but may also serve as directions for subsequent performances, much as a script for a play might function. When we imagine a script for oral performance, we see also the analogy with musical scores, which include such things as notes designating various lengths, rests, signs for repetition, codas for endings, slurring, and staccato, as well as verbal directions for tempo, tone, volume, intensity, and style.[61]

In a similar way, translations that presume performance might use the following in creative ways: punctuation; spacing between words, sentences, and even letters; typing features such as boldface, italics, and underlining; a choice of varying fonts—all as means to suggest pace, volume, emphasis, intensity, and so on. Wendland identifies a number of the following "graphic" signals: "increased type size, distinctive font faces, unjustified right margins, rhythmic lineation, indentation, and judicious use of white space to visually display prominent verbal patterns."[62] Print layout, he argues, "should provide suitable clues for reading."[63] John Miles Foley uses different levels of superscript to convey inflection.[64] Maxey includes also extralinguistic features. He has developed a schema of three columns in which the translation is in the center column formatted to reflect rhythm and pace; to the left are notes on the paralinguistic features illustrating uses

---

60. Hymes, *Now I Know*; Joubert, "Defining"; Fine, *The Folklore Text*; and Tedlock, *Finding the Center*.

61. See Cosgrove, "English Bible."

62. Wendland, *Finding and Translating*, 374; and Wendland, "Duplicating."

63. Ibid., n. 373.

64. Foley, *How to Read an Oral Poem*, 95–108.

of the voice; and to the right are extralinguistic notes identifying gestures and other physical expressions.[65]

Furthermore, the formatting of lines could also reflect identification of utterance units (cola) that facilitate the performer with breathing and pace, and that assist the audience in understanding. The format might also reflect the patterns and structures of oral arts such as parallelism, chiasms, chain formulations, link/stitch words, and various patterns of repetition in words, themes, grammar, syntax, and sound. Some of these patterns of discourse also work as features that assist memory for the performer and enhance memorability for the audience. Furthermore, the translation format might highlight formulaic sayings, proverbs, rhyme, rhythm, onomatopoeic words, ideophones, alliteration, wordplays, unusual words, and the repetition of sounds that structure discourse. Obviously, this can become quite complex, There may be a need to lay out the same passage in different formats to capture all that the translators want to feature.[66] These translation schemes do not limit a performer or a reader to one thing or another, but they do clearly place the printed text in performative space and no doubt make clear that even with specific directions, no two performances will be the same.

As a performer of New Testament writings,[67] I am acutely aware of the limitations of these schemes and notations. I want to add descriptions of what I am doing in performance and note more of the oral arts at work. As aids to translation and performance, we may want to consider performance commentaries or a translation/performance notebook that expresses the multiple physical and verbal things that go into the enactment of each line of what may appear on the surface to be a simple act of storytelling or the oration of an epistle. In addition to providing a translation, a performance commentary might include notes on such matters as voice, physical expressions, movement, memory devices, impact, relevant information from the life world context, issues of power, among other matters. The notes could highlight *diverse* ways by which a composition may be played in performance.

---

65. See Maxey, *From Orality*, 186–88 for a schematic translation of Mark 2:1–12.
66. This is what Wendland does in his analysis of letters, *Finding*.
67. See Rhoads, "Performing," 176–201.

Translating Scripture for Sound and Performance

Power Dynamics of Translation

The dynamics of translation are fraught with complex power issues. Usually a dominant, colonial culture is providing a translation for a suppressed culture, seeking to convert them to Christianity.[68] Recently, translators have begun to be sensitive to issues of power. For example, there are efforts to engage the local culture more fully in the translation process. Wendland, for example, wants translations to be tested and approved by the culture of reception.[69] Maxey is especially sensitive to issues of power and to his own presence and bias as a native of dominant United States culture.[70] He takes into account the power dynamics of the history of translation and seeks to counter an imperialist approach. He is aware that every translation is biased and situated. He knows the complex issues of control negotiated by translation agencies. He is aware also of the bias among translators that privileges writing over orality—how the goal of translation groups is a printed text, how the translation process often involves literacy programs, and how colonializing cultures use writing to dominate.[71] Maxey critiques the sometimes unilateral nature of the translation process.[72]

As expressed by his subtitle, Maxey proposes a "new paradigm of contextual translation." It is based on models of "contextual theology" developed in mission studies.[73] This model seeks to respect the culture for which the translation is being made, entrusts the translation process more fully into the hands of that culture, and seeks for the relationship to be mutually informative. There are two foci to this approach. First, Maxey recognizes both the contextual nature of the biblical materials and the distinct contextual nature of contemporary culture. Therefore, he acknowledges and honors the power of the new culture to develop its own indigenous expressions of biblical translation. Maxey expects to learn and be transformed by his experience. Second, the model is liberationist in putting the oral translation process primarily in local hands so that the new culture can be engaged in the process of translation from the start, and involved in composing their

---

68. On power dynamics in translation, see Bailey and Pippin, "Race"; Sugirtharajah, *Postcolonial Criticism*; West, "African Biblical Hermeneutics"; Yorke, "Bible Translation"; Venuti, *The Translator's Invisibility*; and Bassnett and Trivedi, *Postcolonial Translation*.

69. Wendland, *Finding and Translating*, 374.

70. Maxey, *From Orality*, 42–48.

71. Ibid., 91–2.

72. Ibid., 40.

73. Bevans, *Models*; Gittins, *Life*; and Schreiter, *Constructing*.

translations in and for performance.⁷⁴ The key to this new model is that it takes seriously the *oral* nature of the contemporary culture. While Maxey honors and promotes the literacy of the culture, he has seen how liberating it is for a traditional oral culture to develop translations in their preferred media of performance and song.⁷⁵

Trajectories

I have focused on efforts by key figures to translate for oral or predominantly oral cultures. We may also want to consider what performance translations might look like in print and electronic cultures. Surely performance is one way to get the word off the printed page and away from an electronic text and reinvigorate it in lively, embodied interrelationship with an audience. How can we make the oral arts of the biblical text transparent? How can we make use of techniques of oral performance of literature so as to enliven the printed translation by performances? How can we make the translation relevant in a way that will address and challenge audiences in their context? How can we speak and move and gesture in the ordinary language of various cultures and subcultures of society? How can we translate/perform in such a way as to open up space for interaction with the audience? How can we generate freedom in performance to translate afresh as the performance unfolds?

Where do we go from here in the collaborative efforts of biblical scholarship and translation for orality? I would like to suggest five avenues:

1. Seek to embrace the paradigm shift to an oral medium. This is not easy, because it requires us to imagine anew the early church, reconfigure the biblical writings as oral performances, and rethink translation in terms of orality.

2. Attend carefully to the oral arts and performance arts embedded in the biblical writings. This will require us to develop new tools and learn new methods of analysis

3. Learn how to listen—both to the Hebrew/Greek originals and to translations. And learn how to read the biblical languages aloud with facility. Consider how translations will sound, what their emotional impact might be, how they might impel an audience to action, and

---

74. Maxey, *From Orality*, 51, 231–36.
75. Ibid., 228–31.

what worlds they seek to create. Analyze just what it is about a biblical composition that would generate such effects.

4. Seek to imagine the performance events of the early church: performer, performance, physical location, social context, audience participation, rhetorical impact, and so on. The more concretely we can place biblical writings in performance space, the closer we will get to grasping their persuasive power.

5. Perform biblical materials yourself in translation in your native language. Absolutely, there is no better way to embrace the paradigm shift to orality than to perform a text as an act of persuasion before a live audience. Recently, New Testament scholar Margaret Lee took up the challenge to translate, memorize, and perform the Sermon on the Mount, which she had been studying as oral text for some time. Her comment: "I learned more about the Sermon on the Mount from my few weeks of performance preparation than I have in the entire five years since I wrote my dissertation on that passage. The experience was an awakening for me, replete with new possibilities for my work. . . . I anticipate rich returns on the efforts I intend to lavish in a new scholarly direction."[76]

Conclusion

As a biblical scholar, I have consistently grown through the years in my appreciation for the task of translating. Translation is a demanding and exacting discipline, even while being significantly artful and creative. I have found that the act of translating for performance (and in performance) is one of the most helpful means to understand a biblical text. Translating for performance leads one to grasp in fresh ways the potential meanings of the original composition, the oral arts evident in the text, the significance of sound as a medium for communicating, and the experience of the rhetorical impact on an audience. I believe that translating for orality can enhance the exegetical process such that exegetes become oral translators and that translators become exegetes of the oral—and that both try their hand at performing!

---

76. For more on Margaret Lee's experience of performing, see Lee, "How Performance Changed My (Scholarly) Life."

Bibliography

Bailey, Randall, and Tina Pippin, editors. *Race Class, and Politics of Biblical Translation.* Semeia 76. Atlanta: Scholars, 1996.
Bartsch, Carla. "Oral Style, Written Style, and Bible Translation." *Notes on Translation* 11 (1997) 41–48.
Bassnett, Susan, and Harish Trivedi, editors. *Postcolonial Translation: Theory and Practice.* Translation Studies. London: Routledge, 1999.
Bevans, Stephen. *Models of Contextual Theology.* 2nd ed. Maryknoll, NY: Orbis, 2003.
Boomershine, Thomas. "Bible Translation and Communication Technology." *United Bible Societies Bulletin* 160/161 (1991) 14–19.
———. "A Transmediation Theory of Biblical Translation." *United Bible Societies Bulletin* 170/171 (1994) 49–57.
Botha, Eugene. "Pragmatic Models of Text Interpretation and Bible Translation: Speech-Act Theory and Non-Verbal Communication." Paper presented at the annual meeting of the Society for New Testament Studies, Sibui, Romania, 2007.
Botha, Pieter. "Greco-Roman Literacy as Setting for New Testament Writings." *Neotestamentica* 26 (1992) 195–215.
Cosgrove, Charles, editor. *The Meanings We Choose: Hermeneutical Ethics, Indeterminacy, and the Conflict of Interpretations.* Journal for the Study of the Old Testament Supplement Series 411. London: T. & T. Clark, 2004.
———. "English Bible Translation Postmodern Perspective: Reflections on a Critical Theory of Holistic Translation." In *The Challenge of Bible Translation: Communicating God's Word to the World*, edited by Glen Scorgie et al., 159–74. Grand Rapids: Zondervan, 2003.
Davis, Casey. *Oral Biblical Criticism: The Influence of the Principles of Orality on the Literary Structures of Paul's Epistle to the Philippians.* Journal for the Study of the New Testament Supplement Series 172. Sheffield: Sheffield Academic, 1999.
Dewey, Joanna. "Mark as Oral Narrative: Structures as Clues to Understanding." *Sewanee Theological Review* 36 (1992) 45–56.
———. "The Gospel of Mark as an Oral-Aural Event: Implications for Interpretation." In *The New Literary Criticism and the New Testament*, edited by Elizabeth Struthers Malbon and Edgar V. McKnight, 145–61. Journal for the Study of the New Testament Supplement Series 109. Sheffield: Sheffield Academic, 1994.
———. "Oral Methods of Structuring Narrative in Mark." *Interpretation* 43 (1989) 32–44.
———. "Mark as Interwoven Tapestry: Forecasts and Echoes for a Listening Audience." *Catholic Biblical Quarterly* 53 (1991) 221–31.
Edwards, Mark. *Sound, Sense, and Rhythm: Listening to Greek and Latin Poetry.* Martin Classical Lectures. New Series. Princeton: Princeton University Press, 2002.
Elliott, John H. "A Dog, Shoes, and Subtabular Crumbthrowing: Gestural Communication in the Shift from Oral to Written Communication, with a Focus on the Gospel of Mark." Paper presented at a conference on "Orality and Literacy in Antiquity" in San Anselmo, CA, March 13–14, 2009.
Elliott, Scott S. "Translation and Narrative: Transfiguring Jesus." Atlanta: SBL Publications, 2009. Online: http://www.sbl-site.org/publications/article.aspx?articleId=828/.
Fine, Elizabeth. *The Folklore Text: From Performance to Print.* Bloomington: Indiana University Press, 1984.
Foley, John Miles. *How to Read an Oral Poem.* Urbana: University of Illinois Press, 2002.

———. *The Singer of Tales in Performance.* Voices in Performance and Text. Bloomington: Indiana University Press, 1995.

Fry, Euan M. "An Oral Approach to Translation." *The Bible Translator* 55 (2004) 506–10.

Gittins, Anthony, editor. *Life and Death Matters: The Practice of Inculturation in Africa.* Studia Instituti Missiologici Societatis Verbi Divini 72. Nettetal, Germany: Steyler, 2000.

Harvey, John. *Listening to the Text: Oral Patterning in Paul's Letters.* ETS Studies 1. Grand Rapids: Baker, 1998.

Hymes, Dell. *Now I Know Only So Far: Essays in Ethnopoetics.* Lincoln: University of Nebraska Press, 2003.

Joubert, Annekie. "Defining and Working in an Oral Culture: Between Oral and Written Transmission—The Problems of Textualizing Performance Events." Paper presented at Society for New Testament Studies, University of Birmingham, 2004.

Kelber, Werner H. *The Oral and the Written Gospel: The Hermeneutics of Speaking and Writing in the Synoptic Tradition, Mark, Paul, and Q.* Voices in Performance and Text. Bloomington: Indiana University Press, 1997.

Kuhn, Thomas. *The Structure of Scientific Revolutions.* 3rd ed. Chicago: University of Chicago Press, 1996.

Lee, Margaret Ellen. "How Performance Changed My (Scholarly) Life." *Currents in Theology and Mission* 37 (2010) 304–11.

Lee, Margaret Ellen, and Bernard Brandon Scott. *Sound Mapping of the New Testament.* Salem, OR: Polebridge, 2009.

Levinsohn, Stephen. *Discourse Features of New Testament Greek: A Coursebook on the Information Structure of New Testament Greek.* 2nd ed. Dallas: SIL International, 2000.

Loubser, Bobby. "How Do You Report Something That Was Said with a Smile?—Can We Overcome the Loss of Meaning When Oral-Manuscript Texts Are Represented in Modern Print Media?" *Scriptura* 87 (2004) 296–314.

———. *Oral and Manuscript Culture in the Bible: Studies in the Media Texture of the New Testament.* Stellenbosch: Sun, 2007.

Maxey, James A. "Performance Criticism and Its Implications for Bible Translation." Paper presented at the Society of New Testament Studies, Sibiu, Romania, 2007.

———. *From Orality to Orality: A New Paradigm for Contextual Translation of the Bible.* Biblical Performance Criticism 2. Eugene, OR: Cascade Books, 2009.

Noss, Phillip. "The Oral Story and Bible Translation." *The Bible Translator* 32 (1981) 301–18.

———. "The Ideophone in Bible Translation: Child or Stepchild." *The Bible Translator* 36 (1985) 423–30.

———. "A Translator's Trail: From Engagement to Ideophones to Engagement." In *Translating the Hebrew Bible: From the Septuagint to the Nouvelle Bible Second.* Collection Sciences bibliques 15. Montreal: Mediaspaul, 2005.

Ong, Walter. *Orality and Literacy: The Technologizing of the Word.* London: Routledge, 1982.

Phemister, Marilyn. *Audio Greek New Testament: Westcott and Hort Greek New Testament.* Grand Rapids: Christian Classics Ethereal Library, 2003.

Porter, Stanley E. "Some Issues in Modern Translation Theory and Study of the Greek New Testament." *Currents in Research: Biblical Studies* 9 (2001) 350–82.

———. "Assessing Translation Theory: Beyond Literal and Dynamic Equivalence." In *Translating the New Testament*, edited by Stanley E. Porter and Mark J. Boda, 119–48. McMaster New Testament Studies. Grand Rapids: Eerdmans, 2009.

Porter, Stanley E., and D. A. Carson, editors. *Discourse Analysis and Other Topics in Biblical Greek*. Journal for the Study of the New Testament Supplement Series 113. Sheffield: Sheffield Academic, 1995.

Porter, Stanley E., and Jeffrey T. Reed, editors. *Discourse Analysis and the New Testament: Approaches and Results*. Journal for the Study of the New Testament Supplement Series 170. Studies in New Testament Greek 4. Sheffield: Sheffield Academic, 1999.

Rebera, Basil. "Translating a Text to be Spoken and Heard: A Study of Ruth 1." *Bible Translator* 43 (1992) 230–36.

Reed, Jeffrey T. "Discourse Analysis." In *Handbook to Exegesis of the New Testament*, edited by Stanley E. Porter, 189–218. New Testament Tools and Studies 25. Leiden: Brill, 1997.

Rhoads, David. "Performing the Gospel of Mark." In *Reading Mark, Engaging the Gospel*, 176–201. Minneapolis: Fortress, 2004.

———, editor. *From Every People and Nation: The Book of Revelation in Intercultural Perspective*. Minneapolis: Fortress, 2005.

———. "Performance Criticism: An Emerging Methodology in Second Testament Studies, Part I." *Biblical Theology Bulletin* 36 (2006) 1–16.

———. "Performance Criticism: An Emerging Methodology in Second Testament Studies, Part II." *Biblical Theology Bulletin* 36 (2006) 164–84.

Rohrbaugh, Richard L. "Foreignizing Translation." In *The Social Sciences and Biblical Trans-lation*, edited by Dietmar Neufeld, 11–24. Society of Biblical Literature Symposium Series 41. Atlanta: Society of Biblical Literature, 2008.

Schreiter, Robert. *Constructing Local Theologies*. Maryknoll, NY: Orbis, 1985.

Scott, Bernard Brandon. "A New Voice in the Amphitheater: Full Fidelity in Translation." In *Fidelity and Translation: Communicating the Bible in the New Media*, edited by Paul A. Soukup and Robert Hodgson, 101–18. Franklin, WI: Sheed & Ward, 1999.

Shiell, William David. *Reading Acts: The Lector and the Early Christian Audience*. Biblical Interpretation Series 70. Boston: Brill, 2004.

Shiner, Whitney. *Proclaiming the Gospel: First-Century Performance of Mark*. Harrisburg, PA: Trinity, 2003.

Simon, John. *Greek-Latin New Testament Audio Reading Series*. Austin, TX. Online: http://www.greeklatinaudio.com, 1999.

Small, Jocelyn Penny. *Wax Tablets of the Mind: Cognitive Studies of Memory and Literacy in Classical Antiquity*. London: Routledge, 1997.

Soukup, Paul A., and Robert Hodgson, editors. *Fidelity and Translation: Communicating the Bible in the New Media*. Franklin, WI: Sheed & Ward, 1999.

Sugirtharajah, R. S. *Postcolonial Criticism and New Testament Interpretation*. Oxford: Oxford University Press, 2002.

Sundersingh, J. "Toward a Media-Based Translation: Communicating Biblical Scriptures to Non-Literates in Rural Tamilnadu, India." PhD diss., Fuller Theological Seminary, 1999.

Tedlock, Dennis, translator. *Finding the Center: The Art of the Zuni Storyteller* 2nd ed. Lincoln: University of Nebraska Press, 1999.

Thomas, Kenneth, and Margaret Orr Thomas. *Structure and Orality in 1 Peter: A Guide for Translators*. New York: United Bible Societies, 2006.

Tymoczko, Maria. "Translation in Oral Tradition as a Touchstone for Translation Theory and Practice." In *Translation, History, and Culture,* edited by Susan Bassnett and André Lefevere, 46–55. London: Printer, 1990.

Van Niekerk, A. S., and C. J. Pauw. "Understanding and/or Participation? The Goal of Making the Bible Available in Oral Context." *Scriptura* 74 (2000) 249–57.

Venuti, L. *The Translator's Invisibility: A History of Translation.* Translation Studies. London: Routledge, 1995.

Vries, Lourens de. "Bible Translation and Primary Orality." *The Bible Translator* 51 (2000) 101–14.

Waard, Jan de, and Eugene A. Nida. *From One Language to Another: Functional Equivalence in Biblical Translating* Nashville: Nelson, 1986.

Wendland, Ernst. "Duplicating the Dynamics of Oral Discourse in Print." *Notes on Translation* 7 (1993) 26–44.

———. *Finding and Translating the Oral-Aural Elements in Written Language: The Case of the New Testament Epistles.* Lewiston, NY: Mellen, 2008.

West, Gerald. "African Biblical Hermeneutics and Bible Translation." In *Interacting with Scriptures in Africa,* edited by Jean-Claude Loba-Mkole and Ernst R. Wendland, 3–29. Nairobi: Acton, 2005.

Westfall, Cynthia Long. *A Discourse Analysis of the Letter to the Hebrews: The Relationship between Form and Meaning.* T. & T. Library of Biblical Studies. Library of New Testament Studies 297. Studies in New Testament Greek 11. New York: T. & T. Clark, 2006.

Yorke, Gosnell. "Bible Translation in Anglophonic Africa and Her Diaspora: A Postcolonialist Agenda." *The Bible Translator* 22 (2004) 153–66.

3

Translating the Aural Gospel
The Use of Sound Analysis in Performance-Oriented Translation

Dan Nässelqvist

PHD STUDENT, LUND UNIVERSITY

Introduction

THE EMERGENCE OF PERFORMANCE criticism has brought a much-needed focus to the question of how biblical writings were delivered in antiquity. This development may have more immediate implications for Bible translation than the field of orality at large,[1] since it focuses directly on how biblical texts were read aloud and experienced. However, even as we attest to the importance of performance for translation, there is a difference between translation *of* performance (which aims at finding corresponding ways to express aural features that affected performances in antiquity) and translation *for* performance (which aims at creating a translation that is easy to read aloud today).

---

1. This field is now often referred to as "orality-scribality-memory studies," as in Kelber, "Oral-Scribal-Memorial Arts," 236.

Both these pursuits have their advantages. We can make a translation that captures some important aspects of a New Testament text as an orally delivered text. We can also make a translation that facilitates contemporary delivery, especially if we address how the original oral dimension may be preserved in a new setting.[2] Therefore, a translation *of* performance as well as *for* performance is a realistic ambition. In fact, when we combine these pursuits, we find that they reinforce each other. The best way to translate a biblical text for contemporary performance may be to concentrate on how the text (in its source language) is structured to emphasize, inform, and influence, and then to find corresponding ways of achieving the same effects that are natural to the host language.

If we want to present a translation that captures as much as possible of first-century performance (and use it to facilitate contemporary performance), we have to start with the original written text. During the last decade we have learned a great deal about the delivery of texts in antiquity, especially through the studies of Whitney Shiner and William David Shiell.[3] Even so, the only way of knowing something about how a specific writing was prepared for delivery is by using hints found in the text itself.[4]

Margaret Ellen Lee and Bernard Brandon Scott have shown that an analysis of the aural character of New Testament writings is an effective way of revealing hints about performance.[5] We need to pay attention to how and why a text sounds in a certain way and by what means it structures the sounded text for performance.

I will try to show why an analysis of phonological features of biblical texts is an important aspect of any performance-oriented translation. A sound analysis of shorter passages from John 1 will reveal their aural structure and emphases. After analyzing each passage, I will give an example of how the aural features can be used to create a performance-oriented translation. Note that these translations are intended as illustrations of a single aspect of the text and not as consummate translations in their own right. A final translation will have to consider other aspects, such as syntactic and semantic, to a greater degree.

2. Rhoads, "Performance Criticism," 171.
3. Shiell, *Reading Acts*; Shiner, *Proclaiming*.
4. Maxey, *From Orality*, 135.
5. Lee and Scott, *Sound Mapping*.

Structuring and Translating Sound

Attention to sound and to a graphic representation of a text's structure is at the heart of the sound analysis of Lee and Scott.[6] The same focus is found in the works of Ernst Wendland, who shows how important a thorough understanding of a text's structure is for its translation.[7] While Lee and Scott have deepened our understanding of the sound structure of ancient texts, they do not discuss the implications for translation. Combining the sound analysis of Lee and Scott with Wendland's insight that structure and sound should be reflected in translation provides us with some of the tools needed to make solid performance-oriented translations.

What characterizes the sound analysis of Lee and Scott is the development and interpretation of a sound map of the written text. They describe the sound map as "a visual display that exhibits a literary composition's organization by highlighting its acoustic features and in doing so depicts aspects of a composition's aural character in preparation for analysis."[8] (And, one might add, in preparation for translation.)

A sound map is developed in six steps. The first step is analyzing where each line, or colon, begins and ends. The basic criterion for delineating a colon is vocal articulation: a colon is a complete statement, easy to repeat in a breath.[9] Incidentally, Wendland asserts that one of the most important characteristics of a translation for performance is that it displays the text in this way, line by line.[10] Such a colometric presentation of the text helps the performer memorize and deliver the text more fluently and meaningfully. Thus, the listeners can comprehend it better.[11]

The second step is arranging and analyzing how cola are combined into periods. While a colon is complete in itself, it does not express the entire thought. This is effected by joining cola into periods. Lee and Scott find that depicting the boundaries of each period graphically helps identifying their internal structure.[12] Again, Wendland argues something similar when

---

6. Ibid., 1–2, 167–68.

7. Wendland, "Oral-Aural Dynamics," 20; Wendland, "Performance Criticism," 8; Wendland, "Duplicating the Dynamics," 31, 33.

8. Lee and Scott, *Sound Mapping*, 168.

9. Ibid., 109, 169.

10. He calls the cola "rhythmic speech units" that reproduce "the natural flow of discourse" (Wendland, "Duplicating," 38–39).

11. Ibid., 31.

12. Lee and Scott, *Sound Mapping*, 108–9, 171.

he suggests different ways of presenting a text with formats based on its phonological and intonational patterns.[13]

The third step is identifying and plotting repetitive sound patterns. Repetitions of the quality of sound (for example, through a recurring word or phoneme), as well as of the quantity of sound (for example, through successive cola of the same length), create structure and emphasis.[14]

The fourth step is identifying larger compositional units. Periods are arranged into distinct parts with mnemonic tags. At this macrolevel, sound is still fundamental, although it is intertwined with devices of a more literary nature (such as narrative strategies and indications of time and place).[15]

The fifth step is describing sound quality. This includes identifying hiatus and consonant clashes, instances of especially pleasant or dissonant sounds, the use of different forms of personal pronouns for effects, and significant variations of the verbal aspect.[16]

The sixth and final step is analyzing the relation between the content and the stylistic shape of the text. Lee and Scott point out that stylistic levels are achieved through the structure and character of a composition's cola and periods, as well as through the blending of sounds with significations of words.[17]

Analyzing a text and displaying it as a sound map is a laborious task. However, one need not struggle for long before various implications for translation are revealed. This is especially true when the ambition is a performance-oriented translation. In this field, sound analysis has two important contributions to make. First, sound analysis reveals the aural characteristics of New Testament writings. With the help of a sound map, we can follow the flow and tempo of the discourse and establish where emphasis is directed and effects are applied (for example, verses with assonance, rhyme, or climactic repetitions). These were important features of the oral delivery of texts in the first century CE. With the help of sound analysis we can identify these features and find corresponding ways of expressing them in translation,[18] thereby achieving the above-mentioned

---

13. Wendland, "Duplicating," 32–37.
14. Lee and Scott, *Sound Mapping*, 145–56.
15. Ibid., 174–75.
16. Ibid., 176–79.
17. Ibid., 111–12, 179, 183–88.
18. This is indeed important, as a rigorous commitment to the exact forms of the source language may abuse the host language. The function of these forms have to be

translation *of* performance. As James A. Maxey has stated, "fundamental to biblical performance is the translation of the biblical compositions in a way that brings into relief the performative features of the New Testament and then presents these translations in a script format for performance."[19] This is precisely what we achieve when we make a translation based on a sound analysis of the text. Second, sound analysis provides the starting point for a translation *for* performance. Wendland has reminded us that the goal of a translator with the oral performance of a biblical text in mind is "to reveal the design of the discourse and thus assist the reader in enunciating as well as interpreting it, either for himself or for those to whom he is reading."[20] The "design" that Wendland is speaking about, what Maxey calls "the form" of a text,[21] is the text's structure (including its emphases and effects), which can be readily identified with the help of sound analysis. When David Rhoads considers translation for performance, he identifies at least eight features that distinguish it from translation for silent reading. Of these, seven features have to do with the structure and aural character of the Greek text.[22]

It seems clear that sound analysis is a good starting point for a performance-oriented translation. It provides the basis for translation *of* performance as well as translation *for* performance. Therefore, let us see how sound analysis can provide important clues for a performance-oriented translation of different passages found in John 1.

Sound Analysis and Translation in John 1

When it comes to its aural character and implications for translation, John 1 presents a number of interesting features and passages. I will present only a few of these. Hopefully, they will show that sound analysis can deepen our knowledge about the text and at the same time provide important information for performance-oriented translation.

It is well-known that the prologue of John (1:1–18) contains smoother and more advanced features than most other parts of the gospel. In it, we find a well-structured, narrative-like introduction that makes ample use of

---

understood and translated into compatible forms in the host language (Maxey, *From Orality*, 160).

19. Ibid., 164.
20. Wendland, "Duplicating," 33.
21. Maxey, *From Orality*, 158.
22. Rhoads, "Performance Criticism," 171.

aural features and effects. Thus, it provides fertile ground for sound analysis. The prologue is also one of the best-known and most thoroughly studied parts of the New Testament. Because of this, I will give more attention to the other parts of John 1 and seek to show that new insights for translation can be gained from what at first might seem like quite barren soil.

However, I will begin with a passage found in the prologue. In 1:6–9, the prologue turns from a complete focus on the divine Word to an introduction of John the Baptist and a contrast between him and the Word. John the Baptist is presented as someone who gives witness about the Word (referred to as "the light" in this passage). After the presentation of John in the first two cola, two thematic sounds or morphemes echo throughout the passage: μαρτυρ- and φω-. In the seven cola of 1:7–9, there are no less than ten instances of words that are closely related to μαρτυρία or φῶς. They are presented in varying cases; related verb forms are also used. The result is a striking emphasis on sounds designating "witness" and "light," further stressing the comparison between John and Jesus.

Below, the Greek text is displayed colometrically. To the left of each colon is its colon number, and to the right are the traditional verse numbers. The presentation uses some features of sound mapping of Greek texts found in Lee and Scott,[23] as well as some of the typographical tools that Wendland utilizes on translated texts.[24] The guiding principle is to reveal the sound structure by placing recurring or similar sounds in parallel positions:

1 Ἐγένετο * ἄνθρωπος ἀπεσταλμένος # παρὰ θεοῦ,   [6]
2 ὄνομα * αὐτῷ Ἰωάννης·
3 οὗτος ἦλθεν εἰς   μαρτυρίαν,   [7]
4   ἵνα   μαρτυρήσῃ   περὶ τοῦ φωτός,
5   ἵνα   πάντες # πιστεύσωσιν # δι' αὐτοῦ.
6 οὐκ ἦν ἐκεῖνος #   τὸ φῶς,   [8]
7 ἀλλ'   ἵνα   μαρτυρήσῃ   περὶ τοῦ φωτός.
8 Ἦν #   τὸ φῶς # τὸ * ἀληθινόν,   [9]
9   ὃ φωτίζει πάντα * ἄνθρωπον,
                                              ἐρχόμενον εἰς τὸν # κόσμον.

---

23. Lee and Scott, *Sound Mapping*, 169–171. This and the following sound maps show the result of the first, second, third, and fifth steps of the sound analysis described by Lee and Scott.

24. Wendland, "Duplicating," 33–42.

Displayed in such a way, the parallel expressions and the emphases on the differing forms of μαρτυρία and φῶς are apparent. Read aloud with these markers in perspective, it is also easier to hear the almost rhythmic effect that the repetitions create, as well as how the period is rounded off through the elongation of colon 9. Cola 2–8 each consists of between seven and eleven syllables; colon 9 starts with nine syllables, on to which a subordinate clause of another eight syllables is appended.[25] Moreover, this type of depiction reveals all clashes of vowels (such as hiatus, shown with asterisks) and consonants (shown with pound signs) where words meet. Such clashes affect the tempo and sound quality of the text when it is spoken aloud. Too many clashes of consonants belong to a plain style and were thought of as dissonant if they occurred in writings of higher stylistic intensity. The same is true in the case of clashes of vowels, which force one to make a brief pause between the words, thus breaking the flow of sound. Too many such clashes create a rough and unsteady impression.[26]

The sound map shown above can help us with a translation *of* performance, as it highlights the structure and emphases of a passage. However, it is not a very useful format for displaying translation *for* performance. As Lee and Scott point out, a sound map is merely an analytical tool, not an end in itself.[27] Therefore, a strictly colometric depiction without additional markings in the text is much easier to read:

1	Ἐγένετο ἄνθρωπος ἀπεσταλμένος παρὰ θεοῦ,	[6]
2	ὄνομα αὐτῷ Ἰωάννης·	
3	οὗτος ἦλθεν εἰς μαρτυρίαν,	[7]
4	ἵνα μαρτυρήσῃ περὶ τοῦ φωτός,	
5	ἵνα πάντες πιστεύσωσιν δι' αὐτοῦ.	
6	οὐκ ἦν ἐκεῖνος τὸ φῶς,	[8]
7	ἀλλ' ἵνα μαρτυρήσῃ περὶ τοῦ φωτός.	
8	Ἦν τὸ φῶς τὸ ἀληθινόν,	[9]
9	ὃ φωτίζει πάντα ἄνθρωπον, ἐρχόμενον εἰς τὸν κόσμον.	

---

25. Elongation is one of the three requirements for a particularly well-formed period; see Lee and Scott, *Sound Mapping*, 171–72.

26. Cicero, *Or. Brut.* 77; Dionysius of Halicarnassus, *Dem.* 40; Quintilian, *Inst.* 9.4.37.

27. Lee and Scott, *Sound Mapping*, 2.

With this less complex format, where only the colon and verse numbers are added, other features can be identified in the text. For example, the balancing of cola 2–8 is more evident. One can readily perceive that they are of roughly the same length and at the same time framed by longer first and last cola. Additionally, the repetition of colon 4 in colon 7 as well as the rhymes at the end of cola 8 and 9 are now easier to detect. In fact, one can see that ἀληθινόν in colon 8 not only rhymes with κόσμον at the end of colon 9, but also with ἄνθρωπον and ἐρχόμενον in the middle of colon 9 (just before and after the point where the elongation starts).

This type of colometric presentation can be effectively used in performance-oriented translation. As mentioned above, such a depiction of the text—line by line, echoing the natural flow of discourse—is precisely what Wendland argues for.[28] If it is combined with an effort to render Greek sound structures and effects in corresponding ways in translation, we can produce a good translation *for* performance as well.

How, then, can we find corresponding ways of expressing the sound structures and effects of John 1:6–9 that are natural to English? Let us first state clearly what these structures and effects are:

a. The passage consists of nine clauses, each of them possible to utter in a single breath (that is, it comprises nine cola)

b. Several clauses are subordinated, especially through the use of ἵνα[29]

c. Cola 2–8 are of roughly the same length, while cola 1 and 9 are considerably longer

d. Μαρτυρία and φῶς occur five times each, in different cases and also as verb forms, constantly connected by the repetition of the sound of their basic morphemes (μαρτυρ- and φω-)

e. There are rhymes at the end of cola 8 and 9 (and inside colon 9) and a repetition of colon 4 in colon 7.

f. There are relatively few instances of hiatus (9 %), as compared to John 1 as a whole (17.5 %)

Some of these features, and their effects, are easy to translate. Other, such as the rhymes in cola 8 and 9, are almost impossible to render successfully in English. We are reminded by Maxey that it is the function (or the

---

28. Wendland, "Duplicating," 38–39.

29. This is rather a feature of the syntax, but since it is a structural aspect of the text that affects translation (at least translation *for* performance), it is stated here.

effect) of these features that are to be translated, not necessarily the features as such.[30] The following translation is an illustration of its aural features:

1	There came a man who was sent by God;	[6]
2	his name was John.	
3	He came as a witness,	[7]
4	to witness about the light,	
5	so that through him all might believe.	
6	He was not the light	[8]
7	but [he came] to witness about the light.	
8	The true light,	[9]
9	that lightens every human being, was coming into the world.	

This version diverges slightly from standard translations, chiefly in the choice of words. A comparison with the translation found in the New International Version will make this clear:

> [6] There came a man who was sent from God; his name was John. [7] He came as a witness to testify concerning that light, so that through him all men might believe. [8] He himself was not the light; he came only as a witness to the light. [9] The true light that gives light to every man was coming into the world. (NIV)

The first point of divergence is of course that the NIV presents the text as a continuous stream, while I use a colometric presentation with uneven right margins that seek to display every breathing unit (that is, each colon) and show their hierarchal structure. The basis is an analysis of the aural character of the Greek text (translation *of* performance) and an important goal is a text that is easy to read aloud in the host language (translation *for* performance).

In addition to preserving the colometric and hierarchal structure of the Greek text (features *a* and *b* above), I have also tried to retain somewhat the relative lengths of cola 2–8 in comparison with cola 1 and 9 (feature *c*). That is indeed harder than it seems. Furthermore, I have tried to emphasize and express the stress on "witness" and "light" that is present in the Greek text (feature *d*). I have done this by choosing more concise verb forms (such as "witness" and "lighten") that are phonologically closer to the related nouns of "witness" and "light" than the ones commonly used

---

30. Maxey, *From Orality*, 160.

in translations ("testify" and "give light," in NIV).[31] The justification for this close connection between nouns and related verbs is that the recurring sounds of μαρτυρ- and φω- are an example of the rhetorical figure *polyptoton* (Gr. "many cases"). It is a figure that was used to create strong amplification. One ancient author even cautioned against it because of its labored impression.[32]

If we want to re-create the effect of this Greek way of expressing amplification, we need to find ways to articulate it that are natural to English. This is perhaps best achieved by stressing the aural effect of repeating the two distinct sounds ("witness" and "light") several times in different forms. The result is indeed a somewhat labored impression, which mirrors how it was experienced in antiquity. When it comes to translating the rhymes (feature *e*), however, I have not been able to find a corresponding way of expressing them, or their effect, in English. It should be said that cola 4, 6, 7, and 8 all end with "light" in my translation, and therefore they do rhyme. However, it is hard to hear these endings as rhymes in English; and they do not in any way create the euphonious effect of the rhymes in cola 8 and 9 of the Greek text. I have not tried to re-create any effect of hiatus (feature *f*), due to the fact that the author uses far fewer instances of hiatus in this passage than in John 1 as a whole.

Let us now examine two passages in John 1 that use different effects of sound to emphasize who Jesus is (and who John the Baptist is not). In 1:20, the text stresses that John the Baptist is not the Christ; and, in 1:49, Nathanael says to Jesus that he is the Son of God and the king of Israel. These statements are found in every translation. Yet little of the emphasis of 1:20 and nothing of the force in 1:49 is truly conveyed by the existing translations. In Greek, the aural character of these two verses surpasses the surrounding passages in euphony, emphasis, and effect. Let us begin by examining 1:20:

1	καὶ	*	ὡμολόγησεν			[20]
2	καὶ	*		οὐκ	ἠρνήσατο,	
3	καὶ	*	ὡμολόγησεν ὅτι			
4	Ἐγὼ	*	οὐκ	εἰμὶ * ὁ Χριστός.		

---

31. NKJV uses "bear witness" and "give light," which is closer to the unusually strong stress of the Greek text, yet not as succinct and close to the nouns as "witness" and "lighten."

32. Cicero, *Or. Brut.* 84; *Rhet. Her.* 4.30–32.

With the passage displayed colometrically as a sound map, some of its aural effects are easily discerned. The period is well balanced, with four short cola of almost the same length (cola 1–2 consists of six syllables each and cola 3–4 of eight syllables each). This pattern is reinforced by the assonance of cola 1–3; each of these cola starts with καί followed by a short pause due to hiatus. Then cola 1 and 3 proceed with ὡμολόγησεν, while colon 2 continues with οὐκ, which is later repeated in colon 4 in almost the same position. The result is *paromoiosis*, a powerful rhetorical figure that combines quality (the type) and quantity (the duration) of sound in a strong parallelism. The figure makes this period stand out in comparison with surrounding passages. The fourth unit of John 1, which starts with the witness of John the Baptist in 1:19 and ends in 1:28, mainly contains prose of a quite plain character. John 1:19 and 1:21–23 consist of very simple periods without embellishments or rhetorical figures. In this soundscape, 1:20 certainly stands out.

Besides being euphonious (expressed in part by the complete lack of disharmonious clashes of consonants) and powerful, 1:20 has a distinct pace that further distinguishes it. Among its thirteen words, there are no less than five instances of hiatus. This is more than twice the amount compared to the average number of clashes of vowels in John 1. With five brief pauses in thirteen words, the pace is shortened, even more so in the last colon. Together with the repetitions, the result is a strong emphasis on this passage, especially on John's statement that he is not the Christ.

How, then, could a passage like this be translated? Traditionally, iterations are often revised or removed altogether. The three parallel occurrences of καί in 1:20 can for example be reduced to a single "but," as in the NIV: "He did not fail to confess, but confessed freely, 'I am not the Christ.'" In NKJV, they are expressed with one "and" and one "but," thus completely altering and removing the parallelism and assonance: "He confessed, and did not deny, but confessed, 'I am not the Christ.'" David Rhoads, Kenneth Thomas, and Lee and Scott all stress the importance of translating repeated occurrences of a Greek word with a single word in the host language, wherever possible.[33] This is especially true of translations for performance, since the repetitions themselves are important for building structure and a soundscape where important themes are developed with the help of echoes and recurring sounds. If we want a translation *of* and *for* performance, we

---

33. Rhoads, "Performance Criticism," 171; Lee and Scott, *Sound Mapping*, 143–44, 160 n. 13; Maxey, *From Orality*, 157 (which includes the reference to Kenneth Thomas).

should preserve the parallelism and assonance of the repeated καί in 1:20. The following translation illustrates an attempt to highlight these features:

1   And he confessed.   [20]
2   And he did not deny [it].
3   And he confessed and said:
4   "I am not the Christ."

While this translation[34] retains some of the strong features of the sounded Greek text, others are very hard to achieve in English. While making a full stop at the end of each colon slows the pace of the passage, I cannot find a way of slowing it down even further in the last colon. Even though it has its shortcomings, a translation such as this one undoubtedly changes the pace of the passage and at the same time retains some of the emphasis put on these words compared to the surrounding text.

Moving on to John 1:49, we find that Nathanael says to Jesus that he is the Son of God and king of Israel. While this message is of course significant, translations pick up only the words of the message and nothing of the strong aural emphasis that is conveyed in Greek. For example, the New International Version translates it as follows:

> [49] Then Nathanael declared, "Rabbi, you are the Son of God; you are the King of Israel."

This translation fits well into the style of the preceding passages of the last unit of John 1 (which comprises 1:43–51). In 1:43–48, the periods are plain, neither balanced nor rounded (both of which are important features of a well-formed period),[35] and they lack embellishments, repeated sounds, and rhetorical figures. The problem with translating 1:49 in the same way as the preceding passages is that in the original Greek it truly diverges from them in character. As was the case with 1:20, this verse is much more complex and stylistically audacious:

---

34. Again, the translations are intended as illustrations of phonological features in the biblical text and not as completed renderings. Therefore they are primarily aimed at scholarly readers interested in how performance of biblical writings—in antiquity as well as in our time—affects translation.

35. Lee and Scott, *Sound Mapping*, 171–72.

1   ἀπεκρίθη * αὐτῷ Ναθαναήλ,   [49]
2   Ῥαββί,   σὺ   *   εἶ   *   ὁ * υἱὸς # τοῦ θεοῦ,
3   σὺ βασιλεὺς εἶ   τοῦ * Ἰσραήλ.

The period starts like most of the preceding periods of 1:43–51, with a verb signifying speech followed by a personal pronoun (most often in the dative). This pattern is found in the first or second colon (or both) of ten of the twelve periods in 1:43–51. Thus, 1:49 is well integrated in a very repetitious and clear soundscape. It does, however, evolve beyond anything experienced in the preceding passages of 1:43–48, as can be seen in the sound analysis of the Greek text presented above.

First of all, it rhymes. Ναθαναήλ and Ἰσραήλ in cola 1 and 3 both end with -αηλ; and these words are also placed in the final position of their respective cola. This repetition at the end of a period of a sound heard at its beginning makes the passage rounded. The effect is further reinforced by the fact that the whole period is also balanced, due to the repetition of σὺ and εἶ in cola 2 and 3,[36] and because the three cola are approximately of the same length (cola 1 and 2 each consist of ten syllables and colon 3 of nine syllables). As mentioned above, none of the nine preceding periods of 1:43–48 are either rounded or balanced. Thus, this period is much more well-formed and harmonious compared to the periods that precede it. The effect is more readily appreciated in a strict colometric presentation of the text, stripped of some of the markings of sound analysis:

1   ἀπεκρίθη αὐτῷ Ναθαναήλ,   [49]
2   Ῥαββί, σὺ εἶ ὁ υἱὸς τοῦ θεοῦ,
3   σὺ βασιλεὺς εἶ τοῦ Ἰσραήλ.

Another feature of 1:49 that it has in common with 1:20 is that it includes substantially more occurrences of hiatus (approximately twice as many) compared to the surrounding passages. This slows the pace of the reading and further distinguishes and gives emphasis to it. In 1:49, it is interesting to see that three of the five instances of hiatus are found in colon 2, when Nathanael states that Jesus is the Son of God. The passage slows down in pace, and with the help of rhyme, repetition, and rhythm signals that

---

36. The respective placement of the complements to εἶ is not completely congruent, however. In colon 2 the complement is found after εἶ and in colon 3 it is found both before and after εἶ.

something important is coming. In particular, it points to colon 2 and the important message found in it. Here, content and form are in complete harmony. As the content shifts from a relatively straightforward dialogue to a significant christological statement, the form changes with it and gives the passage a very different sound compared to the preceding passages.

How, then, can we attain effects corresponding to the contrast and emphasis of 1:49 in a performance-oriented translation? This is truly difficult, and the suggestion below is not particularly elegant. Again, these translations are only illustrations of how some of the effects that the Greek text conveys might be expressed in English (in this case at the expense of other aspects of great value).

1	Answer him did Nathanael:	[49]
2	"You are, rabbi, the Son of God.	
3	You are king of Israel."	

This translation aims at four things. First, it presents the text colometrically. Second, it retains the rounded and balanced character of the period. Third, it tries to distinguish this passage and set it in contrast with the preceding periods. Fourth, it tries to slow down the pace of colon 2 and thus to emphasize the proclamation that Jesus is the Son of God. Previous translations have not targeted all, or even most, of these aspects. However, aiming at these four aspects of the soundscape, which sum up both the aural features and the possible effect of the Greek text, means aiming at a translation *of* and *for* performance, while at the same time trying to translate the features and effects in corresponding ways in the host language.

The colometric presentation is easy to achieve, while a rounded and balanced period is harder to produce in translation. My solution is to maintain the end positions of "Nathanael" and "Israel," thereby exploiting the fact that they rhyme in English as well as in Greek and aiming to achieve cola of approximately equal length. When I tried to distinguish the passage from the surrounding text and slow down the pace of colon 2, this was achieved at the cost of natural, contemporary English. Only by rearranging the word order of cola 1 and 2 could I accomplish a significant contrast between how this and preceding passages sound. The transfer of "rabbi" from the beginning to the middle of colon 2 contributed to this, while at the same time it forces the reader to pause briefly before "Son of God." This creates the added emphasis that is found in the sounded Greek text. Thus, the four stated aims are achieved, and the result is a sounded text that functions both as translation *of* and *for* performance. To accomplish this at the cost of natural, contemporary English (and thus, fail to attend to another important aspect of the passage; namely, that it uses ordinary and not archaic Greek) is of course too high a price to pay.[37] Again, these translations are only meant as illustrations of how we can analyze and work with aural features with the future aim of a performance-oriented translation.

Finally, let us turn to a shorter passage, 1:26–27, in order to see how an aural emphasis can be created effortlessly in a very straightforward way. John 1:26–27 is placed at the end of the fourth part of John 1 (1:19–28), which in turn contains the second part of John's testimony. Let us first consult a colometric presentation of the passage:

1	ἀπεκρίθη αὐτοῖς ὁ Ἰωάννης λέγων,	[26]
2	Ἐγὼ βαπτίζω ἐν ὕδατι·	
3	μέσος ὑμῶν ἕστηκεν	
4	ὃν ὑμεῖς οὐκ οἴδατε,	
5	ὁ ὀπίσω μου ἐρχόμενος,	[27]
6	οὗ οὐκ εἰμὶ ἐγὼ ἄξιος	
7	ἵνα λύσω αὐτοῦ τὸν ἱμάντα τοῦ ὑποδήματος.	

It is clear from this depiction that the passage is quite well-formed. It is both balanced and elongated, two of the main features of a well-formed period. The period is balanced due to the fact that several cola are parallel in structure. Cola 2–6 are of approximately the same length (each colon consists of between seven and nine syllables) and cola 4–6 start with a variation of the same sound (an aspirated o). The period is also elongated, as seen in the extended colon 7, which is longer than the other cola (consisting of sixteen syllables). This makes it easy to hear and recognize the end of the period when it is read aloud.

When we augment the colometric presentation with a sound analysis, more information is revealed about the aural character of the passage:

---

37. Nevertheless, translations such as this one can help us recognize and appreciate the soundscape of the Greek text and at the same time remind Bible translators that these aspects should be considered.

Translating Scripture for Sound and Performance

1	ἀπεκρίθη * αὐτοῖς ὁ Ἰωάννης # λέγων,	[26]
2	Ἐγὼ βαπτίζω * ἐν ὕδατι·	
3	μέσος ὑμῶν ἔστηκεν	
4	ὃν ὑμεῖς οὐκ οἴδατε,	
5	ὁ * ὀπίσω μου * ἐρχόμενος,	[27]
6	οὗ * οὐκ εἰμὶ * ἐγὼ * ἄξιος	
7	ἵνα λύσω * αὐτοῦ τὸν ἱμάντα τοῦ ὑποδήματος.	

In the first three cola, the narrative with direct speech proceeds without effects or obstacles. There is only one instance of hiatus in these lines, so that the pace of the reading is not affected. Nor are there any vocal effects, repetitions, or other effects having to do with sound that create attention. Colon 3 ends, however, with an uncertainty about who the subject of ἔστηκεν is. In colon 4, the pattern starts to change. In three short cola, the distinct sound of an aspirated ὁ is repeated in varying forms at the start of each colon. This might be a case of *polyptoton*, just as with μαρτυρ- and φω- in 1:6–9. In this passage, however, the focus is not divided between two different sounds, but is rather intensified by the fact that each colon starts with a variation of a single sound. By referring to Jesus[38] again and again in this way, each time shifting the aural character somewhat, Jesus is placed at the center of the passage with the help of similar sounds. The aural effect of the passage is that the three cola repeat a variation of the same sound and build a sound pattern of repetition and emphasis.[39] When this pattern is confirmed in colon 5 (through the first repetition with variation of ὁ), the many instances of hiatus reinforce the change in intensity and focus. Thus, the pace of these cola is slowed down slightly, and a somewhat rhythmic effect is achieved in the parallel cola of equal length and similar openings.

The effect of the possible *polyptoton* of 1:26–27 has not been preserved in any translation, yet it plays an important role for the aural character of the passage. Traditionally, the period is often translated:

---

38. The reference to the one "who comes after me" (cf. 1:15) makes it clear that the passage is about Jesus.

39. Interestingly enough, the pattern consists of words that are used in syntactically different ways. ὃν and οὗ in cola 4 and 6 are relative pronouns, while ὁ in colon 5 is the definite article of ἐρχόμενος.

[26]"I baptize with water," John replied, "but among you stands one you do not know. [27]He is the one who comes after me, the thongs of whose sandals I am not worthy to untie." (NIV)

If we want to preserve the aural character and emphasis of the Greek text, and if we want to facilitate oral performance and memorization of the passage, we need to find corresponding forms for its characteristic features. A possible performance-oriented translation is this:

1	John answered them and said:	[26]
2	"I baptize in water,	
3	but in your midst stands one	
4	whom you do not know,	
5	who comes after me,	[27]
6	whose sandal strap I am not worthy to untie."	

The first reaction to this translation might be that it consists of only six cola, while the Greek text comprises seven. Since the focus of the text is created by the variation of sounds that gives attention to Jesus, I have let this fact guide the translation. The last two cola are exceedingly hard to keep apart in English, especially if the aim is to begin colon 6 with a relative pronoun. Therefore, I have let colon 6 include the initial repetition of the relative pronoun as well as the elongation that marks the end of the period. Thus, the balanced and elongated effects of the period are achieved even in translation, as cola 1–5 all consist of five or six syllables, while the elongated last colon comprises twelve syllables. Most important, however, is the repetition of pronouns in cola 4–6, which not only helps the memorization of the passage, but also turns the attention to Jesus at the point indicated by the Greek text, and furthermore imparts rhythmicity to the recitation of these lines. English also provides the opportunity to use pronouns that sound slightly different, corresponding to the aural variation of the aspirated ὁ in the Greek text. In short, some aspects of the euphony, emphasis, and aural character of ancient performances are successfully retained in ways that at the same time are natural to English and that thereby facilitate modern performances.

Conclusion

In this chapter, I have focused on the analysis of the aural character of passages in John 1. I have shown that the phonological analysis outlined by Lee and Scott can indeed provide important information about how a biblical text sounded and how it guided the hearer with the help of sound effects and emphases. These are important features of the ancient performance of New Testament writings. Furthermore, I have argued that these insights about how the gospel sounded in the original language are highly relevant for translation, especially if we aim at a performance-oriented translation. The analysis of passages in John 1 has shown that such an undertaking would have to focus on the well-formed passages in particular. These passages often interrupt the flow of sound with a much clearer structure and emphasis, thus changing the soundscape.[40] If we aim at a performance-oriented translation, we should map this soundscape and contemplate how its effects could best be translated in a way natural to the host language.

We must also consider, however, if we want a translation *of* performance or a translation *for* performance. Although I have focused primarily on the aural features of the Greek text and shown its relevance for a translation *of* performance, I have also argued that a combination may be the best way ahead, at least when the aim is contemporary performances of biblical writings. My own translations have aimed at illustrating ways of achieving this and to a large extent have ignored other aspects (such as syntactic and semantic). A final translation will have to involve these other aspects. Further discussion on how to integrate sound and performance analyses in the wider field of Bible translation is truly needed. This study has shown that many features of performance criticism have much to offer in such a discussion.

Bibliography

Cicero. *Rhetorica ad Herennium*. Translated by Harry Caplan. Loeb Classical Library. Cambridge: Harvard University Press, 1954.
Cicero. *Brutus*. Translated by G. L. Hendrickson. Loeb Classical Library. Cambridge: Harvard University Press, 1962.
Dionysius of Halicarnassus. *Critical Essays*. Translated by Stephen Usher. 2 vols. Loeb Classical Library. Cambridge: Harvard University Press, 1939.

---

40. At the very least, they do this in the first chapter of John's gospel. Further research is needed to determine whether this is a distinct stylistic feature of John's gospel.

Kelber, Werner H. "The Oral-Scribal-Memorial Arts of Communication in Early Christianity." In *Jesus, the Voice, and the Text: Beyond "The Oral and Written Gospel,"* edited by Tom Thatcher, 235–62. Waco: Baylor University Press, 2008.

Lee, Margaret E., and Brandon. B. Scott. *Sound Mapping the New Testament*. Salem, OR: Polebridge, 2009.

Maxey, James A. *From Orality to Orality: A New Paradigm for Contextual Translation of the Bible*. Biblical Performance Criticism Series 2. Eugene, OR: Cascade Books, 2009.

Quintilian. *Institutio oratoria*. Translated by Donald A. Russell. 5 vols. Loeb Classical Library. Cambridge: Harvard University Press, 2001.

Rhoads, David. "Performance Criticism: An Emerging Methodology in Second Testament Studies—Part II." *Biblical Theology Bulletin* 36 (2006) 164–84.

Shiell, William David. *Reading Acts: The Lector and the Early Christian Audience*. Biblical Interpretation Series 70. Boston: Brill, 2004.

Shiner, Whitney. *Proclaiming the Gospel: First-Century Performance of Mark*. Harrisburg, PA: Trinity, 2003.

Wendland, Ernst R. "Duplicating the Dynamics of Oral Discourse in Print." *Notes on Translation* 7 (1993): 26–44.

———. "Oral-Aural Dynamics of the Word, with Special Reference to John 17." *Notes on Translation* 8 (1994) 19–43.

———. "Performance Criticism: Assumptions, Application, and Assessment." *T.I.C. Talk: Newsletter of the United Bible Societies Translation Information Clearinghouse* 65 (2008) 1–11.

4

Local Oral-Written Interfaces and the Nature, Transmission, Performance, and Translation of Biblical Texts

Lourens de Vries

VRIJE UNIVERSITEIT AMSTERDAM/UNITED BIBLE SOCIETIES

Introduction

RESEARCH OF THE PAST decades, in anthropological linguistics, classics, and biblical scholarship, resulted in a shift of perspective on orality and literacy, a shift away from the dichotomies of earlier research in the Lord-Parry tradition[1] and toward a perspective in which the complex interaction and interdependence of the oral and the written are emphasized.[2]

The first element in this new perspective was a shift away from a universal, dichotomous characterization of oral cultures versus literate cultures. The perspective shifted toward a range of different local oralities and literacies, with specific, nonuniversal, properties that emerge in unique

1. Lord, *Tales*.
2. Foley, *Anthropological Linguistics*, 417–34; Bakker, "Oral Composition"; Carr, *Tablet of the Heart*.

cultural contexts and historical conditions. In earlier universal dichotomies, as summarized and popularized by Ong,[3] oral cultures were characterized as additive-paratactic, formulaic, redundant, and context-bound. Oral modes of thinking were pictured as situational rather than abstract, aggregative rather than analytic, conservative or traditionalist, and participatory rather than objectively distanced. Such presumably universal properties of orality and oral cultures were then contrasted with the analytic, syntactically complex, abstract, decontextualized discourse and thought patterns of literate cultures.

These dichotomies of oral versus literate cultures were shown to be false by research in linguistics, anthropology, classics, and biblical scholarship. The cognitive effects of writing turned out to differ in crucial ways in different literate cultures,[4] and this supported the idea of different local "literacies." There are oral languages where subordinate structures dominate rather than the predicted predominance of parataxis, and there are oral cultures where formulaic-mnemonic styles (repetition, epithets, rhyme, rhythm, parallelism, stock phrases, chain words, proverbs, and the like) were markedly absent.[5] Highly abstract logic and codification of rules for logical reasoning may emerge in oral religious contexts to establish rules for doctrinal discussions and to detect doctrinal inconsistencies, as in the Buddhist schools of Tibet.[6]

The second element in the new perspective on orality and literacy is the effort to bring them back together again, to break down the almost impenetrable barriers earlier research in the Lord-Parry tradition had erected between the oral and the written, not just between societies but also within societies and within literatures.[7] Research by Biber showed convincingly, on the basis of large digitized corpora of spoken and written English, that the features that people associate with oral and written styles cannot be predicted on the basis of whether a text is spoken or written.[8] Notice that the implication of the research of Biber and others was that there is no basis even for the notion of a oral-written "continuum" or oral-written "spectrum," because such notions maintain a (softened) dichotomous view with

3. Ong, *Orality and Literacy*.
4. Scribner and Cole, *Psychology of Literacy*.
5. De Vries, *Primary Orality*; De Vries, "New Guinea Communities without Writing."
6. Foley, *Anthropological Linguistics*, 419.
7. Carr, *Tablet of the Heart*, 7.
8. Biber, *Variation*.

orality on one end and textuality on the other end of the "spectrum" or "continuum."

Written shopping lists are paratactic and highly concrete; spoken sermons can show abstractness and complex syntax associated with written styles. The oral and the written dimension are intimately connected, have many points of contact, and coevolve such that "societies with writing often have an intricate interplay of orality and textuality, where written texts are intensely oral, while even exclusively oral texts are deeply affected by written culture."[9] This interplay of written and oral dimensions is local in the sense that oral-written interfaces vary in time, place, context, and genre within communities.

The topic of my study concerns local oral-written interfaces in the context of literatures, bodies of long-duration texts that communities highly value and transmit from one generation to another, with each new generation performing these texts anew. Insights into these local oral-written interfaces in relation to literatures turns out to be highly relevant for the field of (Bible) translation studies since these local/written interfaces shaped both Hebrew, Aramaic, and Greek Scriptures and their translations in the languages of the world.

First, I will summarize findings by David Carr in his book *Writing on the Tablet of the Heart: Origins of Scripture and Literature*, a brilliant application of the new orality/literacy paradigm on biblical literatures that shows how local oral-written interfaces in ancient worlds help explain the origin, transmission, nature, and performance of Hebrew, Aramaic, and Greek Scriptures. Then I will look at oral-written interfaces in print and digital cultures where these Scriptures have found a place as translated Scriptures. Third, I will look at the oral-written interface in some primary oral cultures of New Guinea where the Scriptures are the first and often the only written text. Finally, I will look at Neo-Romantic efforts to re-create in modern translations the oral/aural quality of ancient Scriptures, especially the efforts by Buber and Rosenzweig in the German translation *Die Schrift* (1926–1938).

In order to be able to make cross-cultural comparisons, I will use the term "long-duration texts," following Carr, to refer to both oral and written texts that are transmitted from generation to generation within communities that value those texts from ancient times as basic texts, as reflections of culturally or religiously fundamental traditions. From the Gilgamesh epos

---

9. Carr, *Tablet of the Heart*, 7; see also Foley, *How to Read an Oral Poem*.

to Homer's Iliad, and from Israel's Scriptures to origin myths of Korowai Papuans: these are all long-duration texts that are transmitted and performed from generation to generation and that make up the "literatures" of these communities.

Oral-Written Interfaces in Antiquity

According to Carr, the focus in antiquity was on transmission of long-duration texts *from mind to mind* in a process of indoctrination, education, and enculturation of an elite minority of literati.[10] In Egypt, ancient Mesopotamia, and Israel such transmission occurred mostly in a context of fathers teaching sons, fathers who often were priests or royal scribes or otherwise politically, culturally, or religiously prominent figures.[11] Other boys might be taught together with their own sons, and the place of teaching might not be confined to the house of the father-teacher, but the basic model is a father teaching his son in his own house, not in schools in any modern sense.

Greek and Hellenistic transmission of long-duration texts was exceptional in antiquity in the sense that it did not take place primarily in the context of father and son but between a beloved older teacher and younger student, both elite citizens and often with intellectual-homoerotic elements;[12] later we see small-scale, private school-like environments in Greece. Transmission and performance of long-duration texts also took place after the symposium meal where guests would listen to recitation of ancient poetry in Greece and the Hellenistic world.[13]

But the primary mode of existence in all ancient cultures of these constantly evolving text traditions was in the minds and hearts. They were "written on the tablet of the heart,"[14] and the goal was to plant the values and ideals of the ancient texts in those hearts along with the words. "Thus, the minds stood at the centre of the often discussed oral-written interface."[15] Memorization, learning by heart, is therefore central to these traditions; and the oral performance from memory, recitation, is the proof

10. Carr, *Tablet of the Heart*, 6. This section on oral-written interfaces in antiquity is based entirely on Carr's work.
11. Ibid., 5.
12. Ibid., 101.
13. Ibid., 100–101.
14. Ibid, 127.
15. Ibid., 6.

Translating Scripture for Sound and Performance

of mastery of ancient traditions, setting the performer apart from those who have not ingested and internalized the tradition. To be literate does not so much mean knowing your letters and being able to write those letters and copy words or texts—any slave could be taught to perform those chores.[16] Rather, to be (fully) literate in antiquity means that someone has internalized ancient texts and therefore has the ability to recite them and, in the advanced stages of education, to add to the tradition by being able to use the phraseology, motifs, key terms, and style figures in their own speeches and writings. Finally, to be fully literate means finally to have absorbed the moral examples, virtues, and values associated with and communicated through those texts.[17]

Written copies of texts were not designed for instant reading off a page, certainly not for silent reading,[18] but rather "stood as a permanent reference point for an ongoing process of largely oral recitation."[19] This explains many aspects of ancient Bible manuscripts that are alien to print cultures, for example, the absence of word or sentence separation, leaving out vowels or sometimes giving only the first word of a verse in full, with just the first letter of each succeeding word of that verse and other forms of ancient "stenographics."[20] We can only understand these characteristics of Bible manuscripts if we place them in the context of a specific type of local oral-written interface. People orally performed texts they already knew, with the written copy, if it was at all present at the performance scene, functioning as "a musical score does for a musician who already knows the piece."[21]

Written manuscripts that represent words only partially, that do not separate words, and that use very few other visual helps in structuring the text to be read, assume either full memorization, with the written text as reference point in the performative background, or a hybrid of partial memorization and reading off the page. To read a text is a form of recognizing a

---

16. Ibid., 13.
17. Ibid., 19.
18. This does not mean silent reading was unknown; it was known but not the default way to perform a text. See Carr, *Tablet of the Heart*, 4; and Thomas, *Literacy*, 91–92, for the emergence of silent reading and more visually oriented reader-friendly teaching texts for use in early education in the Hellenistic period when literacy became more widespread.
19. Carr, *Tablet of the Heart*, 4.
20. Ibid., 5.
21. Ibid., 4.

known text; it is *anaginoskein* "to recognize anew" in the Greek tradition.[22] Only beginners were given texts with word separation as first exercises in reading and copying texts.[23] The Hebrew verb for reading *qara'* "to call" also reflects the oral-recitative dimension of this oral-written interface. The metaphors of writing on the tablet of the heart found in Greek, Egyptian, and Hebrew sources bring together writing, orality, and memory.[24] The oral, written, and memorization-enculturation dimensions formed an integrated whole, belonged together, and each aspect was valued for its specific contribution to the preservation, transmission, and performance of these literatures. This emphatically includes the written dimension and the reverence for the materiality of the written dimension.[25] The nineteenth and early twentieth-century German (Neo)Romantic conceptualizations of ancient Hebrew orality (e.g., Buber, see below), where the oral dimension is isolated from this oral-written-memorization whole and put on the throne as a kind of *Ur* dimension of these literatures, would not have been understood in antiquity.

Manuscripts that in their visual form assume this type of oral-written hybrid also occur in traditional cultures outside the world of biblical antiquity and have been well documented. The Makassarese of Sulawesi, for example, wrote their long-duration texts on leaves of the Lontar palm. These texts tell the history of six hundred years of one of the most prominent maritime powers of their region in manuscripts where the words not only have no spaces but where each syllable is represented only by the first consonant-vowel, deleting any consonant(s) that close the syllable.[26] No wonder Cumming writes that "only by knowing the subject of a sentence can it be read. According to some Makassarese, the written script only 'becomes' Makassarese when it is spoken aloud."[27] The ability to perform texts in societies with these hybrid oral-written interfaces is therefore always restricted to an elite or specialized minority who has the long-duration texts written on the tablets of their hearts, whether in Makassar or ancient Israel. The central memorization aspect of ancient oral-written interfaces explains a number of other important aspects of ancient literatures as well.

22. Ibid., 180.
23. Ibid., 180, citing Cribiore, *Writing Teachers*.
24. Ibid., 127.
25. Carr, *Tablet of the Heart*, 10.
26. Evans, *Dying Words*, 132.
27. Cummings, *Making Blood White*, xii.

First, there is the link with music, singing, and chanting, because they formed a crucial aid to memorization of these orally performed traditions. Teaching of the *grammata* was in ancient Greece closely associated with and sometimes subsumed under *mousike*.[28]

Second, are the function of *inclusio*, chiasmus, chain words, and other repetitive structures such as parallelism, stylistic features that are not so much oral residues in written texts of earlier purely oral traditions but rather mnemonic and performative aids in the written texts to memorize the text, to inscribe it more easily on the tablet of the heart, and to facilitate the oral performance of written texts by the mouth and lips in recitation. Written prose has these poetic properties to facilitate its memorization and oral recitation. Carr writes in relation to Greek oral-written interfaces: "poetic and formulaic elements often pointed to by the oral-traditional school might be characteristics of *written* Greek epic that evolved to support its *oral* transmission within early Greek society."[29]

Third, the use of acrostics is one of the means in written texts to facilitate memorizing the sequence of passages.[30]

Fourth, the nature of intertexuality in ancient literatures is shaped by this oral-written interface with inscription on the mind at the center. People were not so much looking up passages in written documents to "quote" them or consciously allude to them or interpret them; rather, scribes had ingested the phraseology, styles, idioms, stock phrases, and epithets from the traditions that formed the heart of the scribal curriculum. They were "trained from the outset to write by building on templates provided by earlier texts."[31] So it is dangerous to project onto ancient literatures the kind of intertextuality that we find in print societies,[32] where written texts relate to specific, numbered pages of other written texts via institutionalized quotation, exegesis, and allusion practices. Ancient intertextuality did not represent an exact, verbatim, and traceable relation between written texts; rather, intertextuality was a matter of semiverbatim echoes in the minds of trained scribes of memorized blocks of tradition, of templates, ancient idioms, and epithets. "Many Egyptian and Mesopotamian texts are a patchwork of

---

28. Carr, *Tablet of the Heart*, 94–96.
29. Ibid., 105.
30. Ibid., 73, 125.
31. Ibid., 159.
32. Ibid., 292–93.

distant and closer echoes of other texts, a product of an educational system where people learn to write new texts by internalizing ancient ones."[33]

Fifth, transmission took place in the hybrid of the oral-written interface, and copies of written texts were made in that hybrid of reproducing the text from memory and consulting written texts. The many insignificant variants that combine "semantic overlap with verbal variation"[34] (synonyms, variant word orders, absence of articles and conjunctions in one manuscript, presence of these small words in others, and so on) are consistent with hybrid oral-written transmission and have also been found in other parts of the world in similar oral-written interplay, for example, in mediaeval Europe.

These general features of oral-written interfaces in antiquity should not obscure the very real differences between the ancient traditions of Greece, Egypt, Israel, or Mesopotamia, or the differences over time within these traditions. For example, in pre-Hellenistic and Hellenistic Greek literatures there was an emphasis on the human authors (Homer, Euripides, and so on) absent in other parts of the world of antiquity.[35] For the Greeks, physical exercise and training in the gymnasia were very important alongside training of the mind by memorization of long-duration texts.[36] In Egypt's literacy curricula, wisdom instructions attributed to the great sages played a much more central role in teaching and enculturation than in the Sumero-Akkadian tradition. "The Sumero-Akkadian system did celebrate prediluvian sages, and wisdom literature played a crucial role in the transition from elementary to higher levels of education. Yet, the sages did not achieve the prominence in text, relief, and cult in Mesopotamia that they did in Egypt. In Egypt, wisdom instructions like Amenemhet and Kheti played the central role that sign, name, and lexical lists did in the Sumero-Akkadian system."[37] Of course, all of these traditions coevolved and influenced each other, with ancient Israel, given its geographical position, open for both Egyptian and Sumero-Akkadian influences and later for influences from various parts of the Eastern Hellenistic world.

The oral-written interface developed also within traditions when the political and social contexts changed. For example, in Carr's thinking,

33. Ibid., 159.
34. Ibid., 280.
35. Ibid., 185.
36. Ibid., 191.
37. Ibid., 83.

Hellenistic literacy and orality practices and their interface were crucial to the formation of the emergent Hebrew Scriptures during the second century BCE, not so much in copying Greek models but as a Hellenistic-style, anti-Hellenistic literacy curriculum.[38] With a term from postcolonial studies Carr calls this phenomenon "hybridization."[39] When a community is engaged in political or cultural resistance to a dominant community, it tends to fight the dominant group on its own terms, thereby adopting elements from the same dominant community that the resistance is aimed at. For example, in the Hellenistic world the notion of a transethnic, transnational Greek identity had evolved that allowed ethnically non-Greek persons to become Greek in a cultural sense, the sense of *politeia*, a way of life; the more a non-Greek person had been immersed in the Greek literacy education, the more that person became "Greek."[40] This implied that the person had progressed beyond the mere Greek alphabet into advanced stages of memorizing parts of the Greek textual curriculum. And memorization implied much more than just cognitive internalisation, it meant enculturation with the values and ideals of the ancient Greek texts. Cohen shows how in the Hasmonean period the idea of a transethnic Jewish identity emerged, in opposition to a transethnic Greek identity, yet in a Greek way of identity construction, in Greek terms.[41] Just as becoming Greek meant ingesting a collection of ancient Greek texts, becoming a Jew meant ingesting an increasingly, sharply defined and proto-canonical body of purportedly pre-Hellenistic Hebrew texts.

The early Christians inherited the broad pattern of oral-written processes of education-enculturation and cognitive mastery of a communal tradition, and of the Hellenistic innovation of transethnic and transnational identity just like everyone in the first century, but they placed their own accents.[42] Like their rabbinic counterparts, they memorized Jewish Scriptures, but predominantly in their Greek form. More important, they related to Jewish Scriptures in Greek in a specific way, understanding them as witnessing to a christological reality.[43] The holiness of the memorized traditions resided precisely in their prefiguration of Christ, not primarily

38. Ibid., 253.
39. Ibid., 260, citing Cohen, *Beginnings of Jewishness*, 132–35.
40. Carr, *Tablet of the Heart*, 260.
41. Cohen, *Beginnings of Jewishness*.
42. Carr, *Tablet of the Heart*, 279–85.
43. Ibid., 279.

in the written, Hebrew language form of the scrolls. Moreover, the focus on Greek Scriptures meant a broader range of Scriptures that witnessed to Christ, including texts like the Wisdom of Solomon. Christians used Greek codices in largely oral-liturgical contexts, with "a relative flexibility vis-à-vis the Jewish written tradition."[44]

To become a Christian meant adopting a transethnic and transnational identity that resided in instruction in and memorization of new narrative and gnomic traditions relating to Christ.[45] Carr sees in the variants between versions of Q sayings in Matthew and Luke evidence of the dynamics of gnomic sayings as they functioned in an "intensely oral-written context." They show the type of variants we expect in oral-written transmission of long-duration texts, with inscribing in the hearts as the central aim, namely, verbatim overlap alongside synonyms, variant word orders, and many small, insignificant variants.[46]

Jews and Christians alike inherited two cultural models of education and textuality, the model of the Mesopotamian (and Egyptian) world on the one hand and the model of the Hellenistic world on the other. The Mesopotamian model was the father-son model associated with the home, a small-scale private environment in which the father taught the son first the sign, letters, then very short texts, whether alphabetic name or word list or short sayings or proverbs, and finally inscribed major chunks of ancient textual heritage on the tablet of his sons' hearts, thus indoctrinating them and setting them apart from uneducated masses. The second cultural model was specifically Hellenistic, namely in a context not of fathers and sons but of adults in brotherhoods or associations having their symposium meals.[47]

But although Jews and early Christians inherited those two models of oral-written interfaces, the diverging traditions of rabbinic Judaism and early Christianity placed different accents. The Christians were more Greek in emphasizing the adult education and enculturation connected with symposium meal, in the form of Eucharist, with a ritual function for the recitation of the texts.[48] Rabbinic Jews, on the other hand, continued the model of father-son instruction, leading to a small, private school-like model; by ingesting Jewish Scriptures, the boy was prepared to enter the adult

---

44. Ibid., 279.
45. Robinson, "Logoi Sophon"; Kloppenborg, *Formation of Q*.
46. Carr, *Tablet of the Heart*, 280.
47. Ibid., 284.
48. Ibid.

community in a role similar to that of his father-teacher. Early Christians will also have used the father-son model in instructing new converts, for example, in memorizing gnomic saying and narrative traditions, but they placed a strong emphasis at the same time on "the incorporation of adult coverts into a sacral meal-like fellowship led by a minority of masters of the oral-written Jewish (and early Christian) heritage."[49]

To summarize Carr's main features of ancient oral-written interfaces in relation to their literatures:

a. Memorization is the core of the oral-written interface: written literatures primarily exist in the minds of an educated elite; the primary performance mode is oral-recitative.

b. Memorization is not aimed at cognitive mastery per se but functions in an indoctrination/enculturation context: it makes morally and intellectually different people, different from most others in the community who had not undergone such a formative process of "writing on the tablet of the heart."

c. Written literatures were styled to facilitate memorization and oral recitation (*inclusio*, acrostics, parallelism, epithets, rhyme, rhythm, "poetic prose").

d. The visual design of written manuscripts *scriptio continua*, of writing just parts of words, and of the absence of visual structuring aids is consistent with its background function as a stable reference point of texts known by heart and orally performed from memory.

e. Many small, insignificant variants and verbal variation amid semantic overlap is typical for semiverbatim performance and semiverbatim transmission in hybrid oral-written interfaces with copying (partly) from memory.

f. Quotation is normally from memory, without consulting written sources, semiverbatim, and part of wider intertextuality shaped by template reproduction and echoing as part of learning how to write, in the sense of adding to the tradition by first internalizing its phraseology, set phrases, idioms, motifs, and then the reuse of it in the own writing process, often actualizing or adapting the "quoted" text to the needs of the present context.

---

49. Ibid.

The christological centrality of the Word in the flesh and the concomitant emphasis on the Spirit of Christ rather than Hebrew or Greek letters of a scroll or codex helps us to understand the willingness and motivation to translate Scriptures in the languages of the early Christians.[50] Above all, they wanted to proclaim Christ to everyone. The same flexibility toward issues of language, text form, and letter explains how translations of Christian Scriptures were adapted to new and very different oral-written configurations in later times, to which we now turn.

The Oral-Written Interface in Print Cultures

The invention of printing by Gutenberg in 1440 changed the world in a dramatic way. By 1500, printing presses were all over Europe, and an estimated 20 million volumes had been distributed. Erasmus and Luther's books were distributed by the hundreds of thousands during their lifetime. Written texts entered the lives of very many individuals, and they increasingly read those books individually, in the privacy of their homes. Mass production of the translated Bible created individual reading of the Scriptures from a private copy. Memorization of long-duration texts became an exception, and the primary mode of existence of long-duration texts ceased to be in the hearts and minds.

Compare this to oral-written interface of antiquity where scribes or other literati had memorized texts, recited texts much like a musician plays a piece of Bach, basically from the heart but with the written text functioning as score, as a kind of backup and point of reference. Without a thorough preexisting knowledge of the text, no one could read them out, and indeed the "stenographic" visual form of ancient long-duration texts betrays this specific oral-written interface.

In sharp contrast with this, early modern mass-produced Bible translations of Europe show an explosion of visual elements in the text. A whole new paratextual layer becomes an essential part of Bible translations. All these paratextual features were designed to enable individual readers to pick up the written text and start reading it, just to read it off the page, in private or in church, without the aid of the memorized text stored in the brain, without previous knowledge or familiarity with the text prior to reading it.

---

50. Ibid., 279.

Full literacy in antiquity always was very restricted because ancient societies did not see the point of teaching full literacy to people who never used it in their daily lives and labors, and full literacy distinguished ruling groups from others.[51] By contrast, in early modern print cultures, literacy spreads to middle and even lower classes.

In fact, we see the emergence of a mass reading culture in early modern Europe as the context for the performance of its long-duration texts, a reading culture that had never existed before. Ancient cultures were not reading cultures but memorization-recitation cultures in relation to their literatures. If the ancients had seen such reading, they would have been totally astonished. A lovely example is a page of the *Statenvertaling*, a seventeenth-century Dutch translation full of visual elements to facilitate individual reading of the Holy Scriptures (Figure 4.1):

Figure 4.1: Isaiah 52 in the *Statenvertaling* of 1637, first edition by Van Ravensteyn

51. Ibid.,120.

We see word spacing, indentation, pericopes with titles, chapters, verses, cross references to other texts in Scriptures, annotations and explanations, a massive amount of visual aids to help people read and interpret the written text, silently, instantly, and individually transforming written signs into meaning. In print cultures, books refer to other books, quote them verbatim, precisely mentioning page numbers of the quotation. This creates a very different type of intertextuality, directly connecting one written, printed text to another without mediation of the mind. This is very different from intertextuality in antiquity when people typically inserted memorized bits of long-duration texts in their own speeches and recitations, often adapted to the new contexts, without consulting scrolls or codices, without juggling tablets. Instruction about the printed Bible increasingly also came in the form of other printed books; individuals started to read books about the Book of Books.

The pages of the *Statenvertaling* already show an intense linking system, enabled by printing techniques, where verses of Scripture are linked precisely and exactly to other verses in different books and to theological reflections in the marginal notes. This linking aspect accelerated dramatically in the twenty-first century when the printed Bible moved to digital environments that enabled the Bible translations to be hyperlinked to other places in the same Bible translation, to audiovisual performances of the same texts, to commentaries, glossaries, devotional texts, to other Bible translations, and to editions of the Hebrew, Aramaic, and Greek source texts.

All this amounts to a massive shift away from the primary mode of existence of long-duration texts in the hearts of educated people to a primary mode of existence in the materiality of printed study or the computer screen. The performative conditions changed radically, and the oral-written interface changed with it. Long-duration texts such as the Bible were still heard, were still listened to, still existed in the oral-aural mode, but only in total dependence on the printed or digital Bible where the mouth of the preacher in church transforms the letters on the printed page or screen into sound.

To summarize the oral-written interface of print-digital cultures:
a. The primary mode of existence of long-duration texts is not in the mind but in the printed page or screen; memorization of these texts became a marginal phenomenon, with the significant exception of

traditional Jewish communities where an emphasis on memorization and recitation remained in relation to the Hebrew Bible.

b. Intertextuality developed from a patchwork of memorized, recycled, and semiverbatim echoes of authoritative texts in antiquity to a conscious literary and exegetical technique that created intense webs of links within and between printed texts, with verbatim quotation and precise cross-references to the quoted sources.

c. In digital environments, intertextual linking is taken to a whole new level, and multiple texts become parallel on screen, linked also to pictures and spoken versions of long-duration texts.

d. Intense visual, paratextual manipulation emerges in printed long-duration texts designed to enable instant silent or public reading without memorized, advanced knowledge of the text to be read but also designed to create meaning by internal and external linking of the text.

e. Performance is strictly verbatim; it is not acceptable that readers would vary their wording every time they "performed" the long-duration text by reading it to audiences.

f. Narrative literature emerging after the invention of print loses the "poetic prose" character typical of oral-written interfaces of communities with writing but without print.

g. The stylistic features of texts of antiquity designed to assist in memorizing and reciting the written text (chain words, parallelism, epithets, stock phrases, chiasmus, acrostics and so on) vanish from prose texts, and when these style features are perceived by print culture readers in Bible texts, they are merely seen either as literary and aesthetic features, as embellishment, or as residual features of an *Ur* oral phase.

The Oral-Written Interface in Some Primary Oral Societies of New Guinea

Missionaries from print cultures translated the Bible also for primary oral communities, that is, communities that did not know writing prior to missionization. In order for such Bibles to be usable, literacy programs were devised, and primary oral people were taught how to read and write. It is fascinating to see what happens when the Bible enters yet another world in terms of oral-written interfaces.

How do primary oral cultures deal with long-duration texts prior to the introduction of writing, and how do they deal with the Bible once they have their own translation of the Holy Scriptures? We know relatively little about primary oral cultures because empirical research in purely oral cultures is scarce, and because academic writing about primary oral cultures has been strongly distorted by preexisting false dichotomies and stereotyped ideas on the differences between oral cultures and literate cultures.[52] I had the privilege to live in a primary oral world, the world of the Korowai and Kombai Papuans in the early 1980s and to observe the performative conditions of their oral long-duration texts.[53] Three elements are important:

First, Rumsey and De Vries[54] argued that the distinction between saying something and meaning something is (or was) not made in many oral languages of New Guinea and Australia. One of the consequences of the absence of the distinction between the words produced and the intention behind those words, is that the distinction between direct speech, as a representation of someone's "own words," and indirect speech, as the representation of someone's intention without the pretention that someone is quoted verbatim, is absent in these oral communities. Consider this Kombai example:

(1) *Luwano*   *kho* *mofena*   *yafe.rambo-neno*
     they.said   man that   good.very-QUOTE.PL
     "They praised that man."
     (lit. they said, "That man is very good.")

The reporting Kombai speaker of example (1) does not claim that the words *kho mofena yaferambo* "that man is very good" have been uttered by the reported speakers. He just reports that they have praised that man. Reported speech in Kombai has the *form* of a direct quote, but the quoted words always function as the portrayal of the *intention* of the reported speakers. All speech-act verbs in Kombai require direct speech constructions. Speech acts are actions that require speech in order to be performed. *To promise* is a speech-act verb, *to kill* is not. Consider (1) a reported praise, and (2) a reported promise, both with obligatory direct speech constructions:

---

52. De Vries, "New Guinea Communities without Writing."
53. Van Enk and de Vries, *Korowai of Irian Jaya*; de Vries, *Kombai Language*.
54. Rumsey, "Wording"; de Vries, "New Guinea Communities without Writing."

(2) *Nu wamedefe-ne luwa*
    I come.1SG.FUTURE-QUOTE.SG say.3SG.NON-FUTURE
    "He promised to come."
    (lit. "I will come," he said.)

Since the distinction between wording and intention is not made, reported speech acts always ascribe words to people without claiming that those people uttered those very words occurring in the direct speech constructions. This also happens on a massive scale in Bible translations of New Guinea languages.[55]

Another consequence of the intentionality character is that in the transmission of oral stories, magic formulas, and so on, the intention is transmitted and not the precise wording. Instead of fixed, formulaic wording, we find highly variable wording, something also observed by Goody for other oral cultures.[56] Intentions are transmitted and not the wording of those intentions. In magic formulas it is the names of ancestors and spirits that count, secret names that are very much taboo; these names form the invariable and verbatim, transmitted core of otherwise variable magic spells and chants. In other words, these primary oral cultures seem to be intention-based in their transmission of long-duration texts in the sense that they reproduce meanings and intentions of their long-duration texts rather than the wording. In addition to that, in the absence of a written reference point, there is no emphasis on or concern with the verbatim or semiverbatim repetition of the long-duration text. The long-duration texts exist as meaning and intention in the minds of the tradents of the community.

What this means is that the formulaic, repetitive, musical, rhythmic style with parallelisms, chiasms, rhyme, meter, epithets, proverbs, and so on is *not* characteristic of primary orality, at least as I saw it in operation in New Guinea. This is understandable when a community focuses on the intentions and meanings behind their long-duration texts, does not emphasize the distinction between wording and intention, and has no religious or cultural motivation to transmit the wording of these texts from one generation to the next. Rather, mnemonic-musical-repetitive styles are typical for communities without printing techniques and mass reading cultures and with an oral-written interface with memorization in the center,

---

55. See de Vries, "Quotative Constructions."
56. Goody, *Interface*, 86–105.

communities that are aware of the wording of a text as a separate dimension that needs to be preserved, memorized, recited, and transmitted.

The second characteristic of primary oral performance of long-duration texts in (parts of) New Guinea is (or was) that long-duration texts, such as origin myths, cannot be performed or listened to by just anyone; there are secrecy distinctions in terms of clan, gender, and age. The contents of long-duration texts often have numinous power, and they are connected to notion of origin, identity, and the fear that long-duration texts lose their power if just anyone can listen to them. The style is deliberately vague, and there is indirection, lexical substitution, and so-called ritual languages to prevent secret knowledge and power to leak from the texts.[57]

Third, performance of these primary oral long-duration texts tends to be in one long session rather than by cutting the texts into short sections that are performed separately on separate occasions.

Fourth, intertextuality takes the form of seamless absorption and integration of themes, plots, motifs, and characters of other clans or groups into the own long-duration texts.

Fifth, performance of long-duration texts is always communal, never individual.

When missionary Bible translators translated the Bible in these primary oral conditions, their approaches were shaped by the print cultures they came from, and this includes the perceptions they had of primary orality. Basically, two types of approach were followed:

The first type of approach tried to create a reading culture of the kind they were familiar with in their home countries, reading cultures that emerged in print communities. Literacy programs were organized that were designed to enable people from these primary oral communities to take the printed and translated Scriptures home and read it, individually. But reading cultures cannot be created by literacy programs; they grow under certain conditions, conditions by and large absent in these minority language communities in the interior of New Guinea or elsewhere.

When literacy programs did not have the desired results, the second approach was tried that explained the failure of creating a reading culture in terms of the dichotomy of oral cultures versus literate cultures discussed in the introduction section. Oral cultures were thought to be paratactic, formulaic, concrete, context-bound, prelogic, repetitive, and so on, in

---

57. De Vries, *Genre*.

contrast to literate cultures with abstract, syntactically complex and decontextualized discourse forms, not formulaic-repetitive, and so on.

From the perspective of such dichotomous, juxtaposed views of orality and literacy, it is obvious that the first approach had to fail because it did not take the oral nature of the receptor cultures into account. The solution is then to either "oralize" the style and format of the written Bible translations (making them repetitive-formulaic, avoiding abstractness and syntactic integration, making them paratactic, and so on) or to make sound recordings and films and produce audio-visual Bible translations that people can listen to and watch.

But young churches in minority communities, however pleased with the audiovisual formats, at some point also want a printed, written Bible, as the basis for the life of the indigenous church, at least in my admittedly limited experience in Indonesia. And "oralizing" a written Bible by copying the styles of oral traditional texts in the Bible translation does not work[58] because the underlying dichotomous assumption is false. Bible translations in primary oral communities are a new genre of texts that develop their own stylistic features, which do not correspond to the properties that people with dichotomous views ascribe to oral styles.[59] It does not work to copy properties of specific oral genres in a particular oral culture, for example, copying style properties of oral origin myths into written translations of Genesis, because the cultural and institutional setting and function of oral origin myths is very different from the function of a Genesis translation in a young church in a primary oral community. Genres, with their style features, emerge in specific cultural and institutional environments; and Bible translations are a genre that expresses new institutional contexts of church and Christianity.[60]

---

58 De Vries, *Genre*; Renck, *Contextualization*, 87.

59. De Vries, "The Notion of Genre."

60. See ibid. for a detailed discussion of the stylistic and performative differences between oral origin myths of certain Papuan groups and Genesis translations in Papuan languages, for example, oral origin myths are styled for secrecy, indirection, and vagueness because they are owned by clans and their contents cannot be shared outside the circle of the adult males of the clan lest the myths lose their power. The performative differences are also crucial. Origin myths are performed by adult males of the clan when disastrous or shocking events have happened (e.g., earthquakes, droughts) to restore the cosmos, in all-night sessions. The Genesis text is read in church, in short sessions, in the presence of women and children, and not with the purpose of going back from threatening chaos to cosmic order by performing the Genesis text.

The only real solution is to adjust the Bible translation to the specific local-oral written interfaces that emerge when a primary oral culture becomes (partly) integrated in the course of the years in the wider nation-state and (partly) participates in the literacy practices that come with its institutions of school, shops, government and so on. This creates a small minority of indigenous literati that were exposed to education in the print-dominated environment of the national or majority culture. These literati read out translated Bible texts to listening communities in a liturgical setting, just as they read out and translate government announcements or price lists at shops. In other words, integration in and contact with nation-states creates its own local oral-written interfaces; and translation projects should be designed to function in those specific contexts.

In such contexts, priority should be given to the translation of a *lectionarium* with passages and texts that play a key role in the life of the young churches. Preachers and teachers should practice reading out the *lectionarium* very often, so often that they read the text aloud fluently, based on a strong pretextual knowledge, just as in antiquity; they should know already what they are going to read out. Likewise, the audience should hear the same passages and texts from the *lectionarium* as often as possible. In New Guinea audiences readily and spontaneously pick up passages from translated Scriptures that they then chant and turn into songs, with texts close to the intentions and meanings of the passages read out to them. In that way they memorize and internalize the meanings and intentions of the biblical texts. In later stages, the young churches can expand the *lectionarium* to include other parts of the Bible. Most of these primary oral cultures will sooner or later be integrated into the print cultures of the nation-states where they live, with the concomitant changes in local oral-written interfaces. Bible translation projects should follow and adapt to these changing oral-written interfaces.

Romantically Reclaiming Lost Orality in Modern Print Cultures

Traditional Jewish communities, although now living in print cultures with a very different oral-written interface, always kept elements of the memorization and oral recitation tradition alive in relation to the Hebrew Bible, in personal and communal study of Scripture and in the liturgy. As we saw above, the oral-written interface of antiquity in which this Jewish tradition of memorization and oral recitation has its roots was by no means a specific Israelite element that set Israelite culture or religion apart. On the contrary, "the tablet of the heart" paradigm was all over the worlds of antiquity. But since it persisted in traditional Jewish communities in modern times, the oral-recitative performance tradition (*Miqra*) of Jewish communities started to contrast with Christian interaction with Scriptures as Holy Writ, where memorization and oral recitation lost their central role after the invention of printing.

When the Jewish philosophers Buber and Rosenzweig started their German translation of the Hebrew Bible, *Die Schrift*, in 1926, this oral-aural dimension became a cornerstone of their philosophy and practice of a distinctively Jewish Bible translation that functioned in opposition to the dominant Lutheran Bible translation tradition. Since Buber and Rosenzweig were very influential, both in Bible translation and in theology and philosophy, it is worthwhile paying some attention to their translation views and practices.[61]

Buber and Rosenzweig saw the oral-aural element, *Gesprochenheit* "spokenness," as *die eigentliche Wirklichkeit der Bibel* "the true reality of the Bible."[62] Their central concern is to capture this "spokenness" in their German translation. But this *Gesprochenheit* is something rather different from the oral-aural element that modern scholarship describes as part of the oral-written interfaces of antiquity, including the oral-written interface in which Hebrew Scriptures originated and functioned. Three elements set Buber and Rosenzweig's *Gesprochenheit* apart as typical nineteenth- and early twentieth-century concepts that have little to do with oral-written interfaces of antiquity as described by Carr and others.

First of all, in antiquity, memorization is the core of the oral-written interface. This is memorization broadly understood as "writing on the tablet of the heart," with its associations of small elite groups internalizing and ingesting authoritative traditions including its norms and values, which set them apart from the others who were not so privileged. The ability to recite the traditional texts, the oral performance, is the external manifestation, on the lips, of what is written on the heart. Buber and Rosenzweig focus almost exclusively on the oral dimension, the lips, and seem to cut it loose from

---

61. Clear proof of their continued impact is a very popular Dutch Bible translation, the *Naardense Bijbel,* which was published in 2004. This translation explicitly follows basic principles of Buber and Rosenzweig. In French and English, this tradition was continued by Bible translators such as Chouraqi and Everett Fox.

62. Buber, *Werke*, 1114–15.

its anchor in antiquity, the memorization/enculturation aspect, namely, the heart.

Second, Buber and Rosenzweig conceptualize orality as opposed to and totally separate from the written dimension, with the written form a kind of prison from which to liberate the real spoken word trapped in it. This juxtaposing of orality and literacy was typical for nineteenth- and early twentieth-century thinking and reflects the older paradigm of orality-literacy studies (see the introduction to his volume on the paradigm shift) but alien to the reality of interplay and intimate connectedness of oral and written dimensions in antiquity.

Third, the Buber and Rosenzweig notion of *Gesprochenheit* or "spokenness" of Scripture is filled with theological and philosophical meanings that have their origin in late eighteenth- and nineteenth-century Romantic Germany and have very little to do with the place of the oral dimension in the oral-written interfaces of antiquity. The following German Romantic themes dominated in the Neo-Romantic philosophy and theology of Buber and Rosenzweig, themes that informed and shaped their notion of *Gesprochenheit*:

a. The notion of *Einheit* "unity":[63] for example, unity of form and meaning, unity of the spirit of a people and its language, unity of tradition and canon in the unity of Scripture, in the sense of a hidden *Ur-Midrasch* in Hebrew Scripture,[64] hidden in intertextual links such as recurring roots.

b. A dialogic hermeneutics in which meaning is born in interpersonal encounters.

c. The notion of *Sprachgeist*: "the spirit of a language."[65]

d. The focus on roots and origins, the diachronic, etymologizing and evolutionary dimension to find *Ur* phases, *Ur* meanings and *Ur* realities (e.g., conceptualizing the oral dimension as the *Ur* dimension).

These Romantic themes were absorbed by Buber and Rosenzweig in their formative years[66] and formed their primary, very German and Neo-

---

63. See Schravesande, *Jichud*, for the pervasive role of the *Einheit* theme in Buber's thinking, at all levels.

64. Buber, *Werke*, 1186; see Benjamin, *Tacit Agenda*, 264, for theological agendas packaged in "literary" approaches to Scriptural intertextuality.

65. See Reichert, "It Is Time," 174.

66. See Askani, *Problem*; Schmidt, *Martin Buber's Formative Years*.

Romantic idiom that they employed to reflect on Jewish identity, on the distinctive nature of the Hebrew Bible, and on a distinctive "Jewish" translation of the Bible. The German Romantic theme of *Einheit* was taken up by Buber in his notion of *jichud* ("unification/becoming one"), with its foundation in the ultimate monotheistic unity of the One Master of the Universe.[67] In the notion of a hidden and unifying *Ur-Midrasch* in Scripture, traceable by following the clues of word and root repetition, and linked to notions of unity of form and meaning, of language and "spirit," of *Gesprochenheit* and of etymologizing *Ur* meanings of both Hebrew and German words, Buber and Rosenzweig gave a traditional, postbiblical, rabbinic hermeneutic a strong Neo-Romantic twist.

The notion of *Einheit* occurred very prominently in nineteenth-century Germany, not only in German mysticism but also in German linguistic ideologies. Foley defines linguistic ideology as "that cluster of beliefs that a particular speech community holds about the form and function of language."[68] These ideological beliefs do not form theories of language per se "but rather the background of largely unexamined assumptions that guide the construction of specific theories, be they folk theories or scientific ones." As an influential example of such a linguistic ideology, Foley mentions the emergence of ideas about language in the context of German Romanticism and nationalism of the eighteenth and nineteenth centuries. "These beliefs were clearly articulated by the German Romantic philosopher Herder, who argued for an essential correlation between the language of a community and their mind or spirit (German *Geist*). This was part of a wider German nationalist project of the eighteenth and nineteenth centuries, to forge a unified German nation-state from numerous principalities and kingdoms of central Europe that were German-speaking and this led to a triple equation: the culture of a people is essentially correlated with the language they speak and in turn should ideally correspond to a nation-state."[69]

Every people or *Volk*, homogeneously and "purely" construed, had its own distinctive *Geist*, a spirit expressed in and reflected by their language or *Sprache*. The German *Volk* had a German *Geist*, obviously, and its very own *Sprachgeist*. The almost mystical *Einheit* or unity between *Geist* and *Sprache* became such a widespread and popular Romantic assumption that it surfaces in many places, for example in Romantic thinking on translation

---

67. Schravesande, *Jichud*, 235.
68. Foley, "Personhood," 157.
69. Ibid.

(for example, Schleiermacher). Translation, if it really wanted to capture the *Geist* of another language, was highly problematic in this climate; but some form of translational transfer was possible if one was prepared to insert *fremdes Sprachgeist* ("alien language-spirit") into the receptor language by imposing the spirit of the foreign language as expressed in its grammatical and lexical patterns on the receptor language.[70]

Buber and Rosenzweig connected these Romantic ideas on *Einheit* between *Sprache* and *Geist* to theological ideas on the *Einheit* of tradition and canon. They believed that the Hebrew Bible was a unity, one Book, not many books, as a result of an *Einheitsbewusstsein* ("awareness of unity")[71] or *bibelstiftende Bewusstsein* ("Bible creating awareness")[72] already operative in Scripture itself before it was canonized.[73]

It is against this background that the notion of *Gesprochenheit* or oral-aural spoken *Urwort* dimension of Buber and Rosenzweig must be understood. The ultimate reality of the Hebrew Bible does not reside in written form; rather, the written form is the prison from which the spoken *Ur*-reality must be freed. This liberation takes place when people start to listen (literally) to the Voice that breathes and speaks in the fundamentally oral Hebrew Bible. That is why colometric structuring of the texts is so crucial. Buber and Rosenzweig divided the Hebrew text in cola or breath units, units that could be spoken in one *Atemzug* or breath, units that they saw as breath units and meaning units at the same time.[74]

This fragmentation of the translated text into small breath units is no threat to the underlying Voice or unitary *Botschaft* (message), because the *Einheitsbewusstsein* ("awareness of unity") operative in Scripture creates an intertextual web of audible linkages between these breath units, by repetition of words and of roots, not just within one literary unit (say a psalm or a book) but also across the whole canon, in all directions—from earlier books to later ones and back.[75] These *Leitworte* or repeated leading words

---

70. See Reichert, "It Is Time," for the role of the Romantic notion of *Sprachgeist* in Rosenzweig's approach to translation.

71. Buber, *Werke*, 1113.

72. Ibid., 1186.

73. Schravesande, *Jichud*, 262–63.

74. Buber, *Werke*, 1176–77. Colometric structuring is a distinctive characteristic of all translations in the tradition of Buber and Rosenzweig, e.g., in the United States (Everett Fox), France (Chouraqi), the Netherlands (Oussoren, Waaijman, Ooosterhuis, and Van Opheusden). However, not all translations use pause, breath, and musical criteria as indicated by the Masoretes; instead, syntactic criteria are used to find the cola.

75. Ibid., 1177.

and roots (root concordance) are a dialogic encounter within Scriptures themselves: words in totally different books encounter each other and in doing so create meaning. The listener, in turn, hears the repetitions, ponders on their links, and by doing so becomes partner in and is drawn into the inner scriptural dialogue. He or she then listens to the Voice, the underlying unity in the Hebrew Bible, in a real encounter based on listening to the Word that speaks (both listening and speaking in a nonmetaphorical sense).

The missionary task that Buber and Rosenzweig set for themselves was to capture something of this Neo-Romantically and theologically constructed *Gesprochenheit* in the German translation, in the hope that the Voice would speak to their contemporaries, both Jewish and non-Jewish. The result was a fascinatingly Neo-Romantic translation of the Hebrew Bible, full of *fremdes Sprachgeist* and exemplifying an almost perfect illustration of a basic law of translation, whether foreignizing or naturalizing, namely, that translation cannot escape from what Venuti calls "domestic inscription."[76] Both naturalizing or exoticizing translations are doomed to naturalize or exoticize in domestic terms, in terms of domestic ideologies and expectations, in ways conditioned by the receptor context. Therefore, Buber and Rosenzweig could not escape from exoticizing their Bible in a deeply German way—in this case in ways shaped by the ideologies of Neo-Romantic Germany.

To illustrate some of these points, consider the translation from 1 Kings 12:1 in *Die Schrift*:

> Rechabam ging nach Sichem,
> denn nach Sichem war alles Jissrael gekommen,
> ihn zu königen.

The German verb *königen* that translates the Hifil infinitive הַמְלִיךְ does not exist; it is a neologism. Buber and Rosenzweig created it especially to insert a Hebraic *fremdes Sprachgeist* "foreign language-spirit" into the German translation and to reflect an audible link within the Hebrew Bible, namely, the Hebrew *m-l-k* root consonants that original audiences could hear not only in this infinitive but also in all other words with the same root consonants, for example in the nouns מֶלֶךְ ("king") and מַמְלָכָה ("kingdom") that the listeners had just heard in the preceding passage in chapter 11. The notion of kinghood was one of the major interpretive keys to the Hebrew

---

76. Venuti, *Translation*, 469.

Bible in Buber's views.[77] It is by listening to such audible word and root consonant links, a form of *Gesprochenheit*, that people may encounter the Voice and the *Botschaft* transmitted in these webs of links. However, this is a *Botschaft* that, in true Schleiermacherian fashion, is inseparable from the audible interplay of the words in Scripture; that is, the *Botschaft* "message" defies formulation independent of the intertextual inner scriptural dialogue. Luther uses an existing German verbal expression here: *um ihn zum König zu machen* ("in order to make him king") that, by the way, also creates an audible link to the references to kings and kingship in the preceding chapter.

Buber and Rosenzweig may have tried to capture in their German translation what they saw as the fundamental oral-aural dimension of Scripture, understood in terms of German Neo-Romantic notions. But what about their German audiences and the audiences of modern daughter translations of *Die Schrift*, such as the Dutch *Naardense Bijbel*? These translations came from print and digital cultures; and the way they interact with these translations is shaped by print cultures. Are their ears tuned to listen to these audible intertextual links, and are they hermeneutically equipped to derive significance from such audible links, especially across the boundaries of books or even Testaments? Users of these translations depend on pastors and theologians to point out the intertextual links of recurrent roots and to interpret them as pointers to an underlying unitary message. But such a theological or clerical mediation would be a problem within the views of Buber and Rosenzweig. Their ideal was that people would directly listen to the Voice, without distorting theological mediation, based on the idea that Scripture, once translated in such a way that its *Gesprochenheit* remained intact, would talk to the listener who heard the intertextual links, the inner scriptural dialogue, and would become a dialogue partner in that direct encounter with the Voice. In fact, Buber and Rosenzweig come close in this respect to (some) Protestant hermeneutics of Scripture as essentially self-explanatory, as a unitary whole that reveals itself to the reader who compares the parts and reads one book of Scripture in the light of another.

---

77. Schravesande, *Jichud*, 266.

Conclusion

When we compare the oral-written interfaces of antiquity, of some well-studied oral communities of New Guinea, and of print cultures in relation to their long-duration texts, we see these tendencies and characteristics:

Print Cultures	Antiquity	Primary Orality
strictly verbatim performance	semiverbatim performance	nonverbatim performance
silent and individual reading	silent and individual reading rare	only communal performance
verbatim nonadaptive quotation	semiverbatim adaptive quotation	nonverbatim integrative "quotation"
no emphasis on mnemonic poetic prose	mnemonic poetic prose	no emphasis on poetic prose
long-duration texts primarily exist in written, printed form	long-duration texts primarily exist in mind of literati as form (wording) and meaning	long-duration texts primarily exist as intention in memory
verbatim transmission	many, mostly insignificant variants typical of memory-writing hybrid	very significant variation, adaptive transmission
written form full of intense visual paratextual manipulation	"stenographic" manuscripts; *scriptio continua*, visually poor	no manuscripts; oral-aural paratext
majority can perform (read) long-duration texts	minority, performance from memory written text in background	secrecy restrictions on rights to listen to perform long-duration texts

These characteristics and tendencies are not meant as universal generalizations to make claims about print cultures or primary oral cultures in general. Rather, these are properties of local oral-written interfaces in certain European print cultures, specific cultures of antiquity, and a number of cultures of New Guinea. We do not claim, for example, that all primary oral cultures lack the distinction between wording and intention or that all primary oral cultures focus on transmission of the intentions rather than on the linguistic forms and wording of long-duration texts.

The significance of the presence of primary oral cultures without any emphasis on the distinction between wording and meaning, with markedly less formulaicity than the cultures of antiquity and with a clear focus on intentionality rather than form, is that it refutes false dichotomies that contrast primary oral cultures as formulaic-mnemonic with cultures that have writing. Once people were convinced that all primary oral cultures had formulaic-mnemonic styles (rhyme, rhythm, repetitions, epithets, parallelisms, proverbial forms, and so on), they assumed that all cultures in antiquity must have had an oral *Ur* phase with an abundance of these formulaic-mnemonic characteristics of which a "residue" was still visible in the written literatures of cultures of antiquity. But primary oral cultures of New Guinea such as the Korowai show that the assumption that orality and formulaicity always go together is simply false. Rather, formulaic-mnemonic styles have been found to go together with communities that have writing but that also emphasize memorization and recitative performance.

The Bible emerged as a canonized and at the same time highly heterogeneous body of long-duration texts from antiquity. These were long-duration texts shaped by the specific local, oral-written interfaces of antiquity, as texts written first of all on the tablets of the hearts of literate minorities—fluid and changing text traditions that were part of a curriculum aimed at enculturating and forming new generations of ruling classes.

But once canonized, the Bible started its long journey via societies shaped by rich print and mass reading cultures towards primary oral cultures in remote corners of the world. In doing so, the Bible travelled through a range of different oral-written interfaces.

We can only understand the origin, performance, transmission, and translation of the Hebrew, Aramaic, and Greek Scriptures in the contexts of the ranges of local oral-written interfaces in which the Bible found itself functioning as sacred literature during that long journey. Early modern Bibles such as the Dutch *Statenvertaling* represent one stage in that journey, with their rich visual paratext, including maps, marginal annotations, cross-references, pericopes, and pericope headings. They are a monumental testimony to the adaptive creativity of translators and printers to enable the Bible to continue its journey into a whole new world where the invention of printing had radically changed the ways communities interacted with their literatures.

We cannot re-create the oral-written interface and the performative conditions of antiquity in translations, simply because no translation, as a form of human communication, can escape from domestic inscription. Neo-Romantic German re-creations of *Ur* orality such as Buber's *Die*

Schrift are endearing and fascinating evidence of the impossibility of escaping domestic inscription.

It is equally impossible to impose or transpose the oral-written interface of print cultures, with their reading cultures, upon minority communities that are predominantly oral. The solution is not to assume a universal dichotomy of oral versus literate cultures and then adjust the Bible translation to the features that people from print cultures tend to ascribe to oral cultures. Such "oralizing" efforts are doomed to fail because they have no scientific basis and because they contradict the findings of anthropological linguistics. Bible translations in newly literate communities are a new genre of texts that function in and express the new institution of the Christian church. It is this genre or *Sitz im Leben* that determines its stylistic properties and its relations to texts of the oral tradition.

Bible translations in these contexts should creatively adapt to the specific oral-written interface of newly literate minority communities, or they face failure. As in antiquity there is typically a small group of literati in these communities that can read well-known Bible passages to listening, communal audiences. Pioneer translations in the form of *lectionaria* should be designed to function primarily in that context. When in the course of time such minority groups integrate into wider contexts of nation-states, local oral-written interfaces will change; and revisions of pioneer translations should take such changing interfaces into account.

Bibliography

Askani, Hans-Christoph. *Das Problem der Übersetzung-dargestellt an Franz Rosenzweig: die Methoden und Prinzipien der Rosenzweigschen und Buber-Rosenzweigenschen Übersetzungen.* Hermeneutische Untersuchungen zur Theologie 35. Tübingen: Mohr/Siebeck, 1997.

Bakker, Egbert. "How Oral is Oral Composition?" In *Signs of Orality: The Oral Tradition and Its Influence in the Greek and Roman World,* edited by E. Anne Mackay, 29–47. Mnemosyne Supplementum 188. Leiden: Brill, 1999.

Benjamin, Mara H. "The Tacit Agenda of a Literary Approach to the Bible." *Prooftexts* 27 (2007) 254–74.

Biber, Douglas. *Variation across Speech and Writing.* Cambridge: Cambridge University Press, 1988.

Buber, Martin. *Werke.* Vol. 2, *Schriften zur Bibel.* Munich: Kösel, 1964.

Carr, David M. *Writing on the Tablet of the Heart: Origins of Scripture and Literature.* Oxford: Oxford University Press, 2005.

Cohen, Shaye J. D. *The Beginnings of Jewishness: Boundaries, Varieties, Uncertainties.* Hellenistic Culture and Society 31. The S. Mark Taper Foundation Imprint in Jewish Studies. Berkeley: University of California Press, 1999.

Cribiore, Raffaela. *Writing Teachers, and Students in Graeco-Roman Egypt*. American Studies in Papyrology 36. Atlanta: Scholars, 1996.
Cumming, W. *Making Blood White: Historical Transformations in Early Modern Makassar*. Honolulu: University of Hawaii Press, 2002.
Enk, Gerrit J. van, and Lourens de Vries. *The Korowai of Irian Jaya: Their Language in Its Cultural Context*. Oxford Studies in Anthropological Linguistics 9. New York: Oxford University Press, 1997.
Evans, Nicholas. *Dying Words: Endangered Languages and What They Have To Tell Us*. Language Library. Chichester: Wiley-Blackwell, 2010.
Foley, John Miles. *How to Read an Oral Poem*. Urbana: University of Illinois Press, 2002.
Foley, William. A. *Anthropological Linguistics: An Introduction*. Language in Society 24. Malden, MA: Blackwell, 1997.
———. "Personhood and Linguistic Identity, Purism and Variation." In *Language Documentation and Description* 3 (2005) 157–80.
Goody, Jack. *The Interface between the Written and the Oral*. Studies in Literacy, Family, Culture, and the State. Cambridge: Cambridge University Press, 1987.
Kloppenborg, John S. *The Formation of Q: Trajectories in Ancient Wisdom Collections*. Studies in Antiquity and Christianity. Philadelphia: Fortress, 1987.
Lord, Albert Bates. *The Singer of Tales*. Harvard Studies in Comparative LIterature 24. Cambridge: Harvard University Press, 1960.
Ong, Walter. *Orality and Literacy: The Technologizing of the Word*. New Accents. London: Methuen, 1982.
Reichert, Klaus. "It Is Time: The Buber-Rosenzweig Translation in Context." In *The Translatability of Cultures: Figurations of the Space Between*, edited by Sanford Budick and Wolfgang Iser, 169–86. Irvine Studies in the Humanities. Stanford: Stanford University Press, 1996.
Renck, Günther. *Contextualization of Christianity and Christianization of Language: A Case Study from the Highlands of Papua New Guinea*. Erlanger Monographien aus Mission und Ökumene 5. Erlangen: Verlag der Ev. Luth. Mission, 1990.
Robinson, James M. "Logoi Sophon: On the Gattung of Q." In *Trajectories through Early Christianity*, by James Robinson and Helmut Koester, 71-113. 1971. Reprinted, Eugene, OR: Wipf & Stock, 2006.
Rumsey, Alan. "Wording, Meaning and Linguistic Ideology." *American Anthropologist* 92 (1990) 346–61.
Schmidt, Gerda G. *Martin Buber's Formative Years: From German Culture to Jewish Renewal, 1897–1909*. Judaic Studies Series. Tuscaloosa: University of Alabama Press, 1995.
Schravesande, Hans. *Jichud: Eenheid in het werk van Martin Buber*. Zoetermeer: Boekencentrum, 2009.
Scribner, Silvia, and Michael Cole. *The Psychology of Literacy*. Cambridge: Harvard University Press, 1981.
Thomas, Rosalind. *Literacy and Orality in Ancient Greece*. Key Themes in Ancient History. Cambridge: Cambridge University Press, 1992.
Venuti, Lawrence. "Translation, Community, Utopia." In *The Translation Studies Reader*, edited by Lawrence Venuti and Mona Baker, 468–88. London: Routledge, 2000.
Vries, Lourens de. "Bible Translation and Primary Orality." *The Bible Translator* 51 (2000) 101–13.

———. "Direct Speech, Fictive Interaction and Bible Translation." *The Bible Translator* 61 (2010) 31–41.

———. *Forms and Functions in Kombai, an Awyu Language of Irian Jaya*. Canberra: Australian National University Press, 1993.

———. "New Guinea Communities without Writing and Views of Primary Orality." *Anthropos* 98 (2003) 397–405.

———. "The Notion of Genre and the Nature of Bible Translations." *Notes on Translation* 13/2 (1999) 26–42.

———. "Quotative Constructions and Translation in Papuan Languages." *The Bible Translator* 43/3 (1992) 333–42.

5

Sound and Meaning in the Gbaya Bible
Ideophones, Performance, and Bible Translation

Philip A. Noss

Eugene A. Nida Institute for Biblical Scholarship

Introduction

THE PRIMARY GOAL OF the translator in the current era of Bible translation has been the communication of the message. In English this has been most obviously true for translations like J. B. Phillips's New Testament (1958), *The Living Bible* by Kenneth Taylor (1971), and the *Good News Bible* of the American Bible Society (1976). These versions have all shared the goal of communicating the "good news for everyone."[1] During the latter half of the twentieth century, methods of Bible translation shifted from the preeminence of linguistic theory to communication theory. However, in the Western world, Bible illiteracy began to concern church leaders, Protestant and Catholic alike. In nations where Bibles have been prevalent for centuries,

---

1. Nida, *Good News for Everyone*. Good comprehension was also the goal of the translators of the Authorized Version, better known as the King James Version in 1611 (Rhodes and Lupas, *The Translators*, 2).

Bibles are still distributed in great numbers but appear not to be used. In areas of the world where translations are being produced in languages for the first time, limited use of the newly translated Scriptures has begun to concern Bible translators. As academic inquiry has moved from historical criticism to reader-response criticism, Bible translation agencies have begun to emphasize Scripture use and engagement.[2]

The essence of Scripture engagement is the notion that communication should not be thought to end with a transfer of information, however positive the message might be. Instead, there should be opportunity for a life-enhancing and life-transforming encounter of the listener or reader with the sacred Scripture. In order for this to occur, the Scriptures should be discoverable, accessible, and relevant.[3] Without unduly extending the discussion here, the Bible translator's dilemma came to be determining how to implement the "engagement model."[4] Recognizing the importance of the community of faith in the local interpretation and experience of the Scriptures, James Maxey proposes a new paradigm for Bible translation from the framework of biblical-performance criticism. Since the origins of the Bible were greatly if not dominantly oral, it is logical that the translator should translate from the orality of the Bible to the orality of the new context.[5] This emphasis on translating for orality, according to New Testament scholar David Rhoads, "places both biblical discourse and contemporary translation squarely in the context of the *art of oral performance*" (author's italics).[6]

The resources available to the translator for the creation of a potential communicative event are those of language and, in the case of print, whatever can be made visible on the written page. In an oral setting, the paralinguistic qualities of the performer's voice and the physical presence

---

2. Initially, SIL International emphasized the use of the Bible, while the United Bible Societies developed an approach to Scripture engagement. Since its 2004 annual meetings in Moscow, Scripture engagement has been a major theme of the Forum of Bible Agencies International. For a pedagogical treatment of these issues in the context of the relevance of the Bible for all cultures, see Hill and Hill, *Translating the Bible*.

3. Definition of Scripture Engagement adopted by the UBS Scripture Engagement Project Team meeting at Kota Kinabalu, Malaysia, June 19, 2001.

4. David Rhoads uses the terms, "communication model," "engagement model," and "performance criticism" in "The Art of Translating for Oral Performance" (chapter 2, above).

5. Maxey, *From Orality*, 5.

6. Rhoads, "The Art of Translating for Oral Performance" (chapter 2, above).

of both performer and audience offer additional resources that may enhance or diminish the performative event. Wherever oral communication predominates over the written mode, the translator may dip into the well of oral form and expression. In an African context, perhaps the single most versatile and effective tool in the linguistic repertoire of the communicator is the ideophone. It is this unique linguistic phenomenon that most dramatically enhances the engagement of the listener with the performance narrative.

Ideophones and Perception

The ideophone is recognized as an especially prominent feature of African languages and African language usage. Although it must be defined specifically within the linguistic and cultural domain of a given language, C. M. Doke's characterization of the Bantu ideophone as "a vivid representation of an idea in sound" remains a good starting point.[7] Leteipa O. Sunkuli and Simon O. Miruka, in their concise volume *A Dictionary of Oral Literature*, identify the ideophone as "a sound expression that conveys, for the purpose of intensifying, ideas of color, manner, smell, silence, action, posture, state, etc."[8] Gérard Diffloth observes, "It is in the area of meaning however that ideophones present the most interesting problems,"[9] while Roger Wescott places ideophones in the category of allolanguage and identifies one of their characteristics as "elusiveness".[10]

The ideophone is a form of expressive language that describes, portrays, or depicts anything that a person's senses may feel or observe. It can express a visual image, a sound that can be heard, a smell, a texture, or a taste. It can depict movement or lack of movement, sound or silence, presence or absence, and a great variation in intensity with respect to size, speed, loudness, brightness, emotion, and many other qualities. It may be used singly to express one or more sensations or, in combination, to depict multiple or successive sensations. It may be used metaphorically in creating new images.

The phonological shape of the ideophone may set it apart from other classes of words; it may be characterized by a wide range of processes, such

---

7. Doke, *Bantu*, 118.
8. Sunkuli and Miruka, *A Dictionary*, 40.
9. Diffloth, "Notes on Expressive Language," 441.
10. Wescott, *Sound and Sense*, 30.

as lengthening, doubling, tripling, partial reduplication, and repetition, as well as poetic effects such as assonance, consonance, and vowel and consonant alternation. It may be subject to specific syntactic marking, or it may be optional in grammatical structure. That is, the ideophone is not an obligatory part of speech for complete syntactic structure. The Nigerian literary scholar and critic Isidore Okpwewho observed somewhat dismissively, "Ideophones are not like normal words to which meanings are readily assigned. They are simply sounds used in conveying a vivid impression."[11] However, this is precisely the primary distinguishing feature of the ideophone, namely, that it uses sound to express perception. As the Nigerian linguist Omen Maduka-Durunze hypothesized, "the semantic interpretation of ideophones depends on their sounds and patterns, and on a formal sound-symbolic system of linkages."[12]

George Lakoff draws attention to nonvisual images such as sound images, auditory images, olfactory images, as well as force images, and he distinguishes between image and perception.[13] Gérard Diffloth asserts that "the ideophone is a true gesture-image of the event described," re-creating the event that it is describing.[14] Ideophones evoke the gamut of visual and nonvisual sensory images that are part of the worldview and world experience of every person. Linguistic sound systems are intimately related to perception. As the artist draws on the culture's repertoire of ideophone expressions and uses them in context, whether in conversation or in artistic form, the listener perceives the sensations that are applicable in the context. The meanings are not elusive, but are marked, pertinent, and frequently dramatic.

The phonological shape of the ideophone and its special reliance on sound for meaning invites the question of origin and creativity. Maduka-Durunze states categorically that "new ideophones (including those never heard before) can be constructed as occasion demands, based on a quasi-generative mechanism."[15] However, the Cameroonian poet, comedian, and traditional performer Dogobadomo Béloko declines to make a claim to

---

11. Okpwewho, *African Oral Literature*, 92.
12. Maduka-Durunze, "Phonosemantic Hierarchies," 193.
13. Lakoff, *Women, Fire, and Dangerous Things*, 146, 444.
14. Diffloth, "Notes on Expressive Language," 444.
15. Maduka-Durunze, "Phonosemantic Hierarchies," 193.

coining new ideophones. Rather, the artist picks them up like potsherds and arranges them for creative purposes. In Dogobadomo's own words,[16]

> We don't make them up. We don't make the pretense of inventing them. The Gbaya left them and we gather them up and put them in order. The Grandfathers left them in their abandoned villages and Gbadomo found them and arranged them in order.

Every language has the capacity to create or to borrow and adapt new lexical items. However, ideophones are a very prominent feature of the Gbaya lexicon, whether the vocabulary of each individual Gbaya speaker, or a published dictionary.[17]

Ideophones and the Gbaya Tale

A Gbaya folktale session may be a family affair within the confines of the home, or it may be a public event in which the performer (man, woman, or child) invites the audience to participate in the fun and gravity of the tale.[18] A formulaic song bids the listeners to pay attention:

Narrator:	*Ŋgai nɔ'ɔ, zii to!*	Young men here, listen to a tale!
Audience:	*Too zekeɗe zekeɗe!*	A tale for laughter laughter!
	Zii to, too zekeɗe!	Listen to a tale, a tale for laughter!
Narrator:	*Zɔŋa nɔ'ɔ, zii to!*	Young women here, listen to a tale!
Audience:	*Too zekeɗe zekeɗe!*	A tale for laughter laughter!
	Zii to, too zekeɗe!	Listen to a tale, a tale for laughter!
Narrator:	*Sɔkawi nɔ'ɔ, zii to!*	Old folks here, listen to a tale!
Audience:	*Too zekeɗe zekeɗe!*	A tale for laughter laughter!

---

16. Interview in Meiganga, Cameroon, June 3, 1980.

17. The Gbaya language belongs to the vast Ubangian group of Gbaya-Manza-Ngbaka languages that stretches from northern Congo (DRC) through the Central African Republic into central Cameroon and down into northern Congo-Brazzaville. The majority of its speakers live in rural farming communities. Nearly one-third of the 7321 entries in Paulette Doko-Roulon's Gbaya-French dictionary are ideophones, which she calls adjective-adverbs (2152) and onomatopoeia (60). In the Blanchard-Noss Gbaya-French dictionary of 8544 entries, nearly a quarter (2097) are ideophones.

18. Noss, "Ideas, Phones, and Gbaya Verbal Art," 260ff.

> *Zii to, too zɛkɛɗɛ!*   Listen to a tale, a tale for laughter!

Narrator: *Hirr! Kpiŋgim! Too!* Swiftly it comes! A resounding crash! A tale!

The telling of the tale is for the community—young men, young women, children, and old folks alike! All are invited to listen to a tale and to chuckle (*zɛkɛɗɛ zɛkɛɗɛ!*). But they are also warned that the tale will arrive swiftly, it will come directly (*hirr!*) and will fall upon the audience with a resounding crash *kpiŋgim!* It will be fun, but it will also be weighty and burdensome, and its impact will be felt like the echoing crash of a large bouncing object. An ancient tale received from the ancestors is about to be recounted again. May the listener beware!

At the end of the tale, when the refrain has been sung the last time, and when the moral has been drawn, the performer may end with a formula. It may be as simple as the single word, "Finished!," or a short statement, "My tale is finished," or it may be a traditional formula:

> *To kɔ́'m táŋ tí kóló'í gbat!*
> My tale right under the fig tree *gbat!*
>
> *Bá sɛ́ɛ-tok-mgbara tók nɛ kóló rok!*
> Pierce the fig tree with the warthog-piercing spear *rok!*

The fig tree is a large tree that grows on the waterless plains of savannah country. A welcome sight to a weary traveler, it provides shade from the blazing sun and in season it offers nourishing fruit for the hungry wanderer. The first formula abruptly closes the performance with a crisp snap *gbat!* For the exhausted hunter in the second formula, the fig tree provides a place of rest. As he pauses briefly beside the tree, he stabs the point of his hunting spear solidly into its trunk (*rok*) so that his weapon will be ready at hand when he resumes the chase of the wild boar. In a similar way, the tale will be ready the next time the performer wishes to use it in his or her quest for the bounty of tradition. The audience does not need to be reminded that the fig tree is also a sacred venue where prayers may be brought and sacrifices performed for success in the hunt or for blessings in the life of the village.

The opening and closing formulae in folktale performances are marked by ideophones. Even the Gbaya word for "tale," *to*, is lengthened as it is sung in the refrain and in the narrator's final pronouncement, almost becoming an ideophone in its own right! The ideophones are not supplementary or superfluous in these formulaic structures. They are prominent and are highly marked by syntactic position, as well as by vocal tone and volume. By their essence of sound and imagery, they draw the listeners into the performance, evoking the personal experience and perception of each member of the audience.

In a similar way, a riddling exchange is signaled by an ideophone in an evocation not of the traditional hunting scene but of war. The riddler calls out *Súmgbá!* loudly as a challenge, to which eager opponents reply with equal vigor but in a low tone, *Girimm! Súmgbá* is the Gbaya word for "riddle." *Girimm* represents a thunderous crashing sound like the beat of the great drums of a paramount chief, or the clash of armies in the attack of battle. Here it is metaphorical as it sets in play a riddling session! The challenge of a riddler to his or her peers is a summons to a contest of insight and wit. The act of picking up the gauntlet thrown down by the riddler is signaled by an ideophone.

The frequency of occurrence and the significance of ideophones in a narrative performance depend greatly on the performer's narrative skill and intention. Three performances of a short well-known Gbaya folktale are referred to below. They were told by three different artists at three different times and places. The presence of ideophones is varied among the three versions of the telling of the tale. In one version there are no ideophones, in the second there are five, and in the third there are two.[19] In the song, which is virtually identical in all three performances, an ideophone is repeated prominently in the chorus line; and there are sentence-final vocables in the solo lines.

The plot is presented in a very simple conflict-resolution structure. The central figure in this folktale is most often a young brother-in-law who pays a visit to his recently married sister's new home. His sister's husband goes hunting, kills a red river hog and, when butchering it, sends his sister's young brother with the intestines to wash in the river nearby.[20] There at the riverbank the boy is seized and taken captive by a manatee.[21] When the boy

19. The first tale was recounted by Bèoy Pierre of Mbiboko, Cameroon, on August 5, 1966; the second was told by Belporo Kpokte of Laka Kombo in October 1966; and the third was by Zaoro Ruben in Ngaoundéré on October 11, 1971.

20. The intestines and stomach of the red river hog are to be washed and cleaned so that they can be cooked and eaten like tripe.

21. Manatees (*trichechidae*) are large mammals that live in rivers and lakes. They are herbivores; they may weigh up to a thousand pounds and are usually nonaggressive.

does not return from the river, the villagers go into mourning, thinking that he is dead.

Sometime later a man from the village is cutting rattan in the forest along the river where the manatee has taken the boy.[22] As he is cutting the vines, he hears the voice of the boy singing:

Boy:	Rattan cutter, listen-*ee*!
Chorus:	*Geze-geze listen, listen geze-geze,*
Boy:	Rattan cutter, listen-*oo*!
Chorus:	*Geze-geze listen, listen geze-geze,*
Boy:	My brother-in-law killed a hog-*wa*!
Chorus:	*Geze-geze listen, listen geze-geze,*
Boy:	So I went to wash the stomach-*ee*!
Chorus:	*Geze-geze listen, listen geze-geze,*
Boy:	Manatee took me-*oo*!
Chorus:	*Geze-geze listen, listen geze-geze.*

The rattan cutter rushes back to alert the townspeople to what he has heard. The people bring fishing nets and succeed in rescuing the boy from his apparent riverine fate. The moral of the tale emphasizes the family obligation of taking good care of the brother of one's wife, underscoring the importance of social relationships and ritual in Gbaya culture.

The first version of the tale is a simple recounting of the tale. It is an abbreviated form in which the narrator ends with the song. His greatest interest is to sing the song with his audience as for a dance celebration. Only when the audience requires that he provide a conclusion does he add a brief narrative conclusion to his performance. Apart from the song, there is no ideophone in the tale.

The second version begins with the formulaic opening invitational song with its ideophones *zékédé zékédé* and ends with the formulaic closure and the ideophone *rok*. Ideophones are sparsely but strategically placed throughout the tale. The townspeople expected the boy to come back from the river where he had gone to clean the intestines of the wild hog, but finally, "they went down to the river, *púréemm!* he wasn't there. They went back up and dug a hole for the death drum post and began to mourn." The young boy's disappearance is vividly depicted by the expression *púréemm!*

---

22. Rattan is shoots or vines that are used for wickerwork such as baskets, articles of furniture, and as cord.

signifying a void where something should be visible. The lengthening of the second vowel and of the final consonant provides heightened markedness of the unexpected and tragic nature of the event.

Someone from the village goes into the forest along the river to cut rattan vines, "and as he cut *kpɔɔ kpɔɔ kpɔɔ*, he happened to look up and there *gédéféré!* the boy climbed up and sat on top of a high rock in the middle of the water. The child began singing . . ." The hollow sound of the rattan-cutter's chopping in the forest can be heard (*kpɔɔ kpɔɔ kpɔɔ*). Then suddenly and in sharp contrast to the vacancy portrayed by *púreemm*, there is something visible perched in balancing fashion *gédéféré* on top of a rock in the river. The vine cutter quickly runs up from the valley to the village and tells everyone to stop drumming and mourning, that they should take their fish nets and go to the river valley and see what would happen when he would chop the vines.

At the river he instructs the people to place their nets around the rock that jutted out of the water and then to hide and wait. "He took his machete, and as he chopped the vines, as he chopped the vines *bɔk, bɔk bɔk* twice more, the boy climbed up on the rock again. He sat there and began singing. . . ." The first time the vine cutter had been chopping in the usual manner: *kpɔɔ kpɔɔ kpɔɔ*, but this time his blows are deliberate and solid, first one blow: *bɔk*; and then two blows: *bɔk bɔk*. When the boy reappears and begins singing his song, the people burst (*pemyele!*) out of hiding and pull in their nets and rescue the boy!

In the third version of the tale, the performer uses only two ideophones, placing them at the rescue point in the story—that is, at the climax of the plotline. Instead of focusing on the rescuers bursting out of hiding to save the boy, he describes the motion of the boy's being ensnared, *kelewele*, in the net. The image projected by the ideophone is a smooth rolling motion like that of a fish being turned over in a fishnet. In this way the boy is caught in the nets and, *vup*, he is brought back to fall with a thud onto firm ground. The abruptness of *vup* underscores the certainty of his rescue by the townspeople.

In all three versions, the song begins with the narrator's voice relating the boy's plaintive call for the attention of the rattan cutter. This is immediately answered by the choral participation of the audience. The lines then alternate antiphonally between soloist and audience as the boy successively relates those events that have resulted in his plight, and the villagers repeatedly affirm their presence and attention. The refrain is constituted by an ideophone plus the command to listen to the boy's call. The reduplicated *gɛzɛ-gɛzɛ* depicts a crowd of people standing packed close together. The climax of the tale comes when the people of the village gather at the water's edge to hear the boy's mournful plea for help and take collective action to rescue him. The ideophone may also be understood to represent the sound of cutting rattan. The vine that is being cut by the rattan cutter is commonly used for weaving baskets that are known as *gɛsɛ* or, in some Gbaya dialects, as *gɛzɛ*. Therefore the rattan cutter is actually a basket maker and may be nicknamed "*Gɛzɛ*." The song may thus be understood to mean, "Basket[-maker], Basket[-maker], listen-*ee!*" The ideophone that provides structure to the song simultaneously evokes several images in the minds of the audience participants. In a similar way, the Nigerian linguist Michael Ekere observes that the ideophones in an Ibibio song text "supply the rhythm and create abundant imagery that thrills the listener."[23]

The lines of a song often end with vocables that may be ornamental or that may fill out the rhythm. They are phonologically and structurally similar to ideophones. In this song, each final long vowel is an emotive clause-final particle. The *ee* particle indicates mild emphasis, *oo* is pleading insistence as though speaking from a distance, while *wa* is strong insistence as though in an argument or in giving a forceful command. The most emphatic of the three forms occurs in the line where the boy cites the event that led directly to his fate of being captured by the manatee.

In this very short tale, ideophones have been an available resource for the narrator to use. For the performer whose interest was in the song and not in telling the tale itself, no ideophones were needed, except in the song where they constitute a major part of the text. For the second narrator, ideophones functioned to support and enhance the development and movement of the plot. For the third narrator, ideophones were used exclusively to heighten the drama of the climax. Several of the ideophones are onomatopoeic representing sound and action, while others are visual, revealing absence in one case and movement and presence in another case. The repeated ideophone in the chorus of the song creates associations in the minds of the audience that expand the level of the performance from text to intertext. Indeed, all the ideophones create associations because they may all be used in other tales in different contexts. They are all part of the repertoire of sonic devices that are available to reveal the Gbaya perception of actions, states, attitudes, and events according to their worldview!

23. Ekere, "The Ideophone in Oral Literature," 311.

Ideophones and Biblical Text

The narrator whose creation story is recorded in the first chapter of the book of Genesis imagines what might have been at the beginning of time when God was creating the heavens and the earth. The Hebrew text poetically records that at the time of creation, the earth was *tohu wabohu*.

In the Septuagint, the first translators of the Bible dating two to three centuries BCE understood this Hebrew expression to mean "invisible" and "unformed." The Latin Vulgate of the fifth century CE translated the Hebrew expression with the words *inanis et vacua*, "void and empty." The King James Version renders this as depicting something "without form and void," a place that had neither shape nor content. Contemporary English translations render it a "formless void" (NRSV, JB) or "formless and desolate" (GNB). The modern French translation by André Chouraqui translates the Hebrew conjunction with the French *et*, "and," and transliterates the two Hebrew forms *tohu* and *bohu* without interpretation.[24]

Bishop Samuel Crowther's Yoruba translation of Genesis in 1853 uses the words *jūjū* and *ṣofo* to express the meaning of the Hebrew description. The first is an ideophone for which Abraham's dictionary offers "higgledy-piggledy" as a gloss.[25] The second item is a verbal form with the meaning "be empty." Although the image "higgledy-piggledy" seems anachronistic in the context of an account of creation, the Yoruba term does evoke the concept of disorder and confusion.

Bishop Crowther's translation of the Bible is characterized by an abundant use of ideophones. During a conference presentation, the Yoruba scholar Yiwola Awoyale remarked, "The Yoruba Bible is full of ideophones!"[26] However, the Yoruba rendering of this biblical expression is a marked exception among African language translations. Most translations express the generally accepted denotative meanings of the two Hebrew words as the English translations cited above have done. A Chichewa-speaking seminary student in Zambia proposed a translation that expressed the following: "And the earth was [distant past] *mbalabanda! Pululu!*" The two Chichewa

---

24 This Hebrew expression has been borrowed in contemporary informal French as an invariable masculine noun *tohu-bohu* meaning "confusion, commotion, disorder."

25. Abraham, *Dictionary of Modern Yoruba*.

26. International Symposium on Ideophones, University of Cologne, Germany, January 25–27, 1997.

ideophones depicted a state "without a proper shape and barren [like a desert]." However, this rendering was not retained in the new Chichewa Bible.[27]

The Gbaya Bible translates, "the earth was plain, there was nothing in it."[28] In the account of Jeremiah's vision where the same Hebrew expression occurs, the prophet declares, "I looked, and I saw the earth was *puturu*, there was nothing in it" (Jer 4:23). *Puturu* depicts a flat space, empty and barren. Here its poetic use is appropriate, because it specifies what the speaker saw in the vision. But who was there to witness the act of creation? The poet narrator was attempting to depict a primordial beginning that no human being was present to observe, as God reminded his interlocutor Job with the rhetorical question, "Where were you when I laid the foundation of the earth?" (Job 38:4 NRSV).

What are these two rhyming Hebrew words linked by the *waw* conjunction? Joan O'Brien and Wilfred Major describe them as an "onomatopoeic phrase,"[29] while William Millar refers to "the onomatopoeia of the Hebrew *tohu wabohu*," which he asserts, "captures the turmoil that signals the prelude to the creative act."[30]

Though fairly uncommon in either Old Testament or New Testament texts, onomatopoeia was well known in classical rhetoric. The word is Greek in origin from two words, "name + make," that is, to coin a word; and the specific reference was to create a word that imitated or echoed a specific sound. The term was also applied to a series of words or a phrase that reflected the sound of what was being described. The classic Hebrew example is in the prophet Isaiah's description of the arrogant Assyrian king as he boasts about conquering the world like helpless nestlings flapping their wings, and *potseh peh umetsaptsep*, "not a beak opening, not a chirp" (Isa 10:14 JB).[31]

---

27. Personal communication from Ernst Wendland, April 15, 2000. The new Sango common language Bible translation does not use ideophones for this Hebrew expression either, but it does emphasize the profound darkness that covered the deep with an ideophone: "the place was dark *pitipiti*."

28. *Kalata ko Sɔ*. See Noss, "A Translator's Trail," 372–73.

29. O'Brien and Major, *In the Beginning*, 42.

30. Millar, "In Praise of a Little Chaos," 4. For in-depth treatment of Hebrew onomatopoeia see Weinstock, "Onomatopoeia."

31. Shökel, "Isaiah," 171. In the Sumerian *Epic of Gilgamesh* dating to the second millennium BCE a similar image, both visual and auditory, may be found. The hero Gilgamesh refuses the advances of the goddess Ishtar, reminding her of the beautiful roller bird that she struck, breaking its wing, and "now in the grove he sits and cries, 'kappi, kappi, my wing, my wing'" (*The Epic of Gilgamesh*, 86).

In the New Testament, Paul refers to Lois the *mammē* ("grandmother") of Timothy (2 Tim 1:5), a word that imitates the sounds of a baby. However, this is an example of fossilized onomatopoeia because it is the normal Greek word for "grandmother." Ernst Wendland offers an example of sound play which he identifies as onomatopoeia in James 5:1, *klaúsate 'ololúzóntes* "weep lamenting."[32] The syllables *'ololú* are considered to represent the sound of wailing.

When the biblical text is appreciated as literature, the aesthetic features of the ancient literary form must be recognized. Thus Wendland, writing of the literary-rhetorical approach to translation, draws attention to the "artistry of the Scriptures."[33] He offers as the basic premise of his approach, "If—or better *since*—verbal beauty and power were and are an integral part of the message of Scripture, these dimensions *must* be dealt with in an appropriate, locally determined way in every Bible translation" (author's italics).[34] He speaks of "phonation" as constituting the various techniques used by an author to produce sonic ornamentation—and it is here that we would place ideophones, inclusive of onomatopoeia.[35]

In the drama of prophetic discourse, ideophones are an important device for the translator to employ. The prophet Nahum exploits the power of Hebrew poetic expression through assonance and imagery in depicting the catastrophic destruction of Nineveh and its inhabitants (Nah 2:11/10). The Gbaya translators used their own metaphorical expression heightened by ideophones to convey the drama of the Hebrew text:

> Raid and ravage and ruin!
> Heart fails and knees give way,
> Fear is in the loins of all
> And every face grows pale. (JB)

> Nineveh is undone *kásá-kásá*, to become nothing,
> People are terrified, and they shake *tututu!*
> Fear has tied their stomachs,
> and their faces are pale *kpalili*. (Gbaya Bible)

---

32. Wendland, *Finding*, 97.
33. Wendland, *Translating*, 139.
34. Ibid., 33–34.
35. Ibid., 149. In Wendland's later writing he moves into performance criticism in a search for the oral-aural elements in the written text in which he refers specifically to sound plays, including onomatopoeia (*Finding*, 97).

Translating Scripture for Sound and Performance

The ideophone *kásá-kásá* describes something that is completely taken apart, something that is broken into many pieces. Here it reveals a city in complete ruin, whose inhabitants have scattered and abandoned it. *Tututu* is the motion of trembling or shaking as when one is very cold, or when one is terrified. In their fear, their faces are pale or ashen *kpalili*.

The Gbaya translation of the Psalms features an average of two ideophones each. The psalms are poetic and therefore the dramatic quality of ideophone expression is appropriate as in Ps 20:8 where it highlights the contrastive parallelism of the Hebrew literary form:

> Theirs to crumple and fall,
> But we shall stand, and stand firm. (JB)

> For them it's tumbling falling down *samgbaŋ*,
> For us it's standing firm *kéŋ*. (Gbaya Bible)

Samgbaŋ combines the visual image with the auditory sensation of something great and heavy falling to the ground. Here it is people crashing heavily in unison to the ground. In English, this could be "thud," but the sound of "thud" is not big enough to represent the psalmist's portrayal of the fate of his enemies. We, however, shall stand *kéŋ*, solid, firm, immovable!

The parable of the wise man and the foolish man is recounted by Matthew and Luke. In both Gospels, the consequences of the actions of the two men are portrayed in dramatic fashion. The wise man built his house upon a rock, and when the gale winds hurled themselves against the house, the house stood firm. However, the foolish man built his house on sand and when the gale winds blew and the river rose, his house fell, "and what a fall it had!" according to Matthew (7:27, JB). According to Luke (6:49, JB), "what a ruin that house became!"

The Gbaya translators placed the climax on the ideophone that stood in final position in the sentence. In Matthew, "the house fell to the ground *gété-gété*," while in Luke, "the house broke to the ground completely *mútú-mútú*." The ideophone used for Matthew's house reveals an object that is broken to smithereens. The description of Luke's house is of something being crushed and ground to pieces by overbearing force.[36]

---

36. The revised Krio New Testament of Sierra Leone describes the destruction of the foolish man's house as *patapata* in both Gospels. The Gullah New Testament translates the Matthew version in these words: "*An de house faddown, bam! E smash op!*" The same onomatopoeic word is also used in Luke with only a slight variation in syntax.

Ideophones are fitting devices for depicting the vivid scenes of a vision, as in the Apocalypse where they are used to describe the pure whiteness *kpúŋ-kpúŋ* of the hair of the one like the Son of Man who spoke to John (1:14), the razor sharpness *pédéŋ-pédéŋ* of his two-edged sword (1:16), the prostration of the angels and the four living creatures on the ground *gbéyéŋ* before the throne (7:11), and the scattering *sót-sót* of the islands (16:20), to cite only those examples.

Many Bible translators are hesitant about incorporating ideophones into their rendering of Scripture. They may be convinced that the markedness and creative dynamics of ideophones are incompatible with the norms that govern the form and style of sacred text. A reviewer of the Biakpan translation of the Brotherhood of the Cross and Star of Cross River State in Nigeria labeled the ideophone a "native word" that was not befitting for biblical texts.[37] Its association with informality may cause it to seem unsuitable for the august nature of liturgical discourse.

There may be another factor influencing the translator's decision about whether or not to use ideophones, namely, the nature of the ideophone and its pragmatic meaning. The ideophone represents personal experience and perception and thus introduces the element of the author into the text as an observer or reporter. By its very nature, the ideophone suggests that there was an observer to observe and describe the object or event in question. In the case of creation, there was no one present but the divine Creator himself to proclaim that it was good.

Recognizing the preeminence of ideophones in discourse, the linguist William Samarin wrote, "I dare say that a masterful use of an African's language is probably always correlated with a generous use of ideophones,"[38] to which Ruth Finnegan adds, "A style plentifully embroidered with ideophones is one of the striking characteristics of an effective storyteller."[39]

However, there is a danger! The three versions of a tale presented above revealed variation in quantity from no ideophones to two ideophones to five. But quantity is not the primary consideration. The purpose of the given narration or oration, as well as the text and content, is determinative of

---

37. This statement was made by a reviewer during a committee meeting held to consider language and translation problems in the Bible translation project in the Biakpan language supported by the Brotherhood of the Cross and Star during the 1982–84 period in Calabar, Nigeria. Apostle E. K. Ukpai was the translator appointed by the Brotherhood for the project.

38. Samarin, "Perspective on African Ideophones," 117.

39. Finnegan, *Oral Literature*, 384–85.

style and the occurrence of literary features. In three Old Testament books of approximately the same length, the Gbaya translation team used no ideophones in one book, the book of Ruth, while in Jonah they used, five, reflecting a higher level of drama; and in the poetic prophecy of Nahum they used fifteen ideophones. As Maxey has observed, "Considerably more [ideophones] were used for the performance translation with an abundant use—especially with certain performers—in the actual performances."[40] Ideophones are by nature marked words, bearing a heavily expressive value. If used unwisely, they may detract from the storyline or from the message; if used incorrectly or without circumspection, they may introduce an element of the comic that is inappropriate to the sacred narrative.[41]

Performance and Engagement

The narration of a Gbaya tale is a live communal activity in which the narrator performs for an audience, and the audience participates in the performance. Active participation is confirmed by the audience antiphonal response in the formulaic invitational song, and it continues throughout the performance through audience comment, question, laughter, and sometimes disapproval of a personage in the tale, or of an inept narrator-performer. The most pronounced audience participation is in the singing of the refrain to the song that almost invariably features in the performance of a tale. The narrator must take care that the energy of the song does not carry the audience into dance from which they may not easily be brought back.

The South African scholar Daniel Kunene observes that "the ideophone is a performative speech act *par excellence*, which is often reinforced by body language."[42] The ideophone is often accompanied by a physical gesture, as though the one supplements the other. "The abstraction of speech is reinforced by the concrete presentation of the abstracted act," Kunene writes.[43] Occasionally, the ideophone may be replaced by a gesture that

---

40. Maxey, *From Orality to Orality*, 176.
41. Noss, "The Ideophone," 423–30. See also Samarin, "Appropriateness and Metaphor," in which he reports on an experiment that tested the appropriateness and inappropriateness of specific ideophones in specific contexts.
42. Kunene, "Speaking the Act," 189 (italics original).
43. Ibid., 184.

represents or signals the action or perception that would be evoked by an ideophone.

Linguistically and aesthetically, the ideophone is a focal feature of the performance. It enables the audience to participate "in a happening," as Kunene claims.[44] And he explains, "Having created a surreal world, the ideophone invites the audience to perceive with their senses that which it represents, whether aural, visual, olfactory, etc."[45]

In her book *Sounds Like Life*, Janice Nuckolls describes the sound symbolism of the Quechua language of Ecuador as "a performative technique for expressively communicating the salient sounds, rhythms, and psychophysical sensations that are drawn from perceptions of the environment and bodily experience."[46] It may be equally accurate to state that sound symbolism is a psycholinguistic technique that is used performatively by the artist to draw the audience into the experience of the tale. The key to the significance of the ideophone resides in the fact that all human beings perceive sensations, and these may be evoked through the sound images that each culture shares through its common world view.

Conclusion

The awareness of orality is not new in the history of the Bible and its use. The correct pronunciation of the word *shibboleth* was a matter of life and death for the defeated Ephraimites who attempted to cross the Jordan River in their attempt to flee to safety (Judg 12:5–6). The first account of Scripture translation is found in the book of Nehemiah where the Levites interpreted the Scriptures that were read to the people (Neh 8:7–8). The blessing of Revelation is promised to "the one who reads aloud the words of the prophecy, and blessed are those who hear and who keep what is written in it; for the time is near" (Rev 1:3, NRSV).

Throughout the history of the Christian church, the Bible has been read to the faithful and has been performed liturgically. Liturgical drama is known in the Catholic Church from the Middle Ages. Priests presented the stories of Christmas and Easter dramatically in Latin and in prose. In the later medieval period, Easter drama developed into full-fledged passion

---

44. Kunene, *The Ideophone*, 12.
45. Kunene, "Speaking the Act," 190.
46. Nuckolls, *Sounds Like Life*, 276. See also Nuckolls, "Ideophones in Pastaza Quechua."

plays in which the entire passion of Christ was acted out in vernacular languages and in verse. The tradition of performing passion plays continues in many countries to the present day.

Modern technology offers the possibility of film and multimedia productions of the Bible, or portions of it. The most successful example of docudrama has been *The Jesus Film,* produced by Campus Crusade for Christ. This dramatic presentation of the story of Jesus as written by Luke has been translated into 1050 languages and has had more than six billion showings in 128 countries around the world.

The difference between these performance presentations down through history and the new paradigm that Rhoads and Maxey are proposing is that usually the words are written and then read aloud, as is the procedure in Revelation cited above. The plays of the Middle Ages were based on the Latin Vulgate; and the text of *The Jesus Film* is adapted from a written translation of the Gospel of Luke. In fact, wherever possible, the showing of the film is accompanied by the distribution of printed copies of the Gospel of Luke. Thus, the print mode is the canonical mode. The new paradigm proposes that the oral performance mode should be the privileged mode of a Bible translation and its transmission.

Biblical-performance criticism would suggest that the Bible translator should exegete the orality of the Bible and then translate into the orality of the new performance context.[47] Literary and dramatic features of the translation language should be adopted and exploited in the process of translation in order to enhance engagement with the biblical message. In Nuckolls's words, "This projected involvement, in turn, points the listener to deeper kinds of imaginative, intellectual, and emotional engagement with the narrative."[48] It is these deeper kinds of engagement with the Scripture narrative that the Bible translator in African languages seeks to bring about through the ideophones that the grandfathers and grandmothers left

---

47. In 1971 the Roman Catholic diocese of Pala in western Chad initiated an experiment of oral tradition and memorization of the Gospels among the local Massa community. Having decided that their efforts at evangelization had not been successful, they observed that there were many similarities between the oral setting of the traditional Africa and the oral setting of first-century in Palestine when the Gospels were being developed. Using a technique of editing the Gospel story thematically for easy memorization, they taught the Gospel message to the people. The result was an evangelical renewal, as reported by the Bongor missionary team, in "Une expérience."

48. Nuckolls, "Sound Symbolic Involvement," 51.

behind in their abandoned villages for the artist-translator to pick up and arrange for today's performative event.

Bibliography

Abraham, Roy Clive. *Dictionary of Modern Yoruba*. London: University of London Press, 1958.
La Bible: Traduite et présentée par André Chouraqui. Paris: Desclée de Brouwer, 1985.
Blanchard, Yves, and Philip A. Noss. *Dictionnaire Gbaya-Français: Dialecte Yaayuwee*. Meiganga: Centre de Traduction Gbaya, 1982.
Diffloth, Gérard. "Notes on Expressive Language." In *Chicago Linguistic Society: Papers from the 8th Regional Meeting*, edited by P. M. Peranteau, J. N. Levi, and G. C. Pheres, 440–47. Chicago: Chicago Linguistic Society, 1972.
Doke, C. M. *Bantu Linguistic Terminology*. London: Longmans Green, 1935.
Ekere, Michael. "The Ideophone in Oral Literature." In *Literature and Black Aesthetics*, edited by Dele Orisawayi et al. 300–314. Ibadan, Nigeria: Heinemann Educational Books, 1990.
The Epic of Gilgamesh. Translated by N. K. Sandars. Reading, UK: Penguin, 1960.
Équipe missionnaire de Bongor. "Une experience de tradition orale et de mémorisation des Évangiles en milieu traditionnel africain." *Afrique et Parole* 74 (1974) 9–32.
Finnegan, Ruth. *Oral Literature in Africa*. Oxford Library of African Literature. Oxford: Clarendon, 1970.
Gud Nyus Fɔ Ɔlman (Krio NT). Freetown: The Bible Society in Sierra Leone, 1992.
The Holy Bible (Authorized or King James Version). 1611.
Hill, Harriet, and Margaret Hill. *Translating the Bible into Action*. Carlisle UK: Piquant, 2008.
The Jerusalem Bible. London: Darton, Longman & Todd, 1966. Cited as JB.
Kalata ko Sɔ (Gbaya Bible). Yaoundé: Alliance Biblique du Cameroun, 2009.
Kunene, Daniel P. *The Ideophone in Southern Sotho*. Marburger Studien zur Afrika- und Asienkunde. Series A: Afrika 11 Berlin: Reimer, 1978.
———. "Speaking the Act: The Ideophone as a Linguistic Rebel." In *Ideophones*, edited by F. K. Erhard Voeltz and Christa Kilian-Hatz, 183–91. Typological Studies in Language 44. Amsterdam: Benjamins, 2001.
Lakoff, George. *Women, Fire, and Dangerous Things: What Categories Reveal about the Mind*. Chicago: University of Chicago Press, 1987.
Maduka-Durunze, Omen N. "Phonosemantic Hierarchies." In *Ideophones*, edited by F. K. Erhard Voeltz and Christa Kilian-Hatz, 193–203. Typological Studies in Language 44. Amsterdam: Benjamins, 2001.
Maxey, James A. *From Orality to Orality: A New Paradigm for Translation of the Bible*. Biblical Performance Criticism 2. Eugene, OR: Cascade Books, 2009.
Millar, William R. "In Praise of a Little Chaos: Storytelling and Tradition." Material for a Linfield College course. Accessed May 17, 2004. Online: http://calvin.linfield.edu/~wmillar/2_In_Praise_of_Chaos.html/.
Nida, Eugene A. *Good News for Everyone: How to Use the Good News Bible*. Waco, TX: Word, 1977.

Noss, Philip A. "Ideas, Phones, and Gbaya Verbal Art." In *Ideophones*, edited by F. K. Erhard Voeltz and Christa Kilian-Hatz, 259–70. Typological Studies in Language 44. Amsterdam: John Benjamins, 2001.

———. "The Ideophone and Bible Translation: Child or Stepchild?" *The Bible Translator: Practical Papers* 36/2 (1985) 423–30.

———. "The Oral Story and Bible Translation." *The Bible Translator: Technical Papers* 32/3 (1981) 301–18.

———. "A Translator's Trail: From Engagement to Ideophones through Ideophones to Engagement." In *Traduire la Bible Hébraïque—Translating the Hebrew Bible*, edited by Robert David and Manuel Jinbachian, 351–74. Sciences bibliques 15. Montreal: Médiaspaul, 2005.

Nuckolls, Janis B. "Ideophones in Pastaza Quechua." In *Ideophones*, edited by F. K. Erhard Voeltz and Christa Kilian-Hatz, 271–85. Typological Studies in Language 44. Amsterdam: John Benjamins, 2001.

———. "Sound Symbolic Involvement." *Journal of Linguistic Anthropology* 2/1 (1992) 51–80.

———. *Sounds Like Life: Sound-Symbolic Grammar, Performance, and Cognition in Pastaza Quechua*. Oxford Studies in Anthropological Linguistics 2. New York: Oxford University Press, 1996.

De Nyew Testament (Gullah New Testament). New York: American Bible Society. 2005.

O'Brien, Joan, and Wilfred Major. *In the Beginning: Creation Myths from Ancient Mesopotamia, Israel and Greece*. American Academy of Religion Aids for the Study of Religion Series 11. Chico, CA: Scholars, 1982.

Okpwewho, Isidore. *African Oral Literature: Backgrounds, Character, and Community*. Bloomington: Indiana University Press, 1992.

Rhodes, Erroll F., and Liana Lupas. *The Translators to the Reader: The Original Preface of the King James Version of 1611 Revisited*. New York: American Bible Society, 1997.

Roulon-Doko, Paulette. *Dictionnaire gbaya-français. République Centrafricaine*. Dictionnaires et langues. Paris: Karthala, 2008.

Samarin, William J. "Appropriateness and Metaphor in the Use of Ideophones." *Orbis* 20/2 (1971) 356–69.

———. "Perspective on African Ideophones." *African Studies* 24 (1965) 117–21.

Shökel, Luis Alonso. "Isaiah." In *The Literary Guide to the Bible*, edited by Robert Alter and Frank Kermode, 165–83. Cambridge: Belknap, 1987.

Sunkuli, Leteipa Ole, and Simon Okumba Miruka. *A Dictionary of Oral Literature*. Nairobi: East African Educational Publishers, 1990.

Voeltz, F. K. Erhard, and Christa Kilian-Hatz, editors. *Ideophones*. Typological Studies in Language 44. Amsterdam: John Benjamins, 2001.

Weinstock, Leo Irwin. "Onomatopoeia and Related Phenomena in Biblical Hebrew: A Survey of Certain Correlations between Sound and Meaning in the Lexical and Phonological Levels of a Semitic Language." PhD diss. University of Pennsylvania, 1979.

Wendland, Ernst R. *Finding and Translating the Oral-Aural Elements in Written Language: The Case of the New Testament Epistles*. Lewiston: Mellen, 2008.

———. *Translating the Literature of Scripture: A Literary-Rhetorical Approach to Bible Translation*. Publications in Translation and Textlinguistics 1. Dallas: SIL International, 2004.

Wescott, Roger Williams. *Sound and Sense: Linguistic Essays on Phonosemic Subjects*. Edward Sapir Series in Language, Culture, and Cognition 8. Lake Bluff, IL: Jupiter, 1980.

6

Translating Habakkuk as a Performance

Jeanette Mathews

CHARLES STURT UNIVERSITY

Why Translate? Description of the Project

IN THIS CHAPTER A project of translation is described that was guided by principles of performance criticism. I recently completed a PhD dissertation, bringing together the disciplines of performance studies and Hebrew Bible interpretation. The book of Habakkuk was translated and then analyzed as a "performance." The intention was neither to translate Habakkuk for a contemporary, live performance, nor to seek to understand what an ancient performance of Habakkuk might have looked like in the earliest periods of its transmission. Rather, the aim was to rehabilitate the performance features already embedded in the text in order to show how attending to these might give a new perspective on the text as it has been received. Reading this text as a performance revealed the underlying orality so that shifts in speaker and addressee were noticed, wordplay was highlighted, and attention was given to repetitions and creative improvisations of well-known terms that might have functioned as ready-mades for an attentive audience. It will be evident that I intentionally sought a more literal correspondence with the original forms in the Hebrew text in order to more readily notice any inherently dramatic characteristics. My hope was that any such discoveries would inform future translations.

The starting point for this project was a survey of literature from the discipline of performance studies and the identification of several themes common across the discipline. The field of performance studies is a complex one that incorporates a number of humanities and social-science disciplines as well as the more traditional categories of the visual and performing arts. The breadth of "voices, themes, opinions, methods, and subjects"[1] relating to performance studies means that no single methodology can be appropriated and applied to new situations. Nonetheless, common themes arise as a result of a shared interest in reclaiming the material body in a world that is increasingly dominated by attention to text alone.[2]

The themes that were identified include embodiment, process, and re-enactment. These themes are obvious in live performance: real bodies participate in the action (embodiment); the emphasis is on the actual activity and not just on the completed product (process); and all performance is based upon preexisting scripts or patterns (re-enactment). In relation to Scripture, recognition that a script is not fully realized until it is performed emphasizes the importance of embodiment. The particular "script" of Habakkuk has an open-ended nature, typified by its final verb of movement, well illustrating the theme of process. Its survival as a canonical resource in both the Jewish Scriptures and Christian Scriptures implies that the third theme identified applies to the book. And its colophon, which invites renewed performances, unambiguously calls for re-enactment. The manner in which all three of these performance themes are found within the script of Habakkuk will be further explored later in this chapter.

The project was also informed by the emerging discipline of biblical-performance criticism in which biblical scholars are seeking to develop a methodology that draws out the remnants of oral-aural performance lying behind biblical texts to aid in interpretation. Such studies are interested in the relationship between oral and scribal communities, contextual issues surrounding transmission and reception of text and traditions, and the role that performers and audience played in preserving and passing on biblical traditions. In similar fashion to the broader field of performance studies, biblical performance criticism seeks to move beyond our print-based

---

1. Schechner, *Performance Studies*, 1.
2. Cf. Walker, "Why Performance?," 149.

culture to rehabilitate and celebrate the oral and material foundations of Scripture.

If one were to define *performance*, there would be an emphasis on the carrying out of an action or operation, on the process of that accomplishment, and on the interrelationship between actor, event, and spectator. When a portion of Scripture is read as a script, one is compelled to ask, Who are the actors? Where is the audience? What is the setting of the performance? How does the script present its drama? And what devices are used to engage an audience? Such questions guided my translation of Habakkuk as a script—identification of plural verbs to indicate where the audience is drawn in to the action, attempts to replicate some of the rhetorical and extraverbal devices employed in the original Hebrew, and awareness of how the setting for the drama should influence choices in translation.

What to Translate? Establishing the Text

A fundamental issue arising at the beginning of such a project is the establishment of the text for translation. Scholarly opinion on the state of the text of Habakkuk varies. Some view the Masoretic Text (MT) as authoritative and the best representation of the original text.[3] Others make a distinction between the consonantal and vocalized version of MT, regarding the consonantal text as the authoritative text.[4] Still others see serious problems in the MT and propose a number of significant changes, influenced by the ancient versions including the Septuagint (LXX).[5] Marvin Sweeney comments that the many variant readings found in the ancient manuscripts and versions contribute to the text being regarded as "problematic."[6]

Nevertheless, the MT as presented in BHS was chosen for translation since it has been the most influential text of Habakkuk in Hebrew Bible studies over generations. While recognizing the impact that the Qumran (Q) discoveries have had on textual criticism, given that the Q texts are centuries older than the MT, the fact that Habakkuk 3 was not preserved by

---

3. Brownlee, *Text of Habakkuk*, 113; Robertson, *Books of Nahum, Habakkuk, and Zephaniah*, 40–42; Patterson, "Habakkuk," 132–33; Avishur, *Studies in Hebrew*, 111–12.

4. Bruce, "Habakkuk," 835–36; Haak, *Habakkuk*, 1–11; Margalit, "The Day the Sun Did Not Stand Still," 480–81.

5. See translation note in Roberts, *Nahum, Habakkuk and Zephaniah*; and Hiebert, *God of My Victory*.

6. Sweeney, "Habakkuk, Book of," 2.

Q influenced the choice to base translation on the complete text preserved in the MT. During translation of the text, textual discrepancies were noted. One emendation suggested by the editors of *BHS* and made by many translators was accepted; namely, the redivision of Habakkuk 3:10–11 to place שמש, *sun*, at the end of verse 10 rather than at the beginning of verse 11 as we find in the MT. In other cases the variant readings appear to be the result of theological sensitivities, such as the *tiqqun* in Habakkuk 1:12[7] or the discomfort with the prophet "answering back" in Habakkuk 2:1.[8] It is worth noting that translation from the perspective of performance criticism can positively view discrepancies that exist in the ancient versions as valid interpretive variations that would occur in re-enactments of the material with different audiences.

How to Translate? Translating for Performance

Endeavoring to Present a Literal Translation

One of the consequences of translating a "problematic" text is that the original forms are often altered in order to present a more fluent text for the reader. Especially noticeable in the book of Habakkuk are the attempts to harmonize changes in verbal forms, clarify the identity of speakers, smooth over grammatical forms such as repetitive *waw*-consecutive forms, or alter clauses that are difficult to understand. In my translation, I was careful not to harmonize away inconsistencies but rather to attempt a quite literal translation in order to observe any performative features inherent in such "apparent ungrammaticalities"[9] that might otherwise be ignored. The following examples serve to illustrate how harmonization of the text by translators has resulted in important performative aspects of the text being overlooked or misinterpreted:

---

7. The text in the MT is נמות, "we will not die," but is almost universally translated "you will not die" in recognition of the probable scribal change based on piety.

8. אשיב, "what I will bring back"; compare with the Syriac reading ישיב, "what he returns," and the Aramaic in which the verb is passive.

9. Wendland, "Performance Criticism," 3.

Use of the Definite Article

Adele Berlin notes that Hebrew poetry uses particles infrequently, especially "the definite article (ה, *ha*), the accusative marker (את, *'et*) and the relative pronoun (אשר, *'ăšer*)."[10] The use of these particles should thus be noted by the translator. Almost all translations and commentaries use the parallel terms "the wicked" and "the righteous" in Habakkuk 1:4, while the MT and all versions include a definite article only on the latter. There is also an object marker before "the righteous," which itself is unusual in the poetic script. These particles in conjunction with צדיק suggest that "the righteous" is a specific group or a specific individual. הצדיק may well have been a reference to the prophet himself as a representative of the innocent righteous. Walter Brueggemann notes that prayers of complaint are generated by Israel when the nation thought itself to be innocent and so takes the initiative to put Yahweh "on trial" with the aim of bringing about a restoration of Yahweh's justice.[11] The complaint in Habakkuk 1:2–4 fits this pattern. Repeated instances of צדיק in the script (Hab 1:13, 2:4) can be inferred as additional references to the prophet.

There is no real consensus for the identification of רשע in Habakkuk. Referents that have been proposed include the Assyrians in Habakkuk 1:4 and the Chaldeans in Habakkuk 1:13,[12] the Chaldeans in both instances,[13] or Judeans not upholding justice demanded by the law in Habakkuk 1:4 and the Chaldeans brought as punishment in Habakkuk 1:13.[14] רשע is frequently used as an antonym to צדיק in the Hebrew Bible,[15] and both terms are often used in a generic sense, particularly in the Psalms and Wisdom literature.[16] In order to emphasize the contrast between the use of the definite article for צדיק in Habakkuk 1:4 and the lack of an article for רשע הצדיק was translated to refer to an individual, *the righteous one*, while the corresponding lack of precise identification for רשע allowed for the generic term *wickedness*.

---

10. Berlin, "Introduction to Hebrew Poetry," 303.
11. Brueggemann, *Theology*, 321.
12. Smith, *Book of the Twelve Prophets*, 119–24.
13. Ibid., 118–19; Johnson, "The Paralysis of Torah," 261.
14. Baker, *Nahum, Habakkuk and Zephaniah*, 45–46; Robertson, *Books of Nahum, Habakkuk and Zephaniah*, 34–38; Patterson, "Habakkuk," 127–29.
15. Van Leeuwen, "רשע," 1262.
16. Roberts, *Nahum, Habakkuk, and Zephaniah*, 90.

Another significant example can be seen in Habakkuk 2:2, where a definite article is included to designate הלחות, *the tablets*. This word is used elsewhere for the stones that carried the Decalogue (Exod 24:12). In the same verse is the verb באר, *to make plain*, itself used in only two other places in the Hebrew Bible, both of which are related to the Horeb/Sinai experience (Deut 1:5, 27:8). The use of the definite article in this instance must surely underline the implication that Habakkuk's vision has an affinity with Moses' reception of the law. The mere addition of the article in an English translation would begin to suggest this association, given that very few translations do include the article.[17]

Identification of Speakers

In a performance-critical reading, attention needs to be given to the actors in the drama. Occasionally, however, the identity of the speaker is not clear, perhaps reflecting an original oral communication event that underlies the text in which the identity of speakers would be evident. While a change in verbal forms and subject indicate a break in the discourse at Habakkuk 1:5, there is no introductory formula to identify a new speaker.[18] The Greek translators evidently believed clarification was required and added an "I" into the text on the understanding that the speaker is Yahweh, although the first-person pronoun does not occur until Habakkuk 1:6 in the MT. The NIV and a variety of commentators[19] have followed suit. Habakkuk 1:5–11 is often designated "Yahweh's first response;"[20] but even if it is a response, the verses do not constitute a ready *answer* to the prophet's complaint. In addition to the change in address (plural forms when an individual has asked questions), there is no direct reference to the questions that have been asked. Instead, there is a description of a force being raised that will wreak destruction as it moves through the land. Is mention of this force

---

17. The word "tablets" or "tables" without an article is used in KJV/NKJV, NLT, NIV, RSV/NRSV, ESV, NASB, NJPS, and GNT. The only versions I have come across that do include the definite article are NIrV and *Young's Literal Translation*.

18. Clark and Hatton, *The Books of Nahum, Habakkuk and Zephaniah*, 73, make this observation and suggest that translators "explicitly" introduce Yahweh as the speaker.

19. For example, Ward, *A Critical and Exegetical Commentary*, 8; Robertson, *Books of Nahum, Habakkuk and Zephaniah*, 142; Andersen, *Habakkuk*, 135.

20. For example, Roberts, *Nahum, Habakkuk and Zephaniah*, 91; Hiebert, "The Book of Habakkuk," 634; Andersen, *Habakkuk*, 135.

the prophet's "exasperation"[21] or the deity's announcement? The difficulties in identifying a subject for the phrase פֹּעֵל פֹּעַל can be seen in the versions: the LXX adds ἐγώ, the Syriac also supplies a subject, and the Aramaic and the Vulgate emend the participle to make it passive. Thus, there is ambiguity surrounding the speaker in v. 5 and in the subsequent identification of the "I" in v. 6. Such ambiguity opens possibilities for translation and performance. The speaker in v. 5 could be the prophet himself, reminiscing on an earlier word of Yahweh,[22] or it could be the authoritative voice of Yahweh addressing a wider audience and, as such, effectively ignoring the complaint of the prophet. This interpretation is suggested by Habakkuk's second complaint (Hab 1:12–17). Either option could be effectively "staged" to result in quite different interpretations.

A second example relates to the disparate material that interrupts the woe oracles in the second chapter of Habakkuk. The third woe ends abruptly without a shift to second-person singular verbs, as in the other oracles. It is interrupted by a pious statement: הלוא הנה מאת יהוה צבאות, *Behold! Is it not from Yahweh of Hosts?* (Hab 2:13a). This statement is often considered a marginal gloss with its new terminology and perceived irrelevance to the topic of the woe.[23] Likewise, Habakkuk 2:14 does not logically fit among the woe oracles and has the sound of a slogan that could appear anywhere. Since variations of this verse exist in Numbers 14:21 and Isaiah 11:9, it too is often considered a gloss.[24] As "interruptions," both statements could be viewed as coming from a speaker other than the one delivering the woe oracles. Matthew Anstey characterizes these as "interjections," a performance term, expressing visions that contrast with the taunting of the enemy: an eschatological vision (Hab 2:14) and a liturgical vision (Hab 2:20).[25] While such an understanding could be effectively transmitted in an orally performed version of Habakkuk by using different voices, communicating this idea in translation is more difficult. In my own project, Habakkuk was written in script form, which allowed for divisions with clearly marked headings. Thus, Habakkuk 2 was divided into two scenes,

---

21. Peckham, "The Vision of Habakkuk," 630. Peckham views all of the first chapter of Habakkuk as complaint oracles expanded by a commentary that quotes several sources, including Isaiah 5:12.

22. Cf. Cleaver-Bartholomew, "An Alternative Approach," 216.

23. Andersen, *Habakkuk*, 243; Roberts, *Nahum, Habakkuk and Zephaniah*, 123.

24. Roberts, *Nahum, Habakkuk and Zephaniah*, 123.

25. Anstey, "Habakkuk the Faithful Dissident," 52–53. Anstey adds Habakkuk 2:4b as a third "interjection" expressing an ethical vision.

with the second scene interrupted by a section headed "Interjection" at Habakkuk 2:14. Habakkuk 2:20 was demarcated in the script as an "Interlude," functioning also to mark a transition between Act 1 (Hab 1:1–2:19) and Act 2 (Hab 3:1–19). In retrospect, I wonder if I ought also to have included further interjections at Habakkuk 2:4 and Habakkuk 2:13a since these phrases also form a contrast with the surrounding material.

Plural and Singular Verb Forms

The change to plural imperative for verb forms in Habakkuk 1:5 (ראו, *look*, and תמהו, *be astounded*) is a significant change that is not readily seen in modern English where there is no difference between singular and plural second person pronouns. The change signals the beginning of a new section and, if it is to be understood as a response to the prophet's complaint in Habakkuk 1:2–4, also widens the message to include an audience beyond the prophet. A second example can be seen where the *NRSV* and *NIV* use third person plural forms throughout Habakkuk 1:6–11 despite the predominance of third person singular verbs in the MT. Mention of הכשדים, *the Chaldeans* (Hab 1:6), is quickly replaced by singular references so that the nation is represented by a collective unity. In order to identify an actor who would emphasize this contrast between plural and singular, I understood the reference as the king of the Chaldeans. The lack of a name, however, forms a contrast to Habakkuk the prophet and to Yahweh, suggesting that this is a *persona* that can be fulfilled by any one of a number of enemies perceived by the audience. This deliberate vagueness might therefore be quite significant. A traditional historical-critical reading of the book would attempt an identification of the enemy; however performance readings recognize the potential for new performances in new circumstances to ensure that the message is relevant to each new audience. Such freedom is evidenced by the rendering of this enemy as *Kittim* ("Romans") by the Qumran *Pesher*.

Omission of Recurring Particles

Many translations omit the recurring *waw* at the beginning of clauses. The significance of maintaining these in translation is that they provide a sense of movement and contribute to a building tension, especially in Habakkuk 1:5–11 where the invading enemy is being described.

Shifting Verb Forms

The rhythmic shift between third and second person address in the woe oracles (Hab 2:6–19) is not always faithfully translated (see CEV, NRSV, and *The Message*, all of which harmonize the forms to read consistently as second-person address).[26] Despite a degree of awkwardness in translating with the MT, resulting in the basic pattern "Woe to him who does . . . you do . . . ," the alternation of forms adds vividness and explicitly draws the audience into the action. It raises the question of who is being addressed. Renewal of the audience's attention is one of the reasons for person shifts in prophetic texts, according to Lénart de Regt. Although stated in relation to several other prophetic books, his words apply to the book of Habakkuk also: "Against the background of non-face threatening third person forms, second person forms renew the audience's involvement, addressing Israel anew."[27]

Each of the preceding examples shows that retaining a degree of literalness in translation provides important clues for the performative aspects inherent in the text of Habakkuk.

Lexical Consistency

Another principle followed in my translation is that of lexical consistency. Several studies of performance criticism in relation to translation have stressed the importance of lexical consistency for mnemonic purposes, based on the assumption that original scripts were orally performed.[28] An additional consequence that has been observed, that of making "cognitive connections with the audience,"[29] is of particular relevance to this project. Such connections are made within the performance itself, so that a word or idea repeated later in the performance would form connections to the earlier use in the mind of those listening. An example in Habakkuk is the word פעל, *work* (Hab 1:5, 3:2). Repetition of the word links the first and

---

26. Roberts also translates this way in his commentary, *Nahum, Habakkuk and Zephaniah*, 114.

27. de Regt, "Person Shifts in Prophetic Texts," 231. The term "face-threatening" is used by de Regt (ibid., 218) in relation to Liberia's Bassa language conventions that specify certain situations where second-person address is inappropriate.

28. Thomas and Thomas, *Structure and Orality in 1 Peter*, 1–4; Rhoads, "Performance Criticism, Part II," 171; and Maxey, "Performance Criticism, Part II," 171.

29. Maxey, "Performance Criticism, Part II," 171.

last chapters together (frequently the third chapter is viewed as a later addition to the composition) and raises the question of whether the "work" mentioned in the first chapter is the subject of the prophet's awe in the third chapter. Connections are also made with an audience's cultural register.[30] Such "connections" are often spoken of as examples of intertextuality.[31] Although oral texts can be included when using this term, from the perspective of performance other metaphors might be more effectively utilized. I have referred to these intertextual connections as "ready-mades"—the store of short commonplaces or clichés used by actors or musicians when improvising in performance.

There is an assumption of shared cultural knowledge and references between performer and audience that underlie the use of ready-mades. The creativity of a performance is shown in the way this shared knowledge is modified or challenged by application in a new situation. In Habakkuk, terms such as ישע, *save*; תורה, *Torah*; רשע, *wickedness*; צדיק, *righteous*; and משפט, *justice* could act as ready-mades. Their innovative use in unexpected textual contexts has a shock value that might cause the audience to reassess their understanding of the concepts. For example, תורה, *Torah*, is mentioned in Habakkuk 1:4 but is described as "paralyzed"—an unusual and arresting description. משפט, *justice*, another term familiar to a biblical audience, is used twice to highlight the lack of justice perceived in the presentation of Yahweh at this point in the book. In Habakkuk 1:4, justice is described as "crooked"; and in Habakkuk 1:7, "justice" and "dignity" are qualities attributed to the enemy. The reuse of the term חמס, *violence*, first used in Habakkuk 1:2 and repeated in Habakkuk 1:9, would also be surprising; by translating this word consistently, the audience becomes aware that the very "violence" the prophet had complained about seems to have been engineered by Yahweh. In translation, placing such ready-mades in inverted commas as has been done here would further call attention to their unusual use.

Extraverbal Cues

Translation informed by performance criticism attempts to recognize and replicate the auditory and visual features of the script. If wordplay, assonance, or vivid imagery is present in the Hebrew, there is value in trying to

---

30. Kelber, "Orality and Biblical Studies," 19; Wendland, "Performance Criticism," 3.
31. See, for example, Redditt, "Recent Research on the Book of the Twelve," 52–57.

reproduce those features in translation. As is often emphasized in a discussion of performance criticism, it is the whole event of message transmission that is analyzed. Thus it is important to consider non-verbal and extra-verbal features that are evident in the script when translating. A selection of examples from my translation follows:

- והתמהו תמהו, *and be profoundly astounded* (Hab 1:5). The combination of a *hithpael* and *qal* infinitive absolute of the same root occurs for emphasis, highlighted by consonance in Hebrew. "Be profoundly astounded" is my attempt, via assonance, to imitate this in translation.
- פעל פעל, *a work is being worked* (Hab 1:5) and המר והנמהר, *hurtful and hasty* (Hab 1:6). The alliteration present in the Hebrew text was mirrored in translation.
- ופשו פרשיו ופרשיו, *and they gallop his gallopers and his gallopers come* (Hab 1:8). In order to replicate the onomatopoeic effect of repeated Hebrew words in this phrase, the nouns were translated with the poetic word *gallopers*.
- קיקלון, *shameful shame* (Hab 2:16). This *hapax legomenon* was translated to indicate the wordplay with קלון earlier in the verse. In the second usage, repetition of the first syllable intensified the word; and this was imitated in translation.
- הס, *hush* (Hab 2:20). The serendipity of the onomatopoeic nature of the Hebrew word and a similar sounding English colloquialism allows for this highly iconic translation.

Setting

When reading the entire book of Habakkuk as a performance, I allowed my translation to be guided by the setting of the action. Habakkuk is a book that begins and ends in crisis. The opening words of the prophet (Hab 1:2–4) suggest a situation of turmoil in which injustice reigns and no order is kept, giving rise to bitter complaint. The multitude of negative terms used in three brief verses paints an extremely negative picture: חמס, *violence*; און, *sorrow*; עמל, *trouble*; שד, *devastation*; ריב, *strife*; מדון, *contention*; רשע, *wickedness*; and מעקל משפט, *crooked justice*. An invading army is described in Habakkuk 1:5–11, and it appears invasion is imminent also in Habakkuk 3.16. These descriptions evoke a situation of warfare in which Israel is in a vulnerable position. The closing soliloquy (Hab 3:16–19a) continues to describe a situation of crisis, whether it is a reference to a natural calamity or the devastating result of an invading army. Whatever interpretation is made for this final soliloquy, it is clear that for much of the book the crisis is of a military nature; and this situation guided my choices made in translation. The prophet's expectation of a military invasion suggests that while על־מִשְׁמַרְתִּי (Hab 2:1) is a term used in the Priestly tradition for periods of service in the temple, often translated *duty*, *service*, or *watch* (for example, 2 Chr 7:6, 8:14, 35:2), the setting allows for a translation of *on guard* at *siege works* (Hab 2:1). Plunder (Hab 2:8), violence (Hab 2:8–9, 17), and bloodshed (Hab 2:8, 12, 17) are all mentioned in the woe oracles, compounding the warfare imagery. The military imagery is not limited to Israel's enemies. It is also used in the theophanic description of Yahweh as a warrior with weapons and chariot (Hab 3:3–15).

Despite this pervading military imagery, a turning point in the script and an abrupt change of setting is marked at Habakkuk 2:20—a "pivotal 'silence,'" in the description of Ernst Wendland.[32] Following Wendland and informed by Peter Cotterell's study of Amos[33] I have interpreted this verse as the "peak" of the performance.[34] It suggests that despite the overall setting of crisis and despite the pervading military imagery, the vision of Yahweh in his temple of holiness is the central and dominant vision for the performance. When Yahweh is in his place, all human words, movement, and power are ultimately silenced before him. With a prayer as the opening scenario for the subsequent action, there is a suggestion that worship is the appropriate response by the prophet and the audience to Yahweh's presence in the temple. Worship becomes the context for the rest of the performance and guides the subsequent translation. Along with *the tablets* in Habakkuk 2:2, there are further linguistic and geographical allusions to the Exodus salvation event: mention of "a work" in Habakkuk 1:5 and 3:2;

32. Wendland, "May the Whole World Hush," 113.
33. Cotterell, "A Question of Peak."
34. In discourse analysis, "peak" can be recognized by a number of identifiable features: "*concentration of participants, rhetorical underlining, locus underlining, and grammatical underlining*" (Cotterell, "Discourse Analysis," 156, author's italics). Habakkuk 2:20 conforms to these features insofar as there is a concentration of characters—so that the verse is spoken by the prophet who gives his name to the book but is focused on "Yahweh," the principal character in the drama; the move from a series of woes to a command to be silent has a profound rhetorical effect; a change of locus noted by the sudden introduction of the temple; and the lack of verbs grammatically underline the phrase by giving it an immediate presence.

idols in Habakkuk 2:18; geographical locations from the Exodus tradition in Habakkuk 3:3 and 3:7; and a fourfold reference to Yahweh as a "saving" God in Habakkuk 3:8, 3:13 [x2], and 3:18. These serve to reinforce a context of worship introduced by reference to the temple in Habakkuk 2:20.

Performance Themes That Can Be Found in Habakkuk

The project described here began with a quite literal translation of the MT of Habakkuk. After surveying the literature across the broad discipline of performance studies, I discovered that themes commonly occurring in the literature were also themes that had emerged in the process of translation. The next part of this section introduces three such themes and their significance in a study of the book of Habakkuk.

One of the overriding themes in performance studies is the theme of *embodiment*. For those engaged in performance studies, knowledge is transmitted in holistic, embodied form and involves the researcher in the subject matter. There is a recognized "co-investigative" dynamic in performance studies in which both researcher and subject contribute to meaning.[35] When interpreting Scripture, the investigator is very often not impartial, but instead a faithful reader convinced that the texts are imbued with the spirit of a living God and that they have the potential for transforming knowledge and praxis in the investigator, the faithful community, and the wider world. Reading Scripture as a performance is a reminder that for faithful readers biblical books are scripts to be enacted and lived.

Does the theme of embodiment come to the fore in the book of Habakkuk? I argue that it does, acknowledging that a feature of prophetic literature in general is recognition of the embodiment of the word of Yahweh in the person of the prophet who acts as an intermediary.[36] In the same way that embodiment distinguishes the performance arts from other visual arts such as painting, sculpture and literature,[37] God's message through the prophets distinguishes this form of biblical literature from law codes, narratives, and historiography, because without the prophet the message would not be conveyed. While some of the prophetic experiences described in the Hebrew Bible portray the prophet primarily as a spokesperson passing on a message, the book of Habakkuk portrays the personal struggles

35. Davis, *Cambridge Companion to Performance Studies*, 2.
36. House, "Character of God," 129.
37. Weber, *Theatricality as Medium*, 297.

and responses of the prophet as much as he conveys a divine message. This prophet is present in the midst of the crisis, experiencing Yahweh's revelation visually, audibly, and even viscerally (Hab 3:16). If it is legitimate to identify the prophet Habakkuk as "the righteous one" in this script (Hab 1:4, 1:13, 2:4), then he embodies faithfulness and becomes a model for ancient and contemporary audiences alike. If the questions and complaints of "the righteous one" are not dismissed by Yahweh, then contemporary communities of faith should be confident to bring questions and complaints into the divine presence. If the prophet is instructed to have patience, then contemporary readers should also learn patience. If the prophet models prayer and worship, then these elements are necessary for our ongoing faithfulness.

Several thematic and grammatical features of the book of Habakkuk show that the theme of *process* is integral to the book, particularly the open-ended nature of the text. In performance studies, there is an emphasis on the actual activity of the artist or actor, not just the completion of an event or action. Henry Bial claims, "One of the basic tenets of performance studies is that a performance is not a static finished product. Performances are always in-process, changing, growing, and moving through time."[38] In the book of Habakkuk the questions that the prophet asks at the beginning of the performance are left unanswered. The woe oracles (Hab 2:6–19) and command to "hush" before Yahweh (Hab 2:20) set up an expectation of judgment of the enemy, but this is not resolved, in so far as the script moves to prayer and theophany. Despite the triumphant faith expressed by the prophet at the end of the performance (Hab 3:17–19a), there is also a renewed reference to the crisis of enemy invasion (Hab 3:16). The many *waw*-consecutive forms and the changes in verb tenses at various points throughout the performance give a sense of movement and timelessness. The final word of the script prior to the postlude is an active verb (דרך, *to walk*). By translating with the verb at the end of the sentence (על במותי ידרכני, *on my high places he makes me walk*), a stress on active faithfulness is the lingering impression of the performance.[39] The postlude that completes the script, while uncertain in meaning, gives instruction for

---

38. Bial, *Performance Studies Reader*, 215. This is exemplified by an emerging sub-discipline of performance studies developing at the University of Sydney known as "rehearsal studies"; see McAuley, "State of the Art: Performance Studies," 5–6.

39. A parallel verse in 2 Samuel 22:34 attests על במותי יעמדני, *on my high places he sets me secure*, suggesting passive faithfulness that contrasts with the version in Habakkuk 3:19a.

performers to follow. These observations of the theme of process at work in Habakkuk suggest that it is a text open to renewed performance in our own settings.

A third theme that is common to performance studies is that of *re-enactment*. There is widespread agreement that performances are based upon preexisting models, scripts, or patterns. Therefore performance is understood as the presentation of rehearsed behavior. Nonetheless, it is not mere repetition at work. When past performances are re-enacted in the present, the re-enactment itself results in small revisions of familiar scripts. This theme raises the issue of interpretation. Since re-enactment is not mere repetition, the choices made by the director and performer, the messages conveyed through setting, and the knowledge and experience of the audience will combine to provide a unique experience in each performance. Where "correct" interpretation is made problematic by a lack of clarity in the author's intention or an inability for contemporary interpreters to clearly perceive the original author's intention due to the historical and linguistic gap between us, several different interpretations each may be "faithful performances."

The significant number of *hapax legomena* (ten nouns[40] and five verbs[41]) spread through the book of Habakkuk offers an example of how translation may be understood as re-enactment. Translators must make educated guesses as to the meanings of such words; yet these guesses can still be viewed as faithful renderings of the tradition in the same way that two different actors can faithfully enact a script that will result in very different interpretations.

It is not only *hapax legomena* that require interpretive decisions by translators. The third chapter of Habakkuk is sprinkled with "liturgical instructions," including a prayer form (שגינות, *Shigionoth*), three *Selah* notations, and a colophon similar to those found in the Psalter but unusually placed at the end of the chapter. None of these terms is well understood. The term שגינות, *Shigionoth*, (Hab 3:1) is thought by some to be the plural of שגיון that occurs in Psalm 7:1, the content of which suggests שגיון

---

40. מגמה, "eagerness" (1:9); משחק, "object of derision" (1:10); עבטיט, "heavy debts" (2:6); כפיס, "rafter" (2:11); מעור, "nakedness" (2:15); קיקלון, "shameful shame" (2:16); חביון, "hiding place" (3.4); פרז, "warrior," עליצות, "exultation" (3:14); רפתים, "stalls" (3:17). All references given are in the book of Habakkuk.

41. עקל, "to be crooked" (1:4); נוה, "to abide" (2:5); עור, "to be laid bare" (3:9); רום, [adv] "on high" (3:10); חמר, "to heap up" (3:15). All references given are in the book of Habakkuk.

is a technical name for a sung lament.[42] Apart from the similar annotation, however, Habakkuk 3 does not take the form of a lament, nor is a lament expected in the context, given that the previous scene, which had condemned the Chaldean oppressors and given an expectation that justice would be brought about. Others look to the possible verbal roots and find a meaning based on the root שׁנה, *to stagger*, or שׁגע, *to be mad*, suggesting a wild, passionate song.[43] The similarity to the word נגינות, *Niginoth*, in the Postlude (Hab 3:19b) also suggests it is a musical term. This latter term is equally mysterious, however, since related words elsewhere in the Hebrew Bible suggest the use of stringed instruments (Isa 38:20; Lam 5:14) but at times are indicative of a mocking song (Job 30:9; Ps 69:13; Lam 3:14). In my project, I merely transliterated the Hebrew words, while noting that their presence in the script provides a clear impulse for performance. With greater confidence, a contemporary rendering could be provided in order to allow for a more immediate response from the audience; nevertheless the resulting performance could be very different depending on the nuance of the translation chosen by the translator/director.

Interpretative decisions are raised in a question by Ernst Wendland: "How much 'freedom' did the *transmitter* of a given biblical text (as distinct from the *author*) really have to improvise with regard to the written document that he was commissioned to deliver before a certain audience group in a particular setting?"[44] Noticing the creative use of ready-mades by the author(s) of Habakkuk suggests that such improvisation is already at work in the script itself. As mentioned above, terms such as *Torah*, *justice*, and *violence* arguably depart from any expectation the audience might have had. To give just a few further examples, the prophetic concept of a *day of distress* (Hab 3:16) is used in relation to the enemy rather than to Yahweh's own people.[45] Creation imagery is turned on its head by presenting humankind as the equivalent of the lowlife of creation (*creeping things*, Hab 1:14) rather than the pinnacle (cf. Gen 1:21, 26). Terminology from the liturgical tradition is inserted in Habakkuk 3, but the indeterminate placement of the

---

42. Roberts, *Nahum, Habakkuk and Zephaniah*, 130.
43. Koehler and Baumgartner, *Hebrew and Aramaic Lexicon*, 1414.
44. Wendland, "Performance Criticism," 5, author's italics.
45. According to Francis Andersen, this phrase "never describes the trouble experienced by the wicked when justice is done to them in retribution. It always describes the distress of the LORD's people, caused by an oppressor, a distress from which he should deliver them" (*Habakkuk*, 345).

Selah instruction and the colophon at the end rather than at the beginning of the psalm depart from the norm.

It is clear that choices that have been made by the author(s) of Habakkuk in the representation of older material relate to the circumstances of a people in the midst of crisis and encourage faithfulness under such circumstances. Viewing such changes as "improvisation" emphasizes the possibility of adaptation in every new performance. It is also a reminder that the original "script" of Habakkuk was already a process of improvising inherited and established traditions, making use of ready-mades to surprise and challenge the audience's expectations. The openness that characterizes improvised performance suggests that no text can be assumed to be final. The church's acceptance of canonical scripture as authoritative suggests that new translations should be based on original language scripts rather than building upon earlier adaptations, even though variations amongst the earliest manuscripts already undermine the idea of a pure text. All translation, to an extent, represents a new creation.

The Unsettling Nature of Translation for Performance

Translating Habakkuk as a performance raises some unsettling issues with regard to interpretation and authority. Seeing the biblical text through the lens of performance criticism makes explicit the reinterpretive process that is continually undertaken by faithful readers who read with a presumption that the Scriptures are relevant today. Approaching Scripture as a script that cannot be fully realized until its performance in both its original context and in today's context is appreciated requires both respect for the script *and* preparedness for the dynamism of performance driven by ever-changing settings, actors, and audiences.

Paying attention to performance themes within the book of Habakkuk reveal that the original author(s) played with genres and identities. At times, characteristics usually ascribed to Yahweh are attributed to other characters, including the prophet (righteousness) and the enemy (justice, dignity). In this performance, it was Yahweh, the one expected to stand for justice and righteousness, who was perceived by the prophet to be the instrument of the violence that swept through the nation. The script announces a revelation but launches into a complaint. Later, there is an expectation of judgment, but what follows is prayer. The prophet speaks regularly, but rarely with the prophetic formulae that readers of the prophetic literature might expect. Rather, the words of the prophet include complaint, sarcasm, questions, pain, and lament. Such dissonant texts have been transmitted in this performance despite many opportunities for tempering their impact, as evidenced by textual variations that show such modifications. Their inclusion by the author and their retention by the communities that have preserved the text remind us that through the ages it can be difficult to discern the words of Yahweh amidst human words. This performance preserves not only "God's word through the prophet" but also the prophet's very human questions, confusion, and developing faith.

Finally, translation with an eye to performance puts an increasing demand upon the audience. Noticing places where the audience is explicitly included, speculating about the emotional impact the performance has, and recognition of the liturgical elements all suggest that an audience is essential in this performance. Direct address to the audience (Hab 1:6–11, 2:6–19, 2:20) ensures they do not remain impartial spectators; and the frequent use of present tense verbs means that this performance is not locked in the past but is intended to be reimagined and relived. The shift in verb tenses in Habakkuk and the lack of precise identification of the characters other than the prophet and Yahweh leave openness for those attending to the performance to identify with the events and enable them to use the performance for faithful reenactment in their own time and setting. In effect, when the audience is the faithful community, they become performers themselves, re-enacting the drama in their own setting. When this happens, the interaction between script, actor, and audience that is demanded by the dialogical nature of performance will very likely result in change—in the script, in the interpreter, and in the world inhabited by each.

Bibliography

Andersen, Francis I. *Habakkuk: A New Translation with Introduction and Commentary.* Anchor Bible 25. New York: Doubleday, 2001.

Anstey, Matthew. "Habakkuk the Faithful Dissident: A Performative Hermeneutic for Anglicans in Australia." *St Mark's Review* 203/2 (2007) 47–60.

Avishur, Y. *Studies in Hebrew and Ugaritic Psalms.* Publications of the Perry Foundation for Biblical Research, the Hebrew University of Jerusalem. Jerusalem: Magnes, 1994.

Baker, David W. *Nahum, Habakkuk and Zephaniah.* Tyndale Old Testament Commentary 23B. Leicester, UK: Inter-Varsity, 1988.

Berlin, Adele. "Introduction to Hebrew Poetry." In *The New Interpreter's Bible*, edited by Leander E. Keck, 4:301–15. Nashville: Abingdon, 1996.

Bial, Henry, editor. *The Performance Studies Reader.* London: Routledge, 2004.

Brownlee, William Hugh. *The Text of Habakkuk in the Ancient Commentary from Qumran.* Journal of Biblical Literature Monograph Series 11. Philadelphia: Society of Biblical Literature, 1959.

Bruce, F. F. "Habakkuk." In *The Minor Prophets: An Exegetical and Expository Commentary.* Vol. 2, *Obadiah, Jonah, Micah, Nahum, and Habakkuk*, edited by Thomas E. McComiskey, 831–96. Grand Rapids: Baker, 1992.

Brueggemann, Walter. *Theology of the Old Testament: Testimony, Dispute, Advocacy.* Minneapolis: Fortress, 1997.

Clark, David J., and Howard A. Hatton. *A Handbook on the Books of Nahum, Habakkuk, and Zephaniah.* UBS Handbook Series. New York: United Bible Societies, 1989.

Cleaver-Bartholomew, David. "An Alternative Approach to Hab 1,2—2,20." *Scandinavian Journal of the Old Testament* 17/2 (2003) 206–25.

Cotterell, Peter. "Linguistics, Meaning, Semantics and Discourse Analysis." In *New International Dictionary of Old Testament Theology and Exegesis*, edited by Willem A. Van Gemeren, 134–60. Grand Rapids: Zondervan, 1996.

———. "A Question of Peak." *The Bible Translator* 49/1 (1998) 139–48.

Davis, Tracy C., editor. *The Cambridge Companion to Performance Studies.* Cambridge: Cambridge University Press, 2008.

De Regt, Lénart. "Person Shifts in Prophetic Texts: Its Function and Its Rendering in Ancient and Modern Translations." In *The Elusive Prophet: The Prophet as Historical Person, Literary Character and Anonymous Artist.*, edited by J. C. de Moor, 214–31. Oudtestamentische Studiën 45. Leiden: Brill, 2001.

Haak, Robert D. *Habakkuk.* Vetus Testamentum Supplements 44. Leiden: Brill, 1992.

Hiebert, Theodore. *God of My Victory: The Ancient Hymn in Habakkuk 3.* Harvard Semitic Monographs 38. Atlanta: Scholars, 1986.

———. "The Book of Habakkuk: Introduction, Commentary and Reflections." In *The New Interpreter's Bible*, edited by Leander E. Keck, 6:621–55. Nashville: Abingdon, 1996.

House, Paul R. "The Character of God in the Book of the Twelve." In *Reading and Hearing the Book of the Twelve*, edited by James D. Nogalski and Marvin A. Sweeney, 125–45. SBL Symposium Series 15. Atlanta: Society of Biblical Literature, 2000.

Johnson, Marshall D. "The Paralysis of Torah in Habakkuk 1:4." *Vetus Testamentum* 35 (1985) 257–66.

Kelber, Werner H. "Orality and Biblical Studies: A Review Essay." *Review of Biblical Literature* 12 (2007) 1–24. Online: http://www.bookreviews.org/pdf/2107_6748.pdf.

Koehler, Ludwig, and Walter Baumgartner. *The Hebrew and Aramaic Lexicon of the Old Testament.* Leiden: Brill, 2001.

Leeuwen, C. van. "רשׁע." In *Theological Lexicon of the Old Testament*, edited by Ernst Jenni and Claus Westermann, 3:1261–65. Translated by Mark Biddle. 3 vols. 1971. Peabody, MA: Hendrickson, 1997.

Margalit, B. "The Day the Sun Did Not Stand Still: A New Look at Joshua 10:8–15." *Vetus Testamentum* 42 (1992) 466–91.

Maxey, James A. "Performance Criticism and Its Implications for Bible Translation. Part I: Oral Performance and New Testament Studies." *The Bible Translator* 60/1 (2009) 37–49.

———. "Performance Criticism and Its Implications for Bible Translation. Part II: Challenges and Experiences." *The Bible Translator* 60/3 (2009) 165–82.

McAuley, Gay. "State of the Art: Performance Studies." *SemiotiX* 10 (November 2007) 1–10. Online: http://www.semioticon.com/semiotix/semiotix10/sem-10-05.html/.

Patterson, R. D. "Habakkuk." In *Habakkuk, Nahum, Zephaniah*, edited by K. Barker, 115–272. Wycliffe Exegetical Commentary. Chicago: Moody, 1991.

Peckham, Brian. "The Vision of Habakkuk." *Catholic Biblical Quarterly* 48 (1986) 617–36.

Redditt, Paul L. "Recent Research on the Book of the Twelve as One Book." *Currents in Research: Biblical Studies* 9 (2001) 47–80.

Rhoads, David "Performance Criticism: An Emerging Methodology in Second Testament Studies—Part I." *Biblical Theology Bulletin* 36 (2006) 118–33.

———. "Performance Criticism: An Emerging Methodology in Second Testament Studies—Part II." *Biblical Theology Bulletin* 36 (2006) 164–84.

Roberts, J. J. M. *Nahum, Habakkuk, and Zephaniah: A Commentary.* Old Testament Library. Louisville: Westminster John Knox, 1991.

Robertson, O. Palmer. *The Books of Nahum, Habakkuk, and Zephaniah.* New International Commentary on the Old Testament. Grand Rapids: Eerdmans, 1990.

Schechner, Richard. *Performance Studies: An Introduction.* 2nd ed. New York: Routledge, 2006.

Smith, George A. *The Book of the Twelve Prophets.* Vol. 2, *Zephaniah, Nahum, Habakkuk, Etc.* 8th ed. London: Hodder & Stoughton, 1905.

Sweeney, Marvin A. "Habakkuk, Book of." In *The Anchor Bible Dictionary*, edited by David Noel Freedman, 3:1–6. New York: Doubleday, 1992.

Thomas, Kenneth J., and Margaret Orr Thomas. *Structure and Orality in 1 Peter: A Guide for Translators.* New York: United Bible Societies, 2006.

Walker, Julia A. "Why Performance? Why Now? Textuality and the Rearticulation of Human Presence." *Yale Journal of Criticism* 16/1 (2003) 149–75.

Ward, William Hayes. *A Critical and Exegetical Commentary on Micah, Zephaniah, Nahum, Habakkuk, Obadiah and Joel.* International Critical Commentary. Edinburgh: T. & T. Clark, 1911.

Weber, Samuel *Theatricality as Medium.* New York: Fordham University Press, 2004.

Wendland, Ernst R. "'May the Whole World Hush in His Presence!' (Habakkuk 2:20): Communicating Aspects of the Rhetoric of an Ancient Biblical Text Today." *Journal of Northwest Semitic Languages* 27/2 (2001) 113–33.

———. "Performance Criticism: Assumptions, Applications, and Assessment." *Translation Information Clearinghouse, TicTalk* 65 (2008) 1–11.

7

Comparative Rhetorical Poetics, Orality, and Bible Translation
The Case of Jude

Ernst R. Wendland

CEBITA, University of Stellenbosch

Overview

THIS STUDY EXAMINES THE relatively short epistle of Jude from several distinct but interrelated perspectives. A rhetorical approach is first undertaken to explore how the author organized the discourse in order to carry out a multifaceted strategy of persuasion. His aim was to influence the implied audience to adopt his clearly defined point of view with regard to the letter's predominant topic and goal: a warning against "godless men" (v. 4). Two different rhetorical analyses are comparatively and critically evaluated in this connection. This is followed by the application of a literary-structural methodology that demonstrates how an assortment of artful compositional forms serves to carry out the author's rhetorical objectives on both the macro- and micro-organization of this epistle. It will be further suggested that this hortatory text has been arranged in a distinctly lyric, rhythmic and line-constituted manner that makes it "poetic prose."

During the course of this investigation, the varied oral potential of the original text will be progressively revealed to support the hypothesis that this intense, polemical letter was crafted in writing with a dramatic oral proclamation of the message in view. As a practical conclusion, the challenge of communicating Jude in translation to a contemporary English-speaking audience will be briefly considered, again in a heuristic, comparative manner to illustrate some of the major challenges that must be confronted. In this complex interlingual, cross-cultural endeavor, it will be argued that a "one size fits all" version cannot be the solution. On the contrary, only a rendering that seeks to accommodate to a specific target audience in a well-defined communicative setting can hope to be successful in today's saturated (English) Bible translation market.

What Do We Mean by Rhetoric?

In its classical Aristotelian sense, which is still referenced in the present day, rhetoric is simply the art of argumentation or "persuasion" (*ars rhetorica*)[1] or, to be more specific, "the art of persuasive communication,"[2] which may be expanded somewhat as follows:

> Rhetoric as the art of persuasion encompasses all forms of purposeful communication in the various media available for communication.[3]

Rhetoric thus embraces the notions of textual *form* (literary or oratorical), semantic *content* (that is, a significant issue), communicative *function* (that is, persuasion), and *medium* of transmission (oral, written, audiovisual, etc.). In addition, one must also consider an original *source* (author, orator, composer), an intended or implied *receptor/response group* (e.g., audience,

---

1. Aune, "Rhetoric," 415. Some critics would generalize the definition to simply "the art of speaking" (cf. Soulen and Soulen, *Handbook*, 162), but this is not very helpful.

2. Duke, *Persuasive Appeal*, 30.

3. Phillips, "Rhetoric," 237. Furthermore, "rhetoric as strategic communication attempts to mould another person's view of the world in which he or she lives; it invites its audience to reconsider their existing world view in the light of the world view promoted through strategic communication of one kind or another . . . Biblical rhetoric is first and foremost the art of persuading individuals and communities to accept the Bible's world view" (ibid., 241, 259).

readership), plus a social, psychological, and physical contextual *setting*. All seven of these factors must be included in the analysis and evaluation of any given realization of rhetoric in action.

In practice, rhetoric entails the use of a definite and clearly definable artistic strategy that aims through conventional but skillfully employed means of argumentation to modify (that is, to reinforce, modify, or change) the cognitive, emotive, and/or volitional stance of the intended audience.[4] The term *art* suggests a particular ability or proficiency that one is simply endowed with. *Technique*, on the other hand, implies a compositional skill that can be learned and perfected on the basis of some concrete heuristic principles and procedures. The systematic evaluation or application of this technical art (or artistic technique) with respect to oral and written verbal art forms is known as "rhetorical criticism."[5]

While overlapping in varying degrees with respect to aims and methods, the study of rhetoric may be distinguished from that of artistry in literature (or in "orature" in the case of oral discourse) by its primary focus. An analysis of artistry, or "style," tends to stress the impersonal literary *form* of a given text, whereas the analysis of rhetoric emphasizes the text's interpersonal communicative *function*, or pragmatic intent. Function is progressively realized by means of the form with regard to the twofold goal of cognitive *conviction* coupled with emotive and volitional *persuasion*. Thus, the fact that a person or audience has been cognitively convinced will be manifested correspondingly by a substantial reinforcement or change in some specific thought, attitude, or overt behavior.

There is considerable overlap in the textual realization and the subsequent critical assessment of these two central attributes of recognized literary (or oratorical) discourse—artistry and rhetoric. Many of the same structural and stylistic devices may be involved in their operation and evaluation in a given language, certainly in the ancient Hebrew and Greek biblical literature.[6] Furthermore, both dimensions contribute significantly

---

4. Persuasion involves the formulation of a hortatory argument with the aim of "obtaining or reinforcing the adherence of the audience to some thesis" (Perelman, *New Rhetoric*, 11). Though essentially a written text-based methodology nowadays, it is important to recognize classical rhetoric's foundation in *orality*: "While originally an oral skill used in speeches, rhetoric was later used in written texts as well, particularly in those forms of literature which were meant to persuade" (Webb, "Jude," 612).

5. For a description of two types of rhetorical criticism (diachronic and synchronic) as well as the "procedure of rhetorical criticism," see Aune, "Rhetoric," 417.

6. Mazor argues that "there is no biblical literature" (*Who Wrought the Bible*, 21), but

to the overall *connotative* component of text meaning in terms of impact (verbal power) and appeal (verbal beauty). For this reason, some analysts lump the two together in their classification of artistic technique, for example, in the rhetoric of "composition" and that of "argumentation."[7] In any case, a number of familiar formal features figure prominently in creating the persuasive shape and pragmatic shading of discourse in both secular debate and traditional argument as well as in theological exhortation and encouragement (e.g., with regard to such features as rhetorical questions, hyperbole, irony, figurative language, patterns of repetition, word-order variations for focus and emphasis, direct speech, enigma, allusion, paronomasia, and alliteration). Most of the preceding may be illustrated in the short, but forceful epistle of Jude.

The perception of and response to biblical rhetoric, which acts as an indispensable aid in the expression of a text's religious/theological content, will obviously differ for contemporary, as distinct from the initially intended, receptors of a particular book, pericope, or passage. In addition, for many readers or hearers of the Scriptures in today's world, these two so-called horizons of interpretation (the ancient and modern), which are distinguished by terms such as "source language" (SL) and "target language" (TL) settings,[8] are further complicated by a third. This is the "interposed" horizon that is generated by the use in translation of another translation instead of the original text, thus creating a "secondary version," one that is not based directly upon the original text. On the other hand, there is an increasing number of scholarly tools and resources, in both printed and electronic forms, that are available to bring today's Bible readers and translators back to a conceptual point closer to the original text and its situational (historical, environmental, sociocultural, religious) setting[9]—resources

---

this assertion would seem to be denied by the subtitle of his book: "unveiling the Bible's aesthetic secrets." In short, his claim is that in the case of the Hebrew Scriptures (at least), "What we have is an ideologically driven text, not a literary text, one [ideologically driven text] that enlists complex and enticing aesthetic devices to drive home its message" (ibid., 23). But the latter features are precisely those that characterize "a literary text."

7. Trible, *Rhetorical Criticism*, 32, 41.

8. The term "target language" (cf. "receptor language") may reflect a rather crude and misleading "conduit model" of message transmission, though it is still current in contemporary translation studies (Pym, *Exploring Translation Theories*, 1). "Consumer language," or perhaps "response language," would be more appropriate in that such expressions serve to highlight the active hermeneutical role that a contemporary audience plays in the overall communication process that is activated by translation.

9. For a good overview of the relevant extratextual background of Jude, see Bauckham, *Jude*, 8–16.

such as commentaries, annotated and illustrated study Bibles, specialized book studies, hypertext computer programs, and Internet resources. An understanding of standard Hebrew and Hellenistic literary and rhetorical procedures can also assist then in ensuring that this complex interlingual, cross-cultural, and transhistorical communication activity will be more accurate and hence also profitable to Scripture users and translators as well.

A Greco-Roman Rhetorical Perspective on Jude

A competent Greco-Roman (GR) analysis of the New Testament text, especially an epistle, has many insights to offer Bible exegetes and translators alike. However, as will be suggested below, such an analysis cannot be viewed as the last or the only word on the subject. It may—even must—be complemented by additional perspectives and methodologies, rhetorical and otherwise.[10] In this section I will present a summary of one of the most detailed studies of Jude according to the GR classical method, namely, that of Duane Watson.[11]

A number of features commend Watson's study, for example: the meticulous listing of all the standard rhetorical devices apparently utilized by Jude (along with their GR technical designation and references to the ancient handbooks on rhetoric);[12] a careful listing of the major intertextual citations and allusions within the text, biblical as well as extrabiblical; a specification of the relationship between the putative compositional components of a deliberative speech and the basic formal units of a Hellenistic letter; and a generally perceptive description of the linear movement of the discourse regarding its principal structural segments and their various interconnections. However, it is in connection with this last-mentioned exercise that a rather serious problem comes to light with respect to the larger organization of Jude's epistle. This will be closely considered in the

---

10. I give an overview of a selection of different "rhetorical" approaches in Wendland, "Rhetorical Analysis, 173–86."

11. Watson, *Invention, Arrangement, and Style*. This was the "first full-scale rhetorical analysis of a New Testament book utilizing Kennedy's method" (Watson and Hauser, *Rhetorical Criticism*, 111) and one that "carries Kennedy's methodology about as far as it can go" (Mitchell, *Rhetoric of Reconciliation*, 10). This is in reference to Kennedy's influential work, *New Testament Interpretation through Rhetorical Criticism*.

12. "Although "In the NT the name 'Jude' refers to at least eight different men ... the identification of Jude as the brother of Jesus is the [most] probable" (Webb, "Jude," 616). For further support of this position, see Bauckham, *Jude*, 14–16.

next section, but first Watson's "rhetorical outline of Jude" is reproduced (below) for reference:[13]

I. Epistolary Prescript (Quasi-*Exordium*), vv. 1–2

II. *Exordium*, v. 3

III. *Narratio*, v. 4. Main propositions: 1) the sectarians within the church are ungodly and subject to judgment; 2) the sectarians are the ungodly whose presence and judgment in the last days has been foretold.

IV. *Probatio*, vv. 5–16

    A. <u>First Proof</u>—"The sectarians within the church are ungodly and subject to judgment." An artificial proof based on examples drawn from history, vv. 5–10.

        1. Three historical examples of sinners and their condemnation, vv. 5–7.

        2. Comparison with the sectarians, v. 8.

        3. Amplification by comparison, vv. 9–10.

    B. <u>Second Proof</u>—"The sectarians within the church are ungodly and subject to judgment." An artificial (or inartificial) proof based on examples drawn from judgments of the subtype of supernatural oracle, vv. 11–13.

        1. The prophecy, v. 11.

        2. Application to the sectarians, vv. 12–13.

    C. <u>Third Proof</u>—"The sectarians are the ungodly whose presence and judgment in the last days has been foretold." An artificial

---

13. Watson, *Invention*, 77–78, with slight modifications to the format; all subsequent quotes from this book in the present section are from pages 78–79. The technical GR rhetorical terms referring to the structure of discourse may be briefly defined as follows: *Exordium*—a brief introductory section designed to catch the reader/hearer's attention and goodwill; *Narratio*—a rehearsal or summary of the course of events that are pertinent to the primary goal, or *Propositio*, of the discourse; *Probatio (Argumentatio)*—functions to introduce and develop the various intellectual and affective, deductive and inductive proofs for the central thesis or issue under debate; *Peroratio*—a short conclusion, including some reiteration (*Repetitio*) and perhaps also an emotional appeal (*Adfectus*) (Soulen and Soulen, *Handbook*, 163–64).

proof based on an example drawn from a judgment of the subtype of supernatural oracle, vv. 14–16.

    1. The prophecy of I Enoch 1:9, vv. 14–15.

    2. Application to the sectarians, v. 16.

V. *Peroratio*, vv. 17–23

    A. *Repetitio*—"The sectarians are the ungodly scoffers of apostolic testimony." An artificial proof based on an example drawn from a judgment of the subtype of supernatural oracle, vv. 17–19.

    B. *Adfectus*, vv. 20–23

VI. Doxology (Quasi-*Peroratio*), vv. 24–25

In his concluding "evaluation of the rhetoric" and throughout his study, Watson stresses "the degree of Jude's adherence to conventional rhetorical principles of invention, arrangement, and style." After such an impressive number of examples have been mustered, one actually begins to wonder whether the "New Testament writers sat down with rhetorical handbooks to compose their works."[14] Watson would deny this "false impression,"[15] but his manner of analysis, or at least his presentation of the results, certainly seems to support such speculation. On the other hand, Watson calls attention to one aspect of Jude's rhetorical argumentation that might be regarded as being "deficient," namely, the absence of "any attempt to counter the arguments posed by the sectarians." He explains "this lack of refutation" as an indication that "Jude's response is conditioned by eschatological concerns . . . a conviction [that] makes the need to identify the sectarians primary."[16]

A serious question arises, however, with regard to Watson's conclusion about the main message of Jude's epistle in terms of both theme and purpose. As the preceding outline clearly indicates, this would appear to be predominantly negative in tone and admonitory in intent. In other words:

> To counter the sectarians' word and deed, Jude must convince his audience that the sectarians are ungodly and heading for judgment, and are the ungodly whose presence and judgment were previously predicted.

14. Watson and Hauser, *Rhetorical Criticism*, 112.
15. Ibid., 112.
16. On this point, see also Harm, "Logic Line," 159.

Thus, in order to "meet the needs of the exigence," the reason for writing, Jude "ostensibly addresses his rhetoric to those still loyal to apostolic doctrine and practice." To this end, he employs a deliberative strategy of argumentation to dissuade them from following what will inevitably turn out to their harm (spiritual ruin). This rhetorical approach is supported by an epideictic infrastructure that is intended "to decrease their ethos [that is, that of the sectarians], and to elicit negative pathos."[17]

While not denying the validity of these conclusions, I wish to suggest that they do not tell the whole story, and that, first, an important aspect of Jude's overall message has been either overlooked or ignored. The reason for this error, now one of contemporary interpretation, is closely related to the misconstrual of the larger compositional structure of Jude's letter—a misreading, as it were, of its rhetoric. Second, while I would certainly agree that it is helpful, if not overdone, to analyze this epistle (or any other) "in the light of the conventions of Greco-Roman rhetoric," I do not concur with the stipulation that it "must be interpreted" *only* in this way, that is, solely through the hermeneutical lens of a GR type of methodology.[18] Such a monolithic approach not only leaves one open to possible errors with regard to the interpretation of theme and purpose,[19] but it also ignores the

---

17. To explain, "deliberative rhetoric was the rhetoric of the 'assembly'. . . and was the rhetoric of advice and consent, trying to get one course of action or another, one policy or another voted on in an affirmative manner. The temporal focus of deliberative rhetoric was the future . . . Finally there was epideictic rhetoric, the rhetoric of display . . . the rhetoric of praise and blame . . . Its temporal focus was the present. It did not seek to change beliefs, behaviors, opinions, or attitudes [that is, like deliberative rhetoric], but rather it sought to reinforce existing ones" (Witherington, *New Testament Rhetoric*, 14). Joubert considers Jude to be a classic case of "epideictic discourse," which is followed as a "specific global strategy throughout the letter" ("Persuasion," 79, original italics).

18. Watson, *Invention*, 79.

19. To be more specific, some of the difficulties associated with an overly-strict application of the GR method of analysis may be summarized as follows: "There is the question of the degree that rhetorical theory influenced the epistolary genre . . . and if it is rightly used in analyzing Jewish texts, particularly those from a specifically Palestinian context . . . Greco-Roman rhetorical analysis may leave peculiar features of early Christian rhetoric unappreciated or undiscovered . . . There is the danger of glossing over the changes that rhetoric must undergo in the transition from oral to written form or from one written genre to another . . . There is also the danger of a too rigid application of rhetorical categories to the biblical texts. Black notes 'a disquieting tendency to press oracles or letters into rhetorical schemes of organization'" (Watson and Hauser, *Rhetorical Criticism*, 111; cf. Black, "Rhetorical Criticism"). Other criticisms of a more general nature could be mentioned—for example: the imprecise (hence often debatable) use of detailed technical categories and terminology, the frequent lack of any alternative

oral-aural dimension of the discourse and how the rhetorical (persuasion-motivated) structure and style of the text contributed to its public elocution before a live audience, whether in the original event or subsequently when transmitted via vivid vernacular translation.[20]

A Literary-Structural Corrective

An alternative to Watson's strict GR analysis of Jude's structure and style is offered by Richard Bauckham's comprehensive study of this epistle from a literary-structural perspective. This is not to say that Bauckham ignores the rhetorical dimension, but he does not draw specific attention to it in his discussion. On the other hand, his commentary does give special emphasis to the carefully crafted nature of the discourse as well as its multifaceted structural organization.

This is evident at the very beginning of his study in his thorough overview of matters that pertain to the literary *genre* of Jude.[21] There are no references at all to the terms, conventions, and techniques of classical GR rhetoric, for "the letter of Jude is a real letter." However, it may be more precisely defined as an "epistolary sermon"—a homily "cast in letter form" so that it might be delivered "at a distance" in place of, yet also in the very voice (words) of its apostolic author. Moreover, Jude is a letter whose form and content appear to fall much more under the influence of Hebrew-Semitic rhetorical technique than that of secular Greco-Roman formal

---

perspective on the larger organization of a given discourse, and an often indiscriminate application of the GR framework upon the text, such that one may lose sight of the forest in the description of each and every one of its trees. For a further critique, see Porter, "Theoretical Justification." For a recent defense of the ancient GR methodology as applied to the analysis of New Testament discourse, see Witherington, *New Testament Rhetoric*, especially 216–35.

20. "The art of rhetoric was generally considered to consist of five parts: invention, arrangement, style, memory, and delivery, only the first three of which concern rhetorical criticism of written works" (Watson, *Invention, Arrangement, and Style*, 13). But surely the last two "parts," memory and delivery, also apply to a New Testament epistle that was probably composed orally as it was being written down and was clearly intended to be articulated orally in the hearing of a congregation of believers. These crucial aspects of the compositional process may be briefly described as follows: "Memory (*memoria*) devised mnemonic systems in preparation for oral delivery. It signaled the firm grasp of content and form. Delivery (*pronunciatio* or *actio*) concentrated on aspects of oral presentation appropriate to the subject and the style" (Trible, *Rhetorical Criticism*, 8).

21. Bauckham, *Jude*, 3–5. For more on a "literary-structural" (and rhetorical) approach to the discourse analysis of biblical literature, see Wendland, *Translating*.

speeches.²² We see this, for example, in the opening, "which conforms to the style of the ancient Jewish letter," or indeed, the large middle ("body") section, which manifests a clear "midrashic" development. This involves the use of a series of topically related scriptural references or texts along with an associated brief contemporary commentary—a "method... [that] bears some comparison with the *pesher* exegesis of Qumran."²³ In addition, there are apocalyptic overtones that run throughout the long medial portion of the epistle. As J. D. Charles observes,

> The themes of theophany and judgment, as well as the antithesis of the ungodly and the faithful, constitute a thread running throughout Jewish apocalyptic literature. For the writer of Jude, the borrowing of these motifs serves a useful function. Hereby past paradigms are prophetically linked to the present. They remind the audience of the divine ability to "keep": God reserves the faithful for mercy while reserving the ungodly for certain judgment.²⁴

Finally, there is also the "doxology," which, rather uncharacteristically for letters, closes the work. This doxology clearly reflects a theological *logos* to go along with a prominent divinely focused *ethos*, which characterizes "the literature of Palestinian Judaism."²⁵

---

22. "The NT also has links into Jewish culture and the Hebrew Bible. This means that the conceptualized rhetoric drawn from the Hellenistic milieu is heavily influenced by Hebrew/Jewish non-conceptualized rhetorical forms and styles... In the Pauline corpus and in the NT in general, there is a decidedly mixed approach to rhetoric... [A] living vernacular fusion of primary rhetoric drawn from both Greek and Hebrew rhetorical traditions" (Phillips, "Rhetoric," 250–51). I outline what I term a "rabbinic/Christic" rhetorical technique in Wendland, *Translating*, 193–201.

23. Bailey and van der Broek, *Literary Forms*, 42–45. Midrash "is always commentary on scripture, that is, on a fixed text regarded by the interpreter as the revealed word of God." It may be "either *halakic* (legal, procedural) or *haggadic* (nonlegal, illustrative, etc.) in content; exegetical, homiletical, or narrative in form" (Soulen and Soulen, *Handbook*, 113). "Pesher" is a "technical term from Hebrew meaning commentary" (ibid., 137). Jude is thus, at least in part, an instance of haggadic, homiletical Jewish rhetoric.

24. Charles, "Literary Artifice, 110.

25. Bauckham, *Jude*, 7. "*Ethos* was all about establishing the speaker's character and making clear that he was trustworthy and believable... *Logos* refers to the real meat of the discourse, its emotion-charged arguments. In Greek arguments were called *pistoi*... At the end of the discourse the rhetorician needed to appeal to the deep emotions—love or hate, grief or joy, anger or pity—and so create *pathos* in the audience in order for the hearers to embrace the arguments not merely intellectually but affectively as well" (Witherington, *New Testament Rhetoric*, 15–16). These definitions are fine, but their application is not quite on target with respect to Jude, where we find *pathos*, for example, being appealed to virtually throughout the text.

One of the most obvious and important specific features of Hebrew rhetoric is *repetition*—that is, the exact and analogous reiteration of sound, sense, lexis, and syntax on all levels of discourse structure. Bauckham pays special attention to this aspect of Jude, lexical recursion in particular, which serves to organize the text and to give it cohesion through such devices as catchwords, triple expressions (triplets), and chiastic or parallel patterning. As a result, the discourse arrangement that he proposes differs in several significant respects from that given by Watson, as reproduced above. According to Bauckham then, the "outline of structure" of Jude looks like this:[26]

1–2	Address and Greeting	
3–4	Occasion and Theme of the Letter	
	A The Appeal (summary, 3)	
	B The Background to the Appeal (summary, 4)	
5–19	B' The Background to the Appeal	
	Midrash on the prophecies of the doom of the ungodly	
	5–7	a) Three OT types
	8–10	*plus* interpretation
	9	a') Michael and the Devil
	11	b) Three more OT types
	12–13	*plus* interpretation
	14–15	c) The prophecy of Enoch
	16	*plus* interpretation
	17–18	d) The prophecy of the Apostles
	19	*plus* interpretation
20–23	A' The Appeal (reiterated)	
24–25	Closing Doxology	

A certain simplicity and symmetry of arrangement is much more evident in this outline when compared to that of Watson. The crucial question is: does such patterning have any basis in the text? Which schema is a more accurate reflection of the apparent discourse structure of Jude, and is there any thematic or pragmatic significance to this? The latter factor would include a consideration of the text's transmission. Thus, a simpler, more transparent arrangement of this epistolary sermonette would presumably render it easier to memorize and then to perform publicly before various Christian audiences.

---

26. Bauckham, *Jude*, 5–6 (slightly modified); see also the less detailed proposal of Charles in "Literary Artifice," 120.

There are three major points of difference in this representative pair of structural outlines (Bauckham and Watson); they concern the position and function of verses 3–4, 17–19, and 20–23. These variations concern not only the interpretation of the original text but also its vibrant oral-aural and rhetorical translation today. A lack of space prevents a detailed examination of the various hermeneutical issues involved, but the following is a summary of my reasons for preferring Bauckham's perspective in each case.

Jude 3–4

Watson recognizes that these two verses correspond to the "body-opening of the Greek letter," which consists of "three basic elements: background, petition verb, and desired action."[27] However, due to the constraints of his GR model, he must make a principal division of the text into the *exordium* (3) and the *narratio* (4). The transitional conjunction "for" (γάρ) would clearly suggest a closer linkage between these two verses, as would the "marked alliteration of the 'p' sound in vv. 3–4a."[28] These microlinguistic features are supported by the discourse structure at large, for as Bauckham demonstrates (with considerable precision) "v. 3, the appeal, is the statement of theme for the midrash section, vv. 5–19."[29] A chiastic A–B=B'–A' (shown in boldface on the diagram above), thesis-development (or appeal-motivation) pattern is thus formed to integrate the text topically in a symmetrical manner—a familiar form of Hebrew rhetorical technique, especially where antithesis is concerned.

The interpretation of this point has some important semantic and pragmatic implications: For one, the "main propositions" of this hortatory discourse cannot be limited to v. 4, as in Watson,[30] but must include the content of v. 3 as well. Thus, there *is* such a thing as a definite "body of faith which was once and for all delivered to the saints." This is, in fact, the principal object of Jude's "appeal," without which the motivation supplied in v. 4 (or even the letter as a whole) would have no purpose. In this view, v. 4 and its elaboration in vv. 5–19 is essentially "background" material, a supporting sequence of scriptural testimony, as it were, for the central exhortations of v. 3 and 20–23, and not primary as it seems to appear in Watson's scheme

27. Watson, *Invention*, 47–48. See also White, *Greek Letter*, 15–18; Doty, *Letters*, 34.
28. Bauckham, *Jude*, 29.
29. Ibid., 29.
30. Watson, *Invention*, 77.

of things. A misconstrual of the text's structural organization has several additional consequences, as specified below.

Another noteworthy error that arises in this opening segment of the discourse concerns the function of the so-called *exordium* (v. 3). Following his classical conventions, Watson sees one of the "three aims of the *exordium*" as being "the desire to elicit goodwill through ethos, for . . . the ethos of the rhetor was considered the strongest influence in the case."[31] Thus, he attempts to demonstrate, contrary to the plain sense of the text (and New Testament epistolary literature in general), that "Jude's concentration falls upon himself as rhetor, that is, in establishing his ethos."[32] Now there may indeed be some effort on the part of the author at making the audience more amenable to his message here—perhaps even more approving of his own character. But this is surely no "one-sided emphasis" as asserted,[33] a perception that seems to be yet another instance where the analyst has been directed to a particular interpretation due to the formerly established "expectations" of his specific ("deliberative") rhetorical stance.[34]

Jude 17–19

Both Bauckham and Watson recognize the major transitional function of the vocative "beloved" (ἀγαπητοί) at the onset of v. 17—the question is: transition to what? For Bauckham it begins the last and climactic passage in the series of biblical "proof passages" that Jude has marshaled to bolster his descriptive assessment of the serious situation that he regards his readers to be in. Also involved here is the perhaps unexpected, hence emphatic, shift to early Christian times and the "predictions of the apostles"—men whom at least some receptors may have had personal acquaintance with.[35] Thus, this section is not a mere "recapitulation (or *repetitio*)" of "the main points of the *probatio*" intended to "refresh [the] memory" of the intended

---

31. Ibid., 39.

32. Ibid., 37.

33. One could argue, for example, that the purpose of v. 3 is primary explanatory—that is, it explains why, contrary to the expository doctrinal message that the audience may have expected (that is, "about salvation"), they were instead receiving a rather polemical tract warning against "godless men" (v. 4).

34. Ibid., 37.

35. I fully support Bauckham's argument for an *early* date for this epistle (*Jude*, 13, 103). See Kistemaker, *Jude*, 359–60.

audience.[36] A reappearance of the vocative (cf. v. 3), an imperative form of the key term "remind" (μνήσθητε), plus an explicit personal pronoun, "you-pl." (Ὑμεῖς δέ), is an especially strong instance of structural *anaphora* (marker of a compositional opening, or "aperture").[37] This would be an appropriate way to distinguish this culminating reference to authoritative prophetic-apostolic testimony, that is, vv. 17–19, which serves to contextualize Jude's argument against the apostates in the here-and-now of his receptors' actual hearing. Indeed, the very same issues were at stake, namely, theological skepticism and bestial behavior (vv. 18–19), a point that is underscored by a selective reiteration of vocabulary, for example, the ἀσεβ- "ungodly-" stem (vv. 4, 15, 18).[38]

Jude 20–23

The logic of the preceding argument carries over into this concluding unit of the text's principal medial section (vv. 3–23) with the need to specify its rhetorical function within the whole: Does the "body-closing" of the epistle begin here with a distinct "paraenetic section,"[39] or do these verses constitute the second half of the *peroratio* (or body-closing) that was initiated at v. 17—a portion designated in GR terms as the *adfectus*, or emotional appeal?[40] As already noted above, my preference is for the former interpretation since much more than "pathos" is being appealed to in this section. Indeed, one could argue that the whole purpose of the epistle is being specified or elaborated upon here. Thus, the apostolic charge to "contend for the faith" that concerns the addressees' "common salvation" (v. 3), which has been made possible by "the grace of our God" and "our Lord Jesus Christ" (v. 4), is echoed at this point. This is accomplished through a corresponding exhortation to "build yourselves up in your most holy faith" by "praying in the Holy Spirit" (v. 20), "keep[ing] in the love of God," and "waiting for the mercy of our Lord Jesus Christ" (v. 21).[41]

36. Watson, *Invention*, 69.
37. Wendland, *Translating*, 127.
38. For Watson's counteropinion, see *Invention*, 69.
39. Bauckham, *Jude*, 3; cf. Doty, *Letters*, 34.
40. Watson, *Invention*, 67; or is this the *conquestio* (ibid., 73)? The multitude of GR terms used in this description and analysis is almost overwhelming and hence often confusing.
41. This interpretation foregrounds a threefold topical pattern based on the Trinity, instead of the syntax (a triad of participles).

Complementing this significant topical association is another prominent instance of demarcative structural *anaphora* at the start of this section: ὑμεῖς δέ, ἀγαπητοί (v. 20; cf. v. 17). This feature helps to highlight the importance of Jude's concise summary of "the duties of the Christian life in the Christian community," which is "the main purpose of his letter."[42] Although he recognizes these "injunctions common to primitive Christian catechism and paraenesis," Watson downplays them in order to concentrate on the "emotional appeal" of this segment, in particular, "negative emotion: arousing fear."[43] Once more it appears as if the natural rhetoric and semantic organization of the discourse have been interpreted in a certain way in order to preserve a particular theoretical point of view. While "fear" may indeed be a consideration at the end (v. 23b), to allow this notion to permeate the whole unit seriously distorts the persuasive intention and connotative force that was actually desired by the author with his series of hortatory appeals.

More could be written about the variations between Watson and Bauckham with respect to their different perceptions of Jude's message and organization, but that is not necessary. The point has been simply to illustrate comparatively how such differences in hermeneutical method and focus may affect one's understanding of the overall discourse structure of this epistle and its rhetorical purpose. I do not wish to sound overly critical of Watson's approach and results, for by and large it is a solid study, despite the hyper-reading in favor of a GR model, and it provides many insights into the letter's rhetorical details and dynamics. Such information is valuable also to those who incorporate this dimension of discourse into their contemporary *translation* of Jude.

Furthermore, in my opinion (which itself needs serious testing and evaluation), Bauckham's study too reveals several areas where minor revisions and improvements might be made by taking a closer look at the patterned recursion within Jude as a whole. For example, with regard to the larger organization of Jude, it may be pointed out that the macrochiastic arrangement of the text reflects also a positive-negative, antithetical approach within the argument.[44] Thus, A (v. 3) and A' (20–23) segments deal

---

42. Bauckham, *Jude*, 117.

43. Watson, *Invention, Arrangement and Style*, 71–73.

44. Joubert deals at some length with this point, tying it in to the author's "global strategy" of persuasion: "[This] may be called a 'positive/negative presentation' strategy. On the one hand, *the implied readers are presented in a positive way* . . . In ancient Graeco-Roman rhetoric this technique of praising one's audience by referring to their positive virtues . . . was called *laudatio*. On the other hand, Jude's *opponents are presented in an*

with the reassuring message of the letter, namely, "the salvation we share" that motivates believers to "build yourselves up in your most holy faith." B (v. 4) and B' (5–19), on the other hand, zero in on Jude's major concern, that is, to warn readers against "godless men," whose wickedness has been documented as well as predicted by the Lord's chosen messengers. Jude's challenging tract appropriately begins and ends on an optimistic, constructive note that reaffirms the dependence of all "called ones" (κλητοῖς—v. 1b) upon the God "who is able to keep (φυλάξαι) [them] from falling (caution) and present (στῆσαι) [them] before his glorious presence (comfort)" (v. 24).

Then, on the microlevel of discourse and with respect to the admittedly difficult interpretation of verses 22–23, Bauckham prefers a shorter, two-clause text to a longer threefold arrangement.[45] The latter reading is supported, however, on the basis of a predominant stylistic characteristic, namely, the author's "predilection for arranging his material in groups of three."[46] In fact, one commentator lists "twenty sets of triplets," which display a density that "is unparalleled anywhere else in Scripture."[47] The communicative significance of this prominent stylistic-structural trait in a Jewish contextual setting is that the writer thereby

> exploits the method of a three-fold "witness" [cf. Deut 17:6] to condemn opponents while exhorting the faithful... In essence, the three represent one. A threefold concurrence yields completeness.[48]

---

extremely negative way... The ancient rhetoricians referred to this technique of estranging one's opponents from the audience, by presenting them as negatively as possible, as *vituperatio*" ("Persuasion," 80).

45. Bauckham, *Jude*, 108–11.

46. Metzger, *Textual Commentary*, 659. This reading is supported in turn by Omanson: "Other forms of the text probably arose from scribal carelessness and from confusion regarding the sense of the verb [διακρινομένους] in v. 22. . ." (Omanson, *Textual Guide*, 523). C. Landon presents the case for a "two-clause text" in vv. 22–23 instead of a three-clause reading (*Text-Critical Study*, 131–34). However, his arguments are not very convincing; his strongest point: "if there is a three-clause text at vv. 22–23 involving the relative ὅς, [why] is there not also a three-clause text at v. 10 involving the relative ὅσος?" (ibid., 133). In this case, however, the crucial indicator is not form but content and the three characteristics of the ungodly that are pointed out in v. 10 ("speak abusively... do not understand... [destroyed]"—NIV) in contrast to the three responses of Christians enjoined on behalf of weaker brothers and sisters in vv. 22–23 ("Be merciful to those... others snatch/save... to others show mercy"—NIV). See also the corresponding panels (B and B') in the chiastic structure outlined in the next section.

47. Charles, "Literary Artifice," 122.

48. Ibid., 122.

Such a prominent organizational pattern that runs throughout Jude from beginning to end presumably would also have served to render the content and form of this dramatic text both easier to remember and hence also easier to proclaim from memory. These observations and their implications will be explored more fully in the following sections of this study.

A Paradigmatic Discourse Perspective: Jude's Chiastic Arrangement

In addition to the letter's obvious linear arrangement, which manifests "a remarkably clear structure" that undoubtedly also reflects some "persistent oral techniques,"[49] we find a relatively convincing example of an extended chiastic arrangement that spans the entire text.[50] This formation is not viewed as being in contrast to or as displacing the consecutively-organized, syntagmatic patterns presented above, but rather as constituting a complementary, paradigmatic level of rhetorically shaped textual construction. Among other things, it helps to account for the anomalous v. 9 in Bauckham's proposed outline.[51] The main pragmatic (or functional), lexical, and semantic elements that are viewed as matching each other in corresponding "panels" of the inverted structure of introversion (for example, A and A') are indicated in the following diagram (SA = "speech act"):[52]

A. **Epistolary introduction** (1), participants + a threefold characterization of the "receptors" (addressees): "to those who have been called, who are loved by God the Father, and kept by Jesus Christ," with a focus on divine agency (SA = commendation, encouragement)

B. **Salutation** (2), a threefold benediction—from God through Jude to the addressees: "mercy to you and peace and love" (SA = encouragement)

---

49. Neyrey, *Jude*, 23.

50. The credibility of such chiastic structures increases in proportion to the degree that they are supported by concrete formal means, especially by lexical reiteration and, to a lesser extent, also synonymy.

51. That is, the element designated as [a'] in v. 9 (Bauckham, *Jude*, 6).

52. To be more precise, what I list below as the "speech act" (SA) is actually the "illocutionary force" (primary communicative goal) of the designated utterance (or verse) linking the author, Jude, and his intended audience—that is, as distinct from the utterance itself (the locution) and its desired or observed communicative effect (perlocution) (cf. Wendland, *Translating*, 214–15; see also Brown, *Scripture as Communication*, 32–33).

C. **Purpose** (3), introduced by an appeal with 3 dimensions: "beloved ... the salvation we share[53] ... contend for the <u>faith</u> (πίστει) ... delivered to the holy ones" (SA = exhortation)

D. **Motivation** (4), initial mention of the danger, false teachers: "some ungodly persons" (τινες ἄνθρωποι ... ἀσεβεῖς) + 3 attributes: "forewritten ... perverting ... repudiating" (SA = accusation + admonition/warning +/- informing; this same cluster continues through v. 19)

E. **Reminder** (5–7), warning from OT times (past): δὲ + "I want to remind you" (ὑπομιμνῄσκω) of 3 infamous illustrations (negative exemplification)

F. **Description** (8), the heretics: οὗτοι + 3 attributes: "defile ... flout ... insult"

G. **Extracanonical example** (9), Michael vs. "the devil" (τῷ διαβόλῳ): "may the Lord rebuke you!" —yet no blasphemy

H. **Description** (10), contrasts the heretics: οὗτοι δὲ + 3 attributes: "they blaspheme ... they do not understand ... they are ruined!"

→ I. **WOE oracle** (11), οὐαὶ αὐτοῖς + 3 archetypal instances of ungodliness from the OT: Cain, Balaam, and Korah (SA = warning, condemnation)

H′ **Description** (12–13), οὗτοί + 3x2 (6) attributes (all metaphors of futility): the result is that "they are kept for darkness" (= ruin!)

G′ **Extracanonical prediction** (14–15), Enoch to "these fellows" (τούτοις): δὲ + "the Lord will come ... to rebuke (convict) all the ungodly" for their "ungodliness" (3 uses of the stem

---

53. Although Jude seems to suggest that he will not take up the subject of "salvation" in the present letter, it is clear that any battle for the received faith (doctrine) will ultimately concern the issue of salvation, whether directly or by implication. Thus the appeal to guard their hope of salvation is implicit.

  ἀσεβε-), now including blasphemy ("speaking against God)!

F′ **Description** (16), the heretics: οὗτοί + 3 attributes: "grumblers, complainers . . . followers after their own evil desires"

E′ **Reminder** (17–18), warning from early Christian times (present): δέ + "you must remember" (μιμνήσκομαι) + prediction involving 3 features: "<u>mockers</u> walking according to their own <u>lusts</u> of <u>ungodliness</u>" (negative exemplification)

D′ **Motivation** (19), final mention of the danger, false teachers: Οὗτοί + 3 qualifiers: "divisive . . . carnal . . . not having the Spirit"

C′ **Purpose elaborated** (20–21), a threefold appeal: "beloved . . . build yourselves up in the <u>faith</u> (πίστει) . . . pray in the Spirit . . . keep yourselves in God's love" (SA = exhortation, edification)

B′ **Commission** (22–23), a threefold assignment, the addressees to bless (benefit) others: "mercy some . . . and save others . . . and mercy [still] others" (SA = command, exhortation/admonition)[54]

A′ **Epistolary conclusion** (24–25), a characterization of (= doxology to) God: "to the One who is able to keep/guard you . . . the only God our Savior . . . through Jesus Christ" + a benediction stressing divine agency + a threefold

---

54. By demonstrating "mercy" to the doubtful and fallen among their community (vv. 22–23), believers would significantly reflect the "mercy" that had already been shown to them by God the Father through Christ (v. 2). "These vague references to fellow church members in need of help probably reflect the factual situation within the Christian community where some (most?) members have already accepted the new interpretations of reality as taught by Jude's opponents" (Joubert, "Persuasion," 86). There is also a certain presumption of success in communication here (vv. 20–23): Thus, the author clearly implies that "he has effectively convinced his audience to reject the intruders—in itself a pragmatic tool . . . In other words, his perlocution has succeeded" (ibid., 86). And what might that perlocutionary goal have been? By praising his addressees as "called . . . loved by God the Father and kept by Jesus Christ" (v. 1b) and encouraging them to "build [themselves] up in [their] most holy faith," Jude provides his readers/hearers with the spiritual motivation to overcome in their current struggle with "godless men" (v. 4). "[T]his positive depiction of his audience is obviously to assist the extratextual readers to identify with this intratextual image of themselves and to act in accordance with this role by rejecting the intruders" (ibid., 87). Jude thus reinforces his audience by giving them a positive picture of their character and capacity.

temporal reference: "before all ages, now, and forevermore!" (SA = commendation and praise of God, final encouragement for addressees)

This concentric (paradigmatically arranged) structural pattern overlays, or undergirds, the primary linear (syntagmatically organized) "backbone" of the rhetor Jude's argument. The forward-moving discourse progression, consisting of an alternating sequence of paired constituents involving scriptural example plus contemporary application (thematically: crime-and-punishment), overtly advances the text's argument in typical midrashic style from beginning to end.[55] This is complemented by a simultaneous, but less obvious, retrogressive development, as previously introduced topics, motifs, illocutionary intentions, and emotive elements are recursively recycled, as it were, to reinforce one another as well as the hortatory point and purpose of the message as a whole. This remarkably coherent, artistically shaped arrangement would seem to belie the occasionally alleged hasty manner of composition[56] and rather superficial characterizations, such as the following: "His letter 'is not the work of a literary artist, but of a passionate Christian prophet'"—as if the two were mutually exclusive categories.[57] In any case, Jude's twofold communicative goal (or perlocutionary intention) was, on the one hand, to discredit the godless opponents by drawing attention to their impious, immoral behavior and certain divine judgment (vv. 4, 5–19); on the other, it was to encourage "the saints" (v. 3) to reject the false teachers and remain true to their "most holy faith" (v. 20), which would most surely bring them into "eternal life" (vv. 21, 24).

A few other, more specific issues pertaining to the proposed concentric structure may be noted in passing: In the first place, it is important for the credibility of the introverted framework to observe the unit-initial function words (conjunctions and demonstratives) and potential memory hooks within the succession of chiastically ordered segments, in particular, δὲ "and/but" and οὗτοι "these [fellows]" (pejorative).[58] Only the letter's beginning and ending are excluded from this oscillating sequence, which leads off with the central antithetical agents in the argument, namely, τινες

---

55. Bauckham, *Jude*, 4.

56. For a summary of the reasoning for this conclusion, see Arichea and Hatton, *Jude*, 11–12.

57. Kistemaker, *Jude*, 356, citing Guthrie, *New Testament Introduction*, 927.

58. Kruger, "Jude 7," 121–23.

ἄνθρωποι (v. 4).⁵⁹ The single variation in this alternating pattern occurs, significantly, at its emotive (expressive as well as evocative) climax in the structural center, where there is first a double occurrence, οὗτοι δέ (that is, at "H" in v. 10, where the expected order in the sequence also appears), and then a corresponding zero realization at the midpoint (that is, "I" in v. 11; H' continues normally then with οὗτοι).

The center, or turning point, of the concentric structure (I, v. 11) does not represent the thematic (conceptual) peak of Jude. That is found in vv. 20–21 (C') where we find a reiteration of the letter's principal appeal, coupled with a Trinitarian theological reference. Rather, v. 11 constitutes the work's affective climax as Jude seems to interject himself overtly and personally into the discourse. He appears to adopt the Old Testament prophetic role of a pronouncer of doom in the form of a divine judgment oracle, which typically contains four major structural components:

9. "woe" (οὐαί);

10. identification of the condemned parties;

11. specification of the sin/wickedness (that is, the "reason," introduced by ὅτι "because");

12. pronouncement of punishment (the "result").

As Bauckham observes, "the prophetic character of v. 11 is confirmed by the three aorist verbs, representing the Semitic use of a 'prophetic perfect.'"⁶⁰ A complementary poetic effect is generated by the parallelism in syntactic structure—that is, a threefold pattern of: ([article + noun-Dative] + [article + noun-Genitive] + [verb-aorist]). The rhetor-prophet also heightens the *pathos* here by directly linking the current events of his denunciation with a trio of perhaps the most infamous instances of impiety in the Hebrew Scriptures as well as Jewish rabbinic tradition: Cain, Balaam, and Korah. It is a classic case of *vituperatio*: "Would anyone dare to identify with people who will be damned by God? Certainly not!"⁶¹

---

59. This is also a denigrating reference; thus the troublemakers must not be dignified with a more precise, personal identification (cf. du Toit, "Alienation," 286). "This vagueness is probably deliberate: it is a rhetorical means of portraying them as *incognito* persons who are enemies of the true gospel proclaimed by the apostles" (Joubert, "Persuasion," 82).

60. Bauckham, *Jude*, 78. Similarly, the author's use of the aorist tense (ἦλθεν) in v. 14 is a rhetorical device intended "to dramatically state that the opponent's fate is already sealed" (Joubert, "Persuasion," 84).

61. Du Toit, "Alienation," 286.

The structural-thematic introversion displayed above does not exhaust the impressive inventory of noteworthy recursive elements to be observed in Jude's discourse. It thus provides a convenient framework for organizing them conceptually—for easier memorization and subsequent oral articulation, perhaps? Other prominent correspondences, primarily lexical and phonological, but also illocutionary—that is, pertaining to the letter's "primary motive state [of] reaffirmation"[62]—are found on both the macro- and also the microstructure of the text and will be explored further below.

To conclude this section, I have a final observation concerning the significance of the elaborate structural organization of Jude: The skillfully coordinated overall construction of this letter, coupled with the proliferation of triads and other interwoven instances of recursion, manifests a certain perceptible continuity and regularity in terms of discourse design. This in turn evokes the notions of permanence and stability. Perhaps one might hypothesize then that the text's style and architecture represent a formal "isomorphic equivalent" of the message that it conveys.[63] In other words, the various kinds of repetition, which weave diverse patterns on all levels of composition (phonological, lexical, syntactic, and so forth), constitute a concrete reflection of the main persuasive point that the author wished to make, namely, that faithful constancy—in contrast to the reactionary sort of changes being proposed by the errorists—is a vital aspect of "contending for the faith once delivered to the saints" (v. 3). A corresponding (that is, structural and logical) imperative involves the absolute necessity of adopting that same reliable base or foundation (that is, "objective" faith) upon which to "build" one's personal "faith" (now "subjective") according to Jude's simple, but effective salvific plan (vv. 20–21).[64]

The Poetic, Oral-Aural Features of Rhetoric in Jude

The rhetorical dimension of discourse affects all levels of textual organization—that is, credible and compelling speech, which is amplified through

---

62. Wuellner, "Rhetorical Genre, 117.
63. De Waard and Nida, *From One Language to Another*, 63, 68.
64. By way of contrast then, we also note the high proportion of *hapax legomena* in Jude's epistle, namely, fourteen—plus three more found only in 2 Peter (Charles, "Literary Artifice," 111). Could this perhaps be a subtle literary reflection of the "foreignness" of the licentious teachings that were being promulgated by "godless men" (v. 4)?

varied means, from the phonology of a given composition to its larger syntactic structures. We will pay special attention to the former, the *soundscape* of Jude in this section, but it may be helpful to transition from the latter aspect of the text, its thematic arrangement, by making reference to one of the relevant insights of the well-known twentieth-century Russian linguist and literary critic Roman Jakobson. The intricate manner in which the linear and concentric macrostructures, as shown above, both correspond with and also complement one another would appear to be a discourse-oriented instance of Jakobson's somewhat enigmatic "poetic" function of literature. According to this structural maxim, poetry is manifested by "the projection of the principle of equivalence from the axis of selection to the axis of combination" within the discourse.[65] In other words, various text-defining and integrating patterns of linguistic *parallelism* are progressively formed as categories of static paradigmatic correspondence, based on similarity or contrast. These are developed (by the strategic *selection* of features) and conceptually superimposed upon dynamic continuity as the text unfolds temporally (through *combination*), that is, syntagmatically.[66] The more correspondences there are, along with sufficient novelty and diversity to maintain attention and impact,[67] the more "poetic" a text reads and sounds, and the more meaning-generating connections can be established.

In shorter works like Jude, where the key cognitive categories are relatively limited in number and clearly defined, the text's macrotheme—and its related imperative argument—is rendered rather overtly and emphatically expressed through conceptual reiteration. Considerable interest is developed, however, by means of the addition of associated highly relevant,

---

65. Jakobson, "Closing Statement," 358.

66. "Jakobson established that both prose and poetry, as the fundamental forms of verbal art, depend on two basic axes at work in every type of discourse, namely the axis of selection and the axis of combination . . . These two axes are related, respectively, to the principles of similarity and contiguity . . . As a general principle, both of these forces are present in every speech act" (Pomorska, "Poetics," 171).

67. This pertains to Jakobson's second fundamental principle of poetry, after manifold parallelism—namely, "markedness": "The main concepts underlying this principle are correlation and hierarchy. Two mutually related elements are compared as to the amount of information they carry. The one that carries more information is the marked one, as opposed to the other element bearing less information" (Pomorska, "Poetics," 174). The more parallelism and markedness a text manifests, the greater symbolical potential it has—that is, its capacity to generate new meaning, or to expand existing meaning, through the greater number of realized semantic and emotive connections within the text (ibid., 173).

emotively toned, colorful elements (persons, characteristics, events, images, and allusions), for example, those involving Cain, Balaam, and Korah (v. 11). This contrastive line of reasoning might be hypothetically diagrammed as follows:[68]

> "dear friends" (3): **FIDELITY** [remembrance + retention + resistance + renewal] ➔ **BLESSING** = "salvation" [immediate + eschatological] (1–3, 20–25)
>
> *versus*
>
> "godless men" (4): **SIN** [impiety + immorality] ➔ **POLLUTION** ➔ **PUNISHMENT** (5–19)

Turning then to some of the other poetic features of Jude, we take note of some of the important lexical correspondences that appear throughout the text. There are a number of obvious instances of *reiteration*, such as that involving the verb τηρέω at the beginning and end of v. 6; the three occurrences of βλασφημέω which join vv. 8–10 into a larger topical unit; and the key stem ἀσεβε- which pervades v. 15. As J. Charles observes, "Jude's short but lively polemic is not lacking in 'sound-structure.'"[69] Topically more significant is the extensive word linkage—featuring semantically exact, as well as synonymous and contrastive terms—that runs throughout the text to establish its inverted arrangement, but notably excluding its chiastic core in v. 11. Thus the linear, syntagmatic construction of the text is reinforced by an impressive sequence of "catchwords" such that "[i]n the mere twenty-five verses, *nine* terms occur *five or more* times with five of these appearing *seven or more* times."[70] As a result, "the writer leaves indelibly imprinted on the audience's mind desired images and stereotypes for the purpose of eliciting from them a clear response,"[71] usually one of disgust and aversion with respect to the "godless" interlopers, who are pejoratively introduced at the beginning of the epistle (v. 4).

---

68. See also Harm's attempt to synopsize the content of Jude in syllogistic terms ("Logic Line," 152–53).

69. Charles, "Literary Artifice," 114.

70. Ibid., 111 (italics original). Charles proceeds to list all of these (111–12) and concludes: "By strategic use of catchwords, the writer reflects conscious deliberation in the structuring of his material . . . [which is] further illustrated through his use of connectives" (ibid., 112).

71. Charles comprehensively lists these (ibid., 113–14) and considers them as instances of "parallelism." However, in the normal understanding, parallelism involves synonymous or antithetical, logically-linked lines or utterances, not simply isolated words.

Finally, on the wider plane of discourse organization, we may observe several more subtle lexical-phonological connections that serve to connect the closing verses of the epistle with its beginning: for example, the reference to "mercy" (ἔλεος) in v. 2 and vv. 21–22 (the latter in verbal form); and the related cluster of focal phrases:

"[people] written about beforehand" + "godless" + "our Lord Jesus Christ" (v. 4)

"[words] spoken beforehand" + "our Lord Jesus Christ" + "godlessness" (vv. 17–18)

The close of Jude's hortatory appeal thus plainly (audibly!) resonates with its opening as the apostle reinforces some of his central ideas in rounding out his masterfully crafted, rhetorically motivated, and theologically grounded literary writing. It is a "letter" that ends as positively as it began, with the verbal spotlight firmly fixed on the divine solution for his beleaguered addressees:

"loved by God the Father and kept by Jesus Christ" (v. 2)

"God's love . . . mercy of our Lord Jesus Christ" (v. 21)

But perhaps the most conclusive evidence in support of a poetic, oral-aural perspective on Jude are the many instances of sound- and word-correspondence, or *paronomasia*, which occur within the text. Again, Charles has done us a service by listing these—that is, "instances of alliteration, assonance, homoioteleuton, rhyme, word- and name-play."[72] Two prominent examples toward the beginning and ending of the epistle are as follows:

(v. 3): Ἀγαπητοί, πᾶσαν σπουδὴν ποιούμενος . . . περὶ . . . γράψαι . . . παρακαλῶν ἐπαγωνίζεσθαι . . . ἅπαξ παραδοθείσῃ . . . πίστει.
(vv. 22–23): οὓς μὲν ἐλεᾶτε διακρινομένους,
οὓς δὲ σώζετε ἐκ πυρὸς ἁρπάζοντες,
οὓς δὲ ἐλεᾶτε ἐν φόβῳ μισοῦντες

Below I have delineated the rhythmic, line-based arrangement of Jude according to a literary sense and syntax-based principle.[73] While I would

---

72. Ibid., 114. "*Homoiteleuton* is the name given to a form of artistic prose based on the assonance of the final syllables of certain key words . . . Its presence in the original languages of the Bible is almost always lost in translation" (Soulen and Soulen, *Handbook*, 82).

73. This proposal and its underlying methodology is similar to that outlined in my

not designate the text as "poetry,"⁷⁴ I do feel that it is poetically organized in keeping with the author's rhetorical purpose and in view of the text's ultimate oral enunciation before a congregation of believers, the "called" and "loved" ones (v. 1). The following then would be my suggestion for formatting the first seven verses into semipoetic, cadenced "utterance units" (special typographical devices—for example, boldface type, underlines, italics, have been added in order to highlight selected [*not necessarily all!*] significant phonological features of the original text):⁷⁵

1 Ἰούδας Ἰησ**οῦ** Χριστ**οῦ** δοῦλος,
ἀδελφὸς δὲ Ἰακώβ**ου**,
τ**οῖς** ἐν θεῷ πατρὶ ἠγαπημέν**οις**
καὶ Ἰησοῦ Χριστῷ τετηρημέν**οις** κλητ**οῖς**·
2 ἔλεος ὑμῖν καὶ εἰρήνη καὶ ἀγάπη πληθυνθείη.

3 Ἀγαπητοί, πᾶσαν σπουδὴν ποιούμενος
περὶ τῆς κοινῆς ἡμ**ῶν** σωτηρίας γράφειν ὑμ**ῖν**
ἀνάγκ**ην** ἔσχ**ον** γράψαι ὑμ**ῖν**
παρακαλῶν ἐπαγωνίζεσθ**αι**
τῇ ἅπαξ παραδοθείσῃ τοῖς ἁγίοις πίστ**ει**.

---

earlier study of John 17 "Oral-Aural Dynamics"; this article has been completely rewritten for a forthcoming publication. My approach may be compared to that of Lee and Scott, *Sound Mapping*. Our respective analytical techniques are similar, although I view the dynamics of sound, sense, and syntax as operating more or less on an equal plane to give expression to the author's literary, rhetorical, and thematic objectives, whereas Lee and Scott seem to privilege its sound dimension, for example: "A primary benefit of sound analysis is its power to illuminate a composition's structure. Because New Testament compositions were spoken aloud and processed in real time through listening, sound necessarily served as their primary organizing device" (ibid., 385). While I certainly would not dispute the importance of sound in the process of text composition and transmission, I feel that the grammar and lexis are equally important and must therefore be factored in to a more or less simultaneous perception and construal of the discourse, for example, the nominative appositional string that opens the epistle of Jude: Ἰούδας ... δοῦλος ... ἀδελφὸς.

74. H. J. Cladder claims that Jude is indeed an example of Greek poetry. In an article published over a century ago, he details his postulated "strophic structure" of the text, based on poetic lines (*stichoi*) and half-lines, which is reflected in a number of the ancient manuscripts (codices) ("Strophical Structure"). Cladder identifies fifty-four parallel poetic lines in Jude, all arranged into seven "strophes"—with v. 11 alone functioning as the text's structural midpoint (ibid., 595).

75. These different typefaces are used simply to show repetitions, parallel segments, and other correspondences within the Greek text. They do not have specific or distinct signaling values.

4 παρεισέδυσαν γάρ τινες ἄνθρωπ<u>οι</u>,
οἱ πάλαι προγεγραμμένοι εἰς τοῦτο τὸ κρίμ<u>α</u>,
ἀσεβεῖς, τὴν τοῦ θεοῦ ἡμῶν χάριτ<u>α</u>
μετατιθέντες εἰς ἀσέλγειαν
καὶ τὸ<u>ν</u> μό<u>νον</u> δεσπότη<u>ν</u> καὶ κύριο<u>ν</u> ἡμῶ<u>ν</u>
Ἰησοῦ<u>ν</u> Χριστὸ<u>ν</u> ἀρ<u>ν</u>ούμε<u>ν</u>οι.

5 Ὑπομνῆσαι δὲ ὑμᾶς βούλομαι,
εἰδότ<u>ας</u> [ὑμᾶς] πάντα ὅτι [ὁ] κύρι<u>ος</u>
ἅπ<u>αξ</u> λαὸν ἐκ γῆς Αἰγύπτου σώσ<u>ας</u>
τὸ δεύτερον τοὺς μὴ πιστεύσαντας ἀπώλεσ<u>εν</u>,
6 ἀγγέλους τε τοὺς μὴ τηρήσαντας τὴ<u>ν</u> ἑαυτῶ<u>ν</u> ἀρχὴ<u>ν</u>
ἀλλὰ ἀπολιπόντας τὸ ἴδι<u>ον</u> οἰκητήρι<u>ον</u>
εἰς κρίσιν μεγάλης ἡμέρας
δεσμοῖς ἀϊδίοις ὑπὸ ζόφον τετήρηκεν,
7 ὡς Σόδομα καὶ Γόμορρα
καὶ αἱ περὶ αὐτὰς πόλεις
τὸν ὅμοιον τρόπον τούτοις ἐκπορν<u>εύσασαι</u>
καὶ ἀπελθ<u>οῦσαι</u> ὀπίσω σαρκὸς ἑτέρας,
πρόκεινται δεῖγμα πυρὸς αἰωνίου δίκην ὑπέχ<u>ουσαι</u>.

The preceding analyses would endorse the assumption that Jude is indeed a well conceived literary composition in which the form of the discourse admirably serves the author's intended rhetorical goals and, furthermore, functions to facilitate the text's memorization and ultimate public proclamation. I have argued that this epistle has been "poetically" shaped at least in certain recognizable respects, and this fact must play a role in the text's perception, analysis, and subsequent transmission. Thus, poetry is inevitably enmeshed with orality. Why is this the case? Because a poetic text is always meant to be articulated orally and apprehended aurally.[76] This conclusion lends some important support, in turn, for a rhetorically-toned, "oratorical" translation, a proposal that will be discussed and illustrated further in the next section.

---

76. As the ancient rhetoricians remind us, "A letter is one half of a dialogue or a surrogate for an actual dialogue" (Demetrius)—"The letter is, in effect, speech in written medium" (Cicero) (cited in Charles, "Literary Artifice," 117).

Application to Bible Translation: A Comparison of Two English Versions

Having carefully analyzed the text of Jude from several perspectives in order to reveal its inherent rhetorical and oral-aural potential, a practical application to translation may be made.[77] What difference does all this technical background information about the epistle make in its translation into another language? Just as "the proof of a pudding is in the eating thereof," so also the test of a translation theory is how one reacts or responds to the translation that results from following that theory's recommended principles and procedures.

It is not my intention here to elaborate upon the theory and the practice of Bible translation;[78] rather, it is simply to compare the results of two different methodologies—namely, the so-called "dynamic equivalence" approach,[79] as represented by the *Good News Translation* (GNT), and the "essentially literal" approach,[80] as represented by the *English Standard Version* (ESV). The point of this exercise is to allow readers to judge for themselves which of these two versions most accurately and effectively manifests the embedded rhetoric, literary character, and orality of the biblical text in English, that is, along with the essential content. In addition, readers might also evaluate how well each of these versions has managed to carry out its primary communicative goal, as stated in the following excerpts from their foreword and preface respectively:

> GNT: The *Good News Bible* [now, "Translation"] . . . seeks to state clearly and accurately the meaning of the original texts in words and forms that are widely accepted by people who use English as

---

77. In reality, this interlingual communication process is more cyclical and complementary than linear and unilateral in nature. In other words, exegesis informs translation; and the act of translation can in turn bring further insights as well as questions to the initial exegesis, and so on (I owe this reminder to James Maxey).

78. For an overview of different approaches, see Wendland, *Translating*, 42–79.

79. See Nida and Taber, *Theory and Practice*, 12–32. This approach is also termed "functional equivalence" (ibid., 14), with a somewhat different focus (which is developed further in de Waard and Nida, *From One Language to Another*). In both cases, great emphasis is placed on issues pertaining to orality in the translation process, for example: "The priority of the heard form of language over the purely written forms is particularly important for translations of the Bible . . . [T]here are certain important distinctions between oral and written style" that must be identified and taken into consideration when translating (*Theory and Practice*, 28, 126–27).

80. See Grudem et al., *Translating Truth*, 57–76.

> a means of communication . . . The aim of this Bible is to give today's readers maximum understanding of the content of the original texts.
>
> ESV: As an essentially literal translation then, the ESV seeks to carry over every possible nuance of meaning in the original words of Scripture into our own language . . . Indeed, with its emphasis on literary excellence, the ESV is ideally suited for public reading and preaching, for private reading and reflection, for both academic and devotional study, and for Scripture memorization.

It would seem at first glance that the *brief*, or overall aim, of the ESV is rather more extensive or inclusive than that of the GNT; more will be said about this below. For now, let us assess ESV's claim to have achieved "literary excellence" as well as its suitability for "public reading" and "for Scripture memorization" by comparing its rendering with that of the GNT with respect to several key selections from Jude (that is, vv. 3–4 and 17–23). My own critical remarks will be added along the way by means of footnotes to focus the process of comparison and to elicit evaluative judgments by present readers.[81] The portions of text to be compared and commented on will be marked by corresponding typographical highlights, for example, italics, boldface print, underlines.

---

81. Only selected words, phrases, and features of these two translations have been thus identified for comparison—certainly not all of the differences between them.

Translating Scripture for Sound and Performance

GOOD NEWS TRANSLATION[82]	ENGLISH STANDARD VERSION[83]
False Teachers	**Judgment on False Teachers**
3 *My dear friends*, I was doing my best to write to you about <u>the salvation we share in common</u>, when I felt the need of writing at once to encourage you to **fight on for** the faith which once and for all *God has given to his people.* 4 **For** <u>some godless people</u> have slipped in unnoticed among us, persons <u>who distort the message about the grace of our God in order to excuse their immoral ways, and who reject</u> Jesus Christ, our only Master and Lord. *Long ago the Scriptures predicted the condemnation they have received.*	3 *Beloved*,[84] although I was very eager to write to you about <u>our common salvation</u>,[85] I found it necessary to write appealing to you to **contend for**[86] the faith that was once for all *delivered to the saints.*[87] 4 **For**[88] <u>certain people</u>[89] have crept in unnoticed *who long ago were designated for this condemnation*,[90] ungodly people, <u>who pervert the grace of our God into sensuality and deny</u>[91] our only Master and Lord, Jesus Christ.

82. Scripture quotes from the *Good News Translation* published by The Bible Society, © American Bible Society, 1966, 1971, 1976, 1992—the *Paratext* 7.1 edition; used by permission.

83. Scripture quotations are from The Holy Bible, English Standard Version, copyright © 2001 by Crossway Bibles, a division of Good News Publishers. Used by permission. All rights reserved.

84. Which rendering better conveys the sense and connotation of the Greek ἀγαπητοί? Could "Beloved" possibly be too emotive a term for use in public discourse? Is it too familiar in terms of register?

85. GNT clarifies the potential ambiguity of the adjective "common" (κοινός), which becomes a greater problem when the text is only being heard aloud.

86. The Greek infinitive ἐπαγωνίζεσθαι is in the present text, which the GNT attempts to reflect in "fight on"; this is a more "common language" term than ESV's "contend."

87. GNT makes explicit the agent ("God") of the participle παραδοθείσῃ, which renders the text easier to interpret aurally. For many religious constituencies, the term "saints" (ἁγίοις) is taken to refer to believers already in heaven.

88. The conjunction "for" in English is rather too weak to express the original γάρ here since it has been preceded by two other instances of "for" in v. 3 (in both GNT and ESV). As noted in both the linear discourse outline of Bauckham and my concentric construction, v. 4 expresses the key "motivation" for the "purpose" of the epistle given in v. 3. Thus, a more prominent linkage is desirable, for example, "For this reason."

89. GNT clarifies the double, separated reference to the same group of individuals, namely, τινες ἄνθρωποι + ἀσεβεῖς, by combining them into one, thus making the text easier to process, whether reading or hearing it.

90. GNT reorders v. 4 (*note the italicized words*) in order to present a more logical flow of information. This descriptive participial construction is thus placed at the end of the verse, and the participle προγεγραμμένοι is rendered more explicitly as "the Scriptures predicted."

91. Again, the technique of explicitizing, coupled with a restructuring of semantic

GOOD NEWS TRANSLATION	ENGLISH STANDARD VERSION
Warnings and Instructions	**A Call to Persevere**
17 But remember, my friends, *what you were told in the past* by the apostles of our Lord Jesus Christ. 18 They said to you, "When the last days come, **people will appear who will make fun of you**, people who follow their own godless desires." 19 *These are the people* who cause divisions, who are controlled by their natural desires, who do not have the Spirit. 20 But you, my friends, **keep on building** yourselves up on your most sacred faith. **Pray** *in the power of the Holy*	17 But you must remember, beloved, *the predictions*[92] of the apostles of our Lord Jesus Christ. 18 They said to you, "In the last time[93] there will be **scoffers**,[94] following their own ungodly passions." 19 *It is these who*[95] cause divisions, worldly people,[96] devoid of the Spirit. 20 But you, beloved, **building** yourselves up in your most holy faith and **praying**[97] *in the Holy Spirit*,[98] 21 keep yourselves in the love of God, waiting for the mercy of our Lord Jesus Christ that leads to[99] eternal life.
(continued on next page)	*(continued on next page)*

components in GNT clarifies what is a very complex expression in ESV: "who pervert the grace of our God into sensuality and deny . . ." Very few nonscholarly listeners could comprehend this crucial description as it stands.

92. "The predictions" versus "what you were told in the past"—the issue here is simply one of information density when coupled with "of/by the apostles." The latter would be easier to interpret for a listening audience.

93. The literal "In the last time" (Ἐπ' ἐσχάτου [τοῦ] χρόνου) is not as clear a common-language reference to the "Church-age" period being referred to.

94. "Scoffers" (ἐμπαῖκται) is a term derived from OT prophetic usage that designates wicked people who mock or make fun of God as well as his people; thus the GNT rendering here, "people . . . who will make fun of you," is too narrow in its reference.

95. It is helpful to repeat "people," the antecedent for the demonstrative pronoun Οὗτοί at this point.

96. The term ψυχικοί must be translated contextually: "worldly" is too ambiguous, whereas the GNT paraphrase, "who are controlled by their natural desires," well captures the essential sense.

97. By translating the Greek participles (ἐποικοδομοῦντες . . . προσευχόμενοι) literally, the ESV creates a sentence that is too long (extending through two whole verses) and too dense semantically.

98. The common New Testament command to "pray in the Spirit" (cf. Rom 8:26; Eph 6:18) is often misunderstood. GNT's rendering is an attempt at least to direct listeners to the understanding that the spiritual experience being referred to was (is) under the control/power/guidance/direction of the Spirit of God.

99. ESV's literal reproduction of the original participial construction (προσδεχόμενοι) again results in an unnatural, difficult English wording, that is, believers are to wait for a person (our Lord) to do something (give), rather than for an abstraction (mercy) that simply "leads to" something.

Translating Scripture for Sound and Performance

Spirit, 21 and keep yourselves in the love of God, <u>as you wait for our Lord Jesus Christ in his mercy to give you</u> eternal life. 22 **Show mercy toward** those who have doubts; 23 save others by snatching them out of the fire; and to others show *mercy mixed with fear*, but hate <u>their very clothes, stained by their sinful lusts.</u>	22 **And have mercy on**[100] those who doubt; 23 save others by snatching them out of the fire; to others show *mercy with fear*,[101] hating <u>even the garment stained by the flesh.</u>[102]

Both versions compared above need to be *formatted* more effectively for oral elocution, and at times also verbally modified to better bring out the rhetorical dynamics and poetic beauty of the original in understandable everyday English. The following adaptation of the *The Message* may be critically considered with these specific aims in mind (the same verses from Jude are given below, that is, vv. 3–4 and 17–23):[103]

Dear friends, I've dropped everything to write you
    about this life of salvation that we have in common.
I have to write insisting—begging!—that you fight
    with everything that you have in you
        for this faith entrusted to us
        as a gift to guard and cherish.
What has happened is that some people have infiltrated our ranks
    (our Scriptures warned us this would happen),
    who beneath their pious skin are shameless scoundrels.
Their design is to replace the sheer grace of our God
    with sheer license—
    which means doing away with Jesus Christ,

---

100. The focus of verbal action appears to shift at verse 22, that is, from the addressees themselves ("you yourselves"—ἑαυτοὺς) to "others" (οὕς), thus motivating a paragraph break without a conjunction (GNT).

101. GNT's "mercy mixed with fear" semantically unpacks the original ἐλεᾶτε ἐν φόβῳ to a certain degree.

102. The original text is very difficult to interpret in any case, but a literal translation as in ESV make understanding almost impossible, especially because of the singular references ("garment ... flesh").

103. Peterson, *The Message*. Peterson has these comments with respect to the orality of his translation: "The goal is not to render a word for word conversion of Greek into English, but rather to convert the tone, the rhythm, the events, the ideas, into the way we actually think and speak" (ibid., 8). Note that Peterson does not include verse numbers within his text, only chapter numbers.

our one and only Master.
But remember, dear friends,
    that the apostles of our Master, Jesus Christ,
        told us this would happen:
"In the last days there will be people
    who don't take these things seriously anymore.
They'll treat them like a joke,
    and make religion of their own whims and lusts."
These are the ones who split churches,
        thinking only of themselves.
There's nothing to them,
    no sign of the Spirit!
But you, dear friends, carefully build yourselves up in this most holy faith
    by praying in the Holy Spirit,
    staying right at the center of God's love,
    keeping your arms open and outstretched,
        ready for our Master, Jesus Christ.
This is the unending life, the *real* life!
Go easy on those who hesitate in the faith.
Go after those who take the wrong way.
Be tender with sinners,
    but not soft on sin.
    The sin itself stinks to high heaven!

Perhaps when reading these different translations (*hopefully aloud!*),[104] the question has arisen as to *how* one goes about evaluating them—with regard to accuracy, appropriateness, acceptability, and so forth. Which perspective and approach should one adopt for this purpose? This important issue affects the entire translation process from beginning to end and will be considered by way of summary below in the concluding section of the present study.

104. Other, quite diverse renditions could have been introduced for comparative purposes (the variations among different translations serve to highlight significant translation issues). The following, for example (from Barret, *Funny Things*, 323), is a recent effort to produce a poetic, highly idiomatic contemporary English version (Jude 12b–13):

> *Like clouds that quench no thirst,*
> *Trees that bear no fruit, last or first,*
> *Waves without power but a lot of foam,*
> *And stars destined to call a black hole home,*
> *These bad actors whom he doesn't name,*
> *Are all-star candidates for Jude's Hall of Shame.*

Comparative Critical Judgment—The Need for Oral-Aural Discernment

On the basis of several types of discourse analysis outlined above, I have come to the conclusion that the epistle of Jude gives abundant evidence of having been composed in an excellent literary (or better perhaps, oratorical) style that was ultimately intended to be effectively communicated *aloud* before a listening audience.[105] With respect to its transmission today, whether orally or in writing, via a translated text, we have noted that there are many different options as to how this may be done in a given language—ranging from a wooden literalistic reproduction of the forms of the original text to a free rendering that aims to achieve a basic functional equivalence in terms of contemporary content, impact, and appeal. So which way is the best—that is, the most correct, credible, or effective? Given the large number of variables involved, that is an evaluative question impossible to answer, not without first investigating a number of other queries that pertain to the overall setting of translation reception and use.

One thing is certain—or two things perhaps: First, no translation is perfect and impervious to the need for any further improvement. Thus, just about everyone recognizes the truth of that hard fact of the translation profession—*traduttore traditore* "the translator [is] a traitor," as the Italian saying goes.[106] There will always be some—more or less—semantic and pragmatic "leakage," or loss of communicative significance, in any translation when compared in all respects with the original text from which it is derived, surely in terms of formal stylistic effectiveness, and frequently with

---

105. As was noted earlier, this evaluation of "excellent literary style" is not based purely on ancient Greco-Roman rhetorical norms, but rather in recognition of the felicitous mixture of styles (that is, GR and Semitic) that we see manifested in Jude and many other NT epistles as well (cf. Wendland, *Finding*). Failure to recognize this results in rather negative assessments such as the following: "The letters of Paul are not literary . . . it is plain that the language of the New Testament as a whole does not reflect the *koiné* as it was used by the best educated classes in Hellenistic society . . . Paul's epistolary style was not really 'suited to writing'" (Winter, citing A. Deissmann, M. Thrall, and D. A. Russell, "Revelation versus Rhetoric," 145–46). Such conclusions would appear to be contradicted by Paul himself, for example, in 2 Cor 10:9–10.

106. Actually, the English does not do badly with the original Italian pun; the same is true for Hungarian: *fordítás: ferdítés*, which roughly translates as "translation [is] distortion." Thus, for the competent, creative translator with time, quite a lot can be done to generate matches with regard to interlingual form as well as content and various functional, including rhetorical, implications.

respect to the meaning of the source text as well.¹⁰⁷ The second certainty is this: one cannot achieve all of one's possible consumer-related project goals within the scope of a single translation.¹⁰⁸ That too is true not only with respect to the full author-intended (and tradition-supported) meaning of the original, but it also applies to the envisioned audience (or readership) for whom the version is being prepared.

It is this latter issue that I wish to discuss in somewhat greater detail in this closing portion of my study. Consider, once more, the stated goal of the ESV:

> As an essentially literal translation then, the ESV seeks to carry over *every possible nuance of meaning* of the original words of Scripture into our own language . . . Indeed, with its emphasis on literary excellence, the ESV is ideally suited for public reading and preaching, for private reading and reflection, for *both academic and devotional study*, and for Scripture memorization.¹⁰⁹

In defense of this particular approach, Collins adds, "the essentially literal translation, carefully defined, is the kind of translation that best suits the requirements for an ecclesiastical translation, and for family reading and study."¹¹⁰ The question is, is it actually possible to "carry over every possible nuance of meaning of the original words of Scripture" into English or any other language? If so, it would contradict my first certainty mentioned above. However, most practicing translators and experienced consultants would agree that this goal is *not possible*, simply because a text composed in

---

107. On the other hand, it is also important to point out the possible translational communicative "gain" that is achieved with respect to a given sociocultural setting in terms of certain response language insights that are evoked with respect to the biblical text by means of creative vernacular renditions, for example, Chewa "Ambuye akulange!" "May the Lord punish you!" for the Greek Ἐπιτιμήσαι σοι κύριος at the close of Jude 9 (most major English versions translate the verb ἐπιτιμάω by "rebuke"). I owe this potential corrective with regard to the practice of Bible translation to James Maxey.

108. This brings up the importance of carefully defining the specific audience group for which a translation is intended and the particular purpose and setting of use for which it is being prepared, as highlighted in the functionalist *skopostheorie* of Nord (*Translating as a Purposeful Activity*).

109. ESV, viii (italics added).

110. "What the Reader Wants," 105. This is a translation "that preserves the full exegetical potential of the original, especially as it conveys such things as text genre, style, and register, along with figurative language, interpretive ambiguities, and important repetitions," thus allowing "the reader to listen in on the original act of communication" (ibid.).

one language-culture will never turn out to have the same overall (let alone specific) significance when reproduced exactly (or even closely) in another language-culture, no matter what the method used. Furthermore, can one realistically claim to prepare a version that is equally suitable to serve as a public pulpit Bible (an "ecclesiastical translation") for use in formal worship and also as a text for personal family devotions? Such all-inclusive assertions (and most new translations or revisions seem to make them nowadays) are easy to publish in a version's preface or on its dust jacket, but they are impossible to demonstrate or verify on the basis of comprehensive and credible audience testing procedures.

In fact, it is quite a bit easier to prove the contrary—namely, that a single translation *cannot* satisfy the wishes, needs, and demands of every potential user group. The earlier comparative examination of Jude selections in the GNT and ESV should have adequately confirmed that conclusion, no matter which of the two versions is ultimately preferred. I cannot elaborate upon the principles and procedures of audience testing here,[111] but I will simply point out several factors that need to be taken into account when evaluating one particular translation in relation to another, especially with respect to the oral-aural dimension of discourse.

The fundamental issue to be determined for any current (or projected) translation project is this: *For whom* is it primarily intended? In other words, which identifiable language community, of at least several possible options, is the principal consumer constituency in view? (For example, is the translation intended for those over or under twenty-five years old? Is it intended for those biblically literate or not? For active churchgoers or not? For Protestants or Catholics? For men, women, or both? For fluent speakers of English or for second-language speakers of English?) Once the matter of the consumer constituency has been established through research opinion questionnaires, religious community surveys, requests from individual church bodies, and so on, several associated questions follow concerning other major variables in the wider communication setting, for example:

- *Where*, or in which setting will the proposed translation be primarily used (for example, in public worship or private devotion)?

- *Why*, or for what purpose (for example, to enhance one's appreciation for TL forms or to increase one's understanding of the intended message in TL)?

---

111. For some preliminary suggestions, see Wendland, *Contextual Frames*, ch. 10.

- *How*, or what will be the medium of communication (for example, oral or written, audio alone or audiovisual)?

If the primary medium of message transmission is *oral-aural*, then the term target "audience" becomes especially important, and the appropriate method of assessment must be correspondingly adopted, adapted, or adjusted. For example, from the perspective of the human intermediate source, how readily does a printed translation actually read aloud from the printed page? Does a lector omit, repeat, or mispronounce particular words? Or in the opinion of a listening audience, how easy is the version to understand in terms of its content? On the other hand, how qualitatively and comparatively excellent is the TL text in terms of its language style—diction, rhythm, or euphony in general? If a more verbally vigorous version is desired, say, for a youthful community to use when transposing the text to a sung musical rendition, then a poetic, rhetorically equivalent, "oratorical" ("porhetorical") version may well be the answer.[112] But this question cannot be answered in advance or in isolation. Rather, the issue must be resolved through extensive research and the development of a suitable translation model and method—followed then by extensive trial and testing, revision and re-evaluation—with the whole process being repeated, as needed.

In any case, the significance of the dynamic dimension of orality cannot be denied, and this crucial characteristic of language must be recognized from the very beginning and respected throughout the interlingual, cross-cultural communication process. This methodological imperative and its practical implications are as relevant for analyzing the ancient ("dead") biblical SL text as it is for re-presenting (synthesizing) this text in another ("living") language and some contemporary social setting. Whether the current situation calls for a reassuring message concerning "our common salvation" (κοινῆς ἡμῶν σωτηρίας) or one that is more polemical about "contending for the faith" (ἐπαγωνίζεσθαι τῇ . . . πίστει), the present study has suggested that the soundscape of the text has a great deal to contribute to its overall content, impact, appeal, and to a certain extent also its perceived urgency and relevance as well.

---

112. "Porhetorical" combines the key communicative components of "poetic," "rhetorical," and "oral"; see Wendland, "Expressing," 129.

Bibliography

Agnes, Michael, editor. *Webster's New World College Dictionary*. Cleveland: Wiley, 2006.
Arichea Daniel C., and Howard A. Hatton, *The Letter from Jude and the Second Letter from Peter*. UBS Handbook Series. New York: United Bible Societies, 1993.
Aune, David E. "Rhetoric." In *The Westminster Dictionary of New Testament and Early Christian Literature and Rhetoric*, edited by David E. Aune, 414–17. Louisville: Westminster John Knox, 2003.
Bailey James L., and Lyle D. Vander Broek. *Literary Forms in the New Testament: A Handbook*. Louisville: Westminster John Knox, 1992.
Barrett, Charles D. *Funny Things Can Happen on Your Way through the Bible: Scriptural Oddities and Odd Thoughts about Them in a Book of More Rhyme Than Reason*. Eugene, OR: Resource Publications, 2010.
Bauckham, Richard J. *Jude, 2 Peter*. Word Biblical Themes. Waco, TX: Word, 1983.
Black, C. Clifton. "Rhetorical Criticism and Biblical Interpretation." *Expository Times* 100 (1989) 252–58.
Brown, Jeannine K. *Scripture as Communication: Introducing Biblical Hermeneutics*. Grand Rapids: Baker Academic, 2007.
Charles, J. Daryl. "Literary Artifice in the Epistle of Jude." *Zeitschrift für die neutestamentliche Wissenschaft* 82 (1991) 106–24.
Cladder, H. J. "Strophical Structure in St. Jude's Epistle." *Journal of Theological Studies* 5 (1903) 589–601.
Collins, C. John. "What the Reader Wants and the Translator Can Give." In *Translating Truth: The Case for Essentially Literal Bible Translation*, edited by Wayne Grudem et al., 77–111. Wheaton, IL: Crossway, 2005.
Doty, William. G. *Letters in Primitive Christianity*. Guides to Biblical Scholarship. Philadelphia: Fortress, 1973.
Du Toit, Andreas B. "Alienation and Re-Identification as Pragmatic Strategies in Galatians." *Neotestamentica* 26 (1992) 279–95.
Duke, Rodney K. *The Persuasive Appeal of the Chronicler: A Rhetorical Analysis*. JSOTSup 88. Sheffield: Almond, 1990.
Grudem, Wayne et al. *Translating Truth: The Case for Essentially Literal Bible Translation*. Wheaton, IL: Crossway, 2005.
Guthrie, Donald. *New Testament Introduction*. Rev. ed. Downers Grove, IL: InterVarsity, 1971.
Harm, Harry. "Logic Line in Jude: The Search for Syllogisms in a Hortatory Text." *Occasional Papers in Translation and Textlinguistics* 3/4 (1987) 147–72.
Jakobson, Roman. "Closing Statement: Linguistics and Poetics." In *Style in Language*, edited by Thomas Sebeok, 350–77. Cambridge: Technology Press of Massachusetts Institute of Technology, 1960.
Joubert, Stephen K. "Persuasion in the Letter of Jude." *Journal for the Study of the New Testament* 58 (1995) 75–87.
Kennedy, George A. *New Testament Interpretation through Rhetorical Criticism*. Studies in Religion. Chapel Hill: University of North Carolina Press, 1984.
Kessler, Martin. "A Methodological Setting for Rhetorical Criticism." In *Art and Meaning: Rhetoric in Biblical Literature*, edited by David J. A. Clines et al.,1–19. Journal for the Study of the Old Testament Supplement Series 19. Sheffield: JSOT Press, 1982.

Kistemaker, Simon J. *New Testament Commentary*: Vol. 16, *Exposition of Epistles of Peter and Jude*. Grand Rapids: Baker, 1987.
Kruger, M. A. "τούτοις in Jude 7." *Neotestamentica* 26 (1993) 119–32.
Landon, Charles. *A Text-Critical Study of the Epistle of Jude*. Journal for the Study of the New Testament Supplement Series 135. Sheffield: Sheffield Academic, 1996.
Lee Margaret E., and Bernard B. Scott. *Sound Mapping of the New Testament*. Salem, OR: Polebridge, 2009.
Mazor, Yair. *Who Wrought the Bible?: Unveiling the Bible's Aesthetic Secrets*. Madison: University of Wisconsin Press, 2009.
Metzger, Bruce M. *A Textual Commentary on the Greek New Testament*. 2nd ed. Stuttgart: United Bible Societies, 1994.
Mitchell, Margaret M. *Paul and the Rhetoric of Reconciliation: An Exegetical Investigation of the Language and Composition of 1 Corinthians*. Louisville: Westminster John Knox, 1992.
Neyrey, Jerome H. *2 Peter, Jude: A New Translation with Introduction and Commentary*. Anchor Bible 37C. New York: Doubleday, 1993.
Nida Eugene A., and Charles R. Taber. *The Theory and Practice of Translation*. Helps for Translators 8. Leiden: Brill, 1969.
Nord, Christiane. *Translating as a Purposeful Activity: Functionalist Approaches Explained*. Translation Theories Explained 1. Manchester, UK: St. Jerome, 1997.
Omanson, Roger L. *A Textual Guide to the Greek New Testament*. Stuttgart: German Bible Society, 2006.
Perelman, Chaim. *The New Rhetoric and the Humanities: Essays on Rhetoric and Its Application*. Synthesis Library 140. Dordrecht: Reidel, 1979.
Peterson, Eugene H. *The Message: The New Testament in Contemporary Language*. Colorado Springs: NavPress, 2003.
Phillips, Peter M. "Rhetoric." In *Words &the Word: Explorations in Biblical Interpretation & Literary Theory*, edited by David G. Firth and Jamie A. Grant, 226–65. Downers Grove, IL: IVP Academic, 2008.
Pomorska, Kryotyna. "Poetics of Prose." In *Roman Jakobson: Verbal Art, Verbal Sign, Verbal Time*, edited by K. Pomorska and S. Rudy, 169–77. Minneapolis: University of Minnesota Press, 1985.
Porter, Stan E. "The Theoretical Justification for Application of Rhetorical Categories to Pauline Epistolary Literature." In *Rhetoric and the New Testament: Essays from the 1992 Heidelberg Conference*, edited by Stanley E. Porter and Thomas H. Olbricht, 100–122. Journal for the Study of the New Testament 90. Sheffield: JSOT Press, 1993.
Pym, Anthony. *Exploring Translation Theories*. London: Routledge, 2010.
Soulen Richard N., and R. Kendall Soulen. *Handbook of Biblical Criticism*. 3rd ed. Louisville: Westminster John Knox, 2001.
Trible, Phyllis. *Rhetorical Criticism: Context, Method, and the Book of Jonah*. Guides to Biblical Scholarship: Old Testament Series. Minneapolis: Fortress, 1994.
Waard, Jan de, and Eugene A. Nida. *From One Language to Another: Functional Equivalence and Bible Translation*. Nashville: Nelson, 1986.
Watson, Duane Frederick. *Invention, Arrangement, and Style: Rhetorical Criticism of Jude and 2 Peter*. Society of Biblical Literature Dissertation Series 104. Atlanta: Scholars, 1988.

Watson, Duane, and Alan Hauser. *Rhetorical Criticism of the Bible: A Comprehensive Bibliography with Notes on History and Method*. Biblical Interpretation Series 4. Leiden: Brill, 1993.

Webb, Robert L. "Jude." In *Dictionary of the Later New Testament & Its Developments*, edited by Ralph P. Martin and Peter H. Davids, 611–21. Downers Grove, IL: InterVarsity, 1997.

Wendland, Ernst R. *Finding and Translating the Oral-Aural Elements of Written Language: The Case of the New Testament Epistles*. Lewiston, NY: Mellen, 2008.

———. *Contextual Frames of Reference in Translation: A Coursebook for Translators and Teachers*. Manchester, UK: St. Jerome, 2008.

———. "Expressing Some Extra Sap from a Passage of Scripture." In *Current Trends in Scripture Translation: Definitions and Identity*, edited by Philip Noss, 129–44. United Bible Societies Bulletin. Reading, UK: United Bible Societies, 2005.

———. *Translating the Literature of Scripture: A Literary-Rhetorical Approach to Bible Translation*. Publications in Translation and Textlinguistics 1. Dallas: SIL International, 2004.

———. "Aspects of Rhetorical Analysis Applied to New Testament Texts." In *Handbook of Early Christianity Social Science Approaches*, edited by Anthony Blasi et al., 169–95. Walnut Creek, CA: AltaMira, 2002.

———. "Oral-Aural Dynamics of the Word." *Notes on Translation* 8 (1994) 19–43.

White, John L. *The Form and Function of the Body of the Greek Letter*. Society of Biblical Literature Dissertation Series 2. Missoula, MT: Scholars, 1972.

Winter, Bruce. "Revelation versus Rhetoric: Paul and the First-Century Corinthian Fad." In *Translating Truth: The Case for Essentially Literal Bible Translation*, edited by Wayne Grudem et al., 135–50. Wheaton, IL: Crossway, 2005.

Witherington, Ben III. *New Testament Rhetoric: An Introductory Guide to the Art of Persuasion in the New Testament*. Eugene OR: Cascade Books, 2009.

Wuellner, Willhem H. "The Rhetorical Genre of Jesus' Sermon in Luke 12.1—13.9." In *Persuasive Artistry: Studies in New Testament Rhetoric in Honor of George A. Kennedy*, edited by Duane Watson, 93–118. Journal for the Study of the New Testament Supplement Series 50. Sheffield: Sheffield Academic, 1991.

8

Translation and Performance
Interpreter-Mediated Scriptures in Manjaku

Jill Karlik

UNIVERSITY OF LEEDS

Introduction

THE FIRST THREE BOOKS in this series discuss the significance of performance to audience appreciation of the original biblical texts in ancient times and identify parallels for the communication of Scripture in translated biblical discourse today,[1] moving from "text as referent" to a new paradigm of "text as medium for generating an experience" through performance.[2] This chapter draws upon their findings to shed light on the interpreter-mediation of Scripture into Manjaku,[3] a Guinea-Bissau language in which

---

1. Hearon and Ruge-Jones, eds., *The Bible in Ancient and Modern Media*; Maxey, *From Orality*; and Wire, *The Case for Mark Composed in Performance*.

2. Bartholomew with Rhoads, in Hearon and Ruge-Jones, eds., *The Bible in Ancient and Modern Media*, xviii.

3. Manjaku belongs to the West Atlantic/Northern/Bak language group. See Jan Karlik, *A Manjaku Grammar*.

179

there are only a few written Scripture portions and few other instances of written use. The practice is barely mentioned in Bible-translation literature, but investigation into the social dynamics of these live performative events and analysis of features of performance in the interpreted product may hopefully contribute something of relevance to the "conversation" that Rhoads envisages for this series.[4]

My pathway towards research into this topic began, as Maxey describes for his own journey,[5] from an assumption that written translation plus literacy and the hearing of read-aloud texts would be the principal method of communicating Scripture to a realization that the primary orality of Manjaku culture provides other, more effective means.[6] This led me eventually to an awareness of the sociocultural and interpretive significance of the oral translations of Scripture typically carried out in churches across the region, wherever the seeds of the gospel have been sown by mother-tongue preachers and interpreters who did not have access to any carefully thought-out translation, written or otherwise. If we overlook their role, we ignore a formative element in the development of a vernacular hermeneutic within their local communities. Anecdotal evidence suggests that in the region as a whole, interpreter-mediation of Scripture is probably more common than the reading aloud of written Scriptures in the vernacular, even in languages where these exist. Yet as far as it has been possible to ascertain, my ongoing study is the first empirical research into the practice.

For scholars of biblical-performance criticism, the significance of interpreter mediation of Scripture lies in the fact that the translation itself arises dynamically in the presence of the congregation/audience. This chapter accordingly examines some sample texts in the light of the communication situations and expressions of opinion by participants, and identifies presentational and textual features that may be of particular interest to performance criticism. The data collection took place mainly in a group of Methodist congregations serving an immigrant community in the Gambia, where interpreters relay Scripture into Manjaku from an English version. What I found was a high value placed by end-users and leaders alike on lively performance, as well as an expectation of fidelity to the source text.

---

4. Rhoads, "What is Performance Criticism?," 100.

5. Maxey, *From Orality*, 5–10, 167–70.

6. Ong (*Orality and Literacy*) coined the term "primary oral culture" to indicate cultures that make little or no use of literate communication, in which the nature and significance of orality differs from that of orality in more literate cultures.

Mikkelson has researched the somewhat analogous situation of untrained court interpreters in minority languages (including some of little or no written use) in immigration hearings in Canada,[7] where the absence of a definitive resource casts the interpreters on each other for support. She describes the benefits of a series of training seminars designed for them, in expectation of their services being needed for many years to come, even while hoping for an eventual ideal solution (in this case, when the next generation produces professionally trained interpreters).

The church interpreters could similarly do with help. Several written translation projects in Manjaku have been started and discontinued over the past forty-five years. Three years into a current translation project,[8] no Bible books produced in it had yet passed the community review stage for publication. Meanwhile, the churches continue to rely on their interpreters and mother-tongue preachers. Even if congregations embrace the use of written Scriptures at some future date, the older practice is likely to continue alongside it, though possibly in new forms or settings. As previous contributors to this series point out, "when new communication media come along, the old media do not vanish."[9] In view of this, I suggest that help for those delivering the "old media" would be worthwhile, even while efforts continue towards production of well-thought-out Scriptures.[10]

Personal Journey

Two experiences contributed to opening my eyes to the significance of the oral communication of Scripture. The first occurred in the early 1970s when my late husband[11] was sight-interpreting the book of Acts from English into his native Czech for his mother, at a period when there was no modern Bible version available in Czech. Her reaction was to say, "It's more

---

7. Mikkelson, "Relay Interpreting," 373.

8. Backed by three Bible translation agencies and employing three translators, with an expenditure of US$82,000 over the first three years.

9. Fowler, "Why Everything We Know," 7. The same point is made also by Dewey, *Women on the Way*, 36.

10. Parts of this chapter were first presented in a paper titled "Interpreter-Mediated Scriptures in a group of Gambian Churches" at a conference on "The Bible in Africa," at the University of KwaZulu-Natal in Pietermaritzburg, South Africa, September 2005, and in an article on audience-design in the text data, "Interpreter-Mediated Scriptures," published in *Interpreting*, 2010.

11. John (Jan) Karlik.

exciting than a radio serial." I remember telling him, "Then you must have been doing something right."

The second occurred in a translation workshop with the Evangelical Church of Guinea-Bissau in 1994 when we were trying out new Manjaku translators with a view to restarting (written) Bible translation in Manjaku after a gap of nearly thirty years. One of my husband's original translation colleagues from the 1960s was present as we discussed Mark 1:2, "Make straight paths for Him." He suddenly said, "I liked it better the way we had it before," and quoted verses 2 and 3 virtually verbatim from a 1966 version—as I was able to check it in an old typewritten copy.

My husband had always regretted that translations from that period were never circulated in writing, after political upheaval led to his expulsion and his translation colleagues fled (and illness prevented his subsequent return). But I came to see that most of the key terms and many modes of expression in use in the churches were from those early translations: elements of the texts had passed into oral memory. As the translators and other believers scattered, they had passed them on through preaching and teaching in related churches in the diaspora in Senegal and The Gambia, as well as in various regions of Guinea-Bissau. The translation team's working methods undoubtedly contributed to facilitating this. They used to study a passage in the morning and draft a translation, then go out in the evenings to village churches where they would teach or preach on the passage; and feedback on the way home brought about revisions. In light of recent studies in performance, we may see performative factors in the dynamic of preaching on the texts as the likely means by which so much passed into oral memory, both for the translators who did the preaching and for their hearers.

Eventually, we established a three-year translation project in 1998–2001 under the direction of a gifted mother-tongue translator. The aims were to lay a foundation for any future Bible translation by checking and developing key terms and testing orthographical conventions, while translating Luke and the script of the feature film *Jesus*, based on Luke, for dubbing. Because of civil war in Guinea-Bissau, the project took place among the Methodist congregations in The Gambia: a town church and five associated village churches where services are monolingual in Manjaku or bilingual in English and Manjaku. The translator, himself a preacher, worked with a group of Manjaku preachers to prepare the passages and gain feedback from them. Halfway through the project, I started thinking about an exit strategy—something we should probably have done in advance.

As I pondered how we might leave the churches in a stronger position than when we started, it dawned on me that they would simply go back to using their mother-tongue preachers and interpreters to relay Scripture, as they had been doing for the previous fifty years. It would be a long time before they would have enough written Scriptures to adopt a regular practice of reading them aloud in services; and in a language with no history of written use, the variety of dialects in this immigrant community were presenting a real hurdle to reading aloud. So we switched part of the translator's time to experimenting with helping the interpreters prepare passages in advance.

Interpreters eagerly attended fortnightly seminars, for which the translator intuitively adopted cognitive apprenticeship and reflective practice as training methods—the most common methods in use on professional interpreter training courses,[12] as I later discovered. There was in fact a two-way benefit: the texture of the translator's written Luke text became more geared toward public performance as he approached the task from the interpreters' perspective.

Divergent Attitudes to the Practice

Recognizing the significance of the role that these interpreters were likely to play for many years to come, I wrote around in 1999, asking what helps might be available for them. The responses ranged from, "This is exactly what we try to avoid because it leads to error" (from a Bible translation consultant) to, "Mostly we just start storying and the interpreter does his or her best" (by a leader in the chronological Bible storying movement). It was this divergence of attitude, coupled with the absence of prior research, which led me to undertake a study of the practice.

There are few references to interpreter-mediation of Scripture in the extensive literature on Bible translation, except as a prior practice that the written Scriptures are expected to replace, when they become available. Such mention as occurs at conferences is generally negative, based on perceived shortcomings in the interpreted product at the levels of both texture and lexical fidelity. For example, it was described from the platform at a major "Scripture Use" conference as "this dreadful practice." In surveys on the use of Bible translations, it is entirely discounted. Nor is it mentioned in the first three books in this series, although it may be supposed that

---

12. Pöchhacker, *Introducing Interpreting Studies*, 178.

Scriptures sight-interpreted by African preachers underlie a good deal of the vernacular hermeneutics referred to by Maxey when he quotes African theologians such as Pobee:[13]

> Africans come to church with all their skills of oral communication inherited down the ages . . . There is a living oral tradition which gives direction to a people who do not read or write.

Koops makes one of the few substantive references to interpreter-mediation of Scripture:[14]

> This is what happens in many places where there is no written translation in the local language but the people want a "translation" so they do it orally, off the cuff, from the reading of the Bible passage in the major language of the area. The result ranges from partially successful in the case of simple narratives to outrageously bad in the case of poetical and epistolary materials.

The sample texts examined in this chapter include epistolary and poetical text-types, so that readers may judge for themselves where they fall between "partially successful" and "outrageously bad"—and whether they are sufficiently successful, and on what levels, to make it worthwhile offering the interpreters help. We may also see that "off-the-cuff" needs qualification in an oral culture where social memory becomes a strong influence in the context of a regular congregational practice.

Low Take-Up of Written Scriptures

Getting written Scriptures into use in minority languages in Africa has generally proved very difficult.[15] Maxey notes that the Vuté people of Cameroon seemed "uninterested" in their language's written form.[16] Margaret Hill comments:[17]

---

13. Pobee, "Oral Theology," 88. Quoted, with other quotations from African theologians, in Maxey, *From Orality*, 70.

14. Koops, "From Moses to Dilbert," 193, footnote. Koops writes from his perspective as a Bible translation consultant.

15. Sterk and Muthwii, "Publishing of Christian Scriptures," 150.

16. Maxey, *From Orality to Orality*, 11.

17. Hill, "Challenge of Acceptability of the Translation by the Target Language Community," 1: unpublished paper, Bible in Africa Conference, University of KwaZulu-Natal, September 2005. Margaret Hill is a senior consultant in Scripture Engagement.

Often [the Bibles] represent the life's work of an African translator, yet now the results of their labours are being left to the termites and the rats.

My inquiries among churches in Guinea-Bissau as to why New Testaments in two other local languages were not in use produced a variety of common reasons in relation to orthographies and dialects, but one in particular intrigued me: "Our people prefer to listen to interpreters." [18] This comment spurred me to investigate whether there were factors inherent in the interpreter-mediated Scriptures that made them acceptable.

Translation as a Cultural Act

The first step was to recognize the practice of oral interpretation as "translation." Support was found in Toury's view that "any target language utterance which is presented as such, or regarded as such, within the target culture, on whatever grounds," may be regarded as a translation, and thus a suitable subject for analysis as translation.[19]

In the *Routledge Encyclopedia of Translation Studies*, under the heading, "African Tradition," Bandia comments (and in this context we should understand "interpreting" for "translation")[20]:

> The practice of translation in sub-Saharan Africa is virtually as old as communication through the spoken word . . . Given the multiplicity of ethnic communities in the region . . . translation always has been, and still is, the order of the day.

In this region, where interpreting is thus an everyday practice, we may see interpreter-mediation of Scripture as an indigenous solution by means of which the local Manjaku congregations have "appropriated" the Bible.[21] This accords with Toury's notions of translation as a cultural act,[22] the translational product as a fact of the target culture, and "translatorship" as a cultural role. Toury's view of the translator's role can also account for

---

18. The mission I was associated with took Manjaku Bible translation off their list of goals in response to the non-use of New Testaments in these other languages.

19. Toury, *Descriptive Translation Studies*, 19.

20. Bandia, "African Traditions," 313.

21. West, "Trajectories and Trends," 106. West describes "ordinary readers and hearers" in Africa as being not simply recipients but appropriators of the Bible.

22. Toury, *Descriptive Translation Studies*, 53.

the rise of certain interpreters within the congregations: "'translatorship' amounts first and foremost to being able to play a social role, that is, to fulfill a function allotted by the community in a way which is deemed appropriate in that community's own terms of reference." This view goes some way towards accounting for a similarity of style observed between interpreters functioning in the same congregation: it becomes, as Wadensjø puts it,[23] the "normal, adequate, correct etc. way to act."

Interpreter-Mediated Scriptures as a "Non-Book" Format of Scripture

Maxey notes that it has been assumed throughout much of modern history that literacy would accompany Bible translation. He continues:[24]

> I suggest that literacy not be the presupposed medium for biblical translation ... First, the anthropological model of contextualisation suggests that one discover *what is already available* in a given context. Oral communications continue to be predominant throughout much of the world—even when literacy is available. Second, historically, the first-century world consisted of a predominantly oral setting in which the New Testament was composed.

"*What is already available*" in the Manjaku church contexts—and in many other churches across the region—happens to be interpreter mediation of Scripture. It is also what was available historically in the early church as the gospel spread,[25] modeled on the practice of interpreter-mediation of Old Testament texts within Judaism, which dated at least from the time of Ezra around four centuries earlier.[26] By the first century, the Old Testament renderings were often from the Septuagint Greek translation, rather than from the original Hebrew, just as the Manjaku interpreters' renderings are from a translation in a language of wider distribution. Fowler speculates as

---

23. Wadensjø, *Interpreting as Interaction*, 5.

24. Maxey, *From Orality to Orality*, 47 (italics added). This view was put forward by Klem in *Oral Communication of Scripture* (1972) and "Dependence on Literacy Strategy" (1995) but was not taken much into account in the Bible translation movement as a whole until the last decade.

25. Metzger, *Early Versions of the New Testament*, 286; Hermann, "Interpreting in Antiquity," 20.

26. Kaufmann, "Interpreters in Early Judaism," 2; Kaufman, "Contribution à l'histoire de l'interprétation consécutive," 976.

to whether Jesus was able to read the Hebrew Scriptures;[27] more relevant to this chapter might be whether Jesus rendered them into Aramaic, as we may suppose he did, when expounding them.

Once the interpreted Scriptures are recognized as a particular (non-book) format of Scripture, they can be accommodated to models of Bible translation. Wilt's "frames of reference" model can accommodate any target text format, including interpreted Scriptures, although they are nowhere mentioned in his book. His diagrammatic representation of the model (see Figure 8.1) highlights the disparity between the frames of reference in which the source text (text X) and target text (text Y) arise, and the fact that the translator's own frames of reference may differ from both, all of which can give rise to translational problems.

The arrows represent the construction of meaning by negotiation between speaker/writer and receptors in terms of their respective frames of reference, an insight informed by Relevance Theory.[28] With the interpreter as the "in-between," the communication model is exemplified by the communication-situation for biblical discourse in the Manjaku congregations, through which vernacular hermeneutics arises in the community of practice. The diagram also usefully identifies the audience as a community; church congregations are more than an audience of disparate hearers, forming instead an interpretive community.[29]

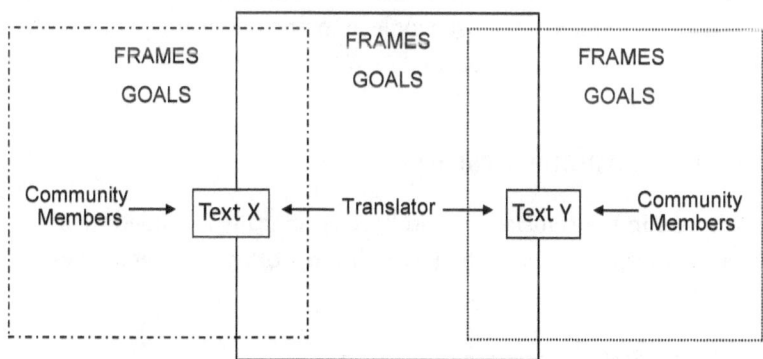

Figure 8.2: Diagram showing translation as mediation, after Wilt[30]

27. Fowler, "Why Everything We Know about the Bible Is Wrong," 7.
28. Gutt, *Translation and Relevance*, 35.
29. Soukup, "Understanding Audience Understanding," 103–105.
30. Adapted from Wilt, "Translation and Communication," 79.

Translating Scripture for Sound and Performance

The notion of interpreter-mediated Scripture readings as a format of biblical discourse may be easier to entertain if we set them alongside other "nonbook" formats, such as storytelling, and dramatized or graphic Scriptures. This entails recognition that the difference in format gives rise to differences beyond a mere change of medium, as in any transmediatization. Just as oral communication uses different prosodic and syntactic structures from written communication,[31] so interpreted discourse has its own characteristic features and should be evaluated as interpreting, not as written translation, although valid comparisons can be made. This does not imply a lower view of fidelity but, as Fry points out in relation to other nonbook formats, evaluation of fidelity has to take account not only of the text itself but of "wider discourse and communication factors which relate to the presentation of the message as a whole."[32]

For Manjaku congregations, interpreter-mediated Scripture has historically been the *only* format available for church services. In Sunday school lessons, sermons, and informal situations, biblical discourse is frequently communicated in storytelling mode, but in formal services, interpretation from a version in a language of wider distribution is recognized as the most appropriate mode to fill the "reading slot"; that is, if the passage is delivered in Manjaku at all. Many churches in Guinea-Bissau have dropped the practice of delivering Scripture in the vernaculars since the introduction in 2000 of the whole Bible in Kiriol (Portuguese Creole), the lingua franca, on the grounds that most people in their congregations "understand something" of the reading in Kiriol.[33]

Interpreting Studies Research

Few scholars in the translation field have specifically extended their ideas to include interpreting, and the research tools of translation studies have

---

31. Halliday, *Spoken and Written Language*, 97.

32. Fry, "Faithfulness," 8.

33. The Kiriol Bible is well-translated into the culture in general ways, but many of the key biblical terms, such as "salvation," "sanctification," and so on, are Portuguese borrowings, so even those people for whom Kiriol is a mother tongue might not grasp the biblical concept, except for theological education within the churches.

A general decline in interpreting in these and related churches in Guinea-Bissau may also in part be attributed to a view of Kiriol as a vehicle for national unity and identity in the aftermath of the civil war of 1998–2000.

generally been found inadequate for processing interpreting data.[34] Interpreting did not become the subject of empirical research until the late 1940s with the Nuremberg Trials, when simultaneous interpreting (SI) attracted attention from cognitive psychology because it provided exciting insights into cognitive processes.

At first, attention was mainly focused on conference interpreting, both consecutive and simultaneous. However, in the last fifteen years, there has been a burgeoning of studies on interpreting in community situations, driven largely by interest in the legal, medical, and social-service domains in Western countries, where it used to be common—and to some extent still is—for interpreting to be carried out by untrained interpreters. Among these is the work of Wadensjø on "Interpreting as Interaction,"[35] highlighting the social relationships involved. Particularly useful insights for the present study come from a body of research into community sign language interpreting, because of similarities at the sociocultural level.[36] These arise from the face-to-face communication situation of the sign-language interpreter, the preference for highly communicative style in the communities, and the tendency for interpreters to become well-known figures in the Deaf communities. There are further similarities in the existence of sign languages in many microdialects, and the fact that the interpreters function at the interface with the print world.

The short-segment mode of interpreting as commonly practised in churches has only recently attracted any research attention, even in relation to sermons.[37] The mode is ostensibly consecutive, but the delivery of source text (ST) input and the cognitive processes involved seem to me to have more in common with SI than with consecutive conference interpreting, which is typically carried out in segments of several minutes, making the rhetorical structures of the ST accessible to the interpreter. Although the short-segment interpreter is given a gap for production of the target text (TT) and has some control over its length, inferencing from the ST and formulation of the TT overlap as in SI, since the interpreter must be ready to say something as soon as the reader pauses, even if only a filler when

---

34. Pöchhacker, *Introducing Interpreting Studies*, 41.

35. Wadensjø, *Interpreting as Interaction*.

36. For example, Cokely, *Interpretation: A Sociolinguistic Model*.

37. Downie at Heriot-Watt University is collating information on use of interpreters in churches and researching intervention length in sermons.

faced with an underdetermined input. Not being able to choose when to initiate the next TT segment adds to this pressure.

The inaccessibility of the ST rhetorical structure and full context, combined with the lack of time for reflection, gives the interpreter an enormous disadvantage compared with a translator working in whatever mode, who has time to consider inferences from the ST and find equivalents in the TT. However, in terms of the translational act itself, there is an inherent advantage in the ephemeral nature of the ST. The linguistic forms of the ST quickly drop out of the interpreter's working memory and the focus is on the inferences drawn from it, which is conducive to production of a natural-sounding TT, not only conveying propositional meanings but, more significantly, evoking the emotive force. Llewellyn-Jones's diagram of the cognitive processes in interpreting (Figure 8.2), based on Cokely's work in American Sign Language (ASL) and his own in British Sign Language (BSL), highlights the crucial significance of the working memory, to carry ST input just long enough for the interpreter to draw inferences in terms of source culture frames of reference, or "Memory Organization Packets" (MOP's).[38]

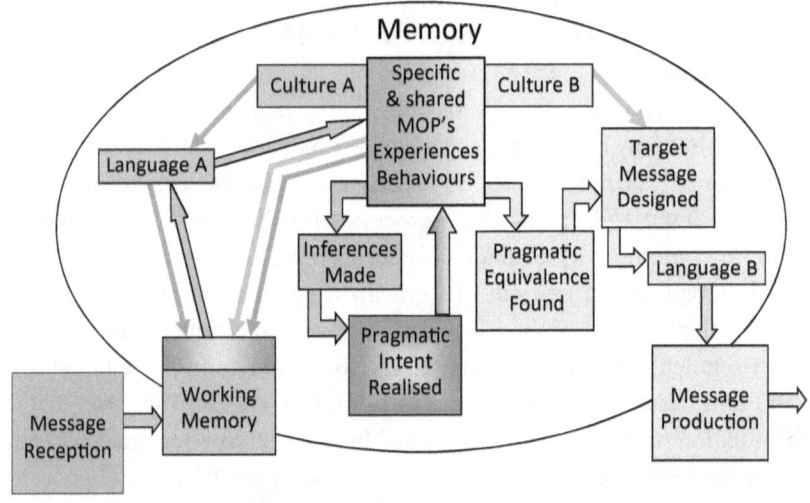

Figure 8.1: Llewellyn-Jones's diagram of the Interpreting Process Model[39]

---

38. Schank, *Dynamic Memory Revisited*, 123–54.

39. Llewellyn-Jones, in lectures, 2008; developed from Cokely, *Interpretation: A Sociolinguistic Model*, 124.

In the case of sight-interpretation, the Manjaku TT's are segmented by gaps in which the interpreter silently reads a sentence or whole verse in the English ST before rendering it into Manjaku. Although this produces a fragmented effect, each sentence is produced in a natural-sounding way. The main difference for an interpreter between this and the short-segment mode is the opportunity to return briefly to a sentence to check it and maybe clarify a point before continuing. On the other hand, a mother-tongue preacher may spend some time considering the text and looking up references for the sermon, before rendering the biblical passage by sight-interpretation.

The Gambian Community of Practice[40]

I am grateful to the Methodist Church of the Gambia for permission to record church events during a six-month period in 2004, and especially to the congregations and interpreters who took part in interviews, seminars, and focus groups. The naturally-occurring text examples cited here mostly come from a corpus of forty-five interpreter-mediated Scripture readings by fourteen interpreters, eight male and six female, recorded in their Sunday services and midweek neighborhood Bible studies. The whole of each event was recorded in order to facilitate analysis of the interpreters' performances in relation to the communication situations and against the wider sociocultural and organizational background; it also provides a corpus of naturally occurring Manjaku speech in the same domain and broadly the same register.

The village congregations are drawn from small Manjaku settlements, each made up largely of immigrant families originating from a particular Guinea-Bissau village and retaining the homeland village dialect. The Manjaku members of the town congregation, however, are from various dialect groups, coming mostly from families in one or another of the surrounding village settlements. The whole group of churches functions as an organizational unit. They come together for joint activities and share the same preachers on a rotation, with the effect that the various dialects are familiar even in the more homogeneous village congregations. They use the same terms for biblical concepts and ecclesiastical practice. The group thus constitutes a "community of practice" although they are not a speech

---

40. Described in more detail in Karlik, "Interpreter-Mediated Scriptures," 164–70.

community in the traditional sense, being drawn from a variety of dialects.[41] As a worshiping community, the whole group of churches also constitutes a "community of interpretation," sharing a (biblical) textual foundation;[42] the interpreters and mother-tongue preachers are themselves members of this community.

The settlements retain close links with the homeland villages and with related immigrant communities in Senegal, France, and other regions of The Gambia,[43] where they live under Portuguese, French, or English as the languages of education. Local languages of wider distribution—all of them, like Manjaku, having little written use—are Portuguese Creole (Kiriol) in Guinea-Bissau, and Wolof and Mandinka in The Gambia and Senegal. At the interface with the wider social environment, interpreting practices are a well-established part of language use in the general community. Some individuals, including all the regular church interpreters, have grown up interpreting from childhood or their early teens. Some are seen as having a particular skill in it, and some are recognized as having gifts in public performance. Professor Francine Kaufmann has pointed out that this situation parallels that of Yemenite Jewish communities in both the Yemen and Israel, which are probably the only contemporary Jewish communities that continue the ancient practice of interpreter mediation of the Old Testament Scriptures.[44]

To assess expectations as to performance, I set up focus groups in which participants could compare presentational factors in interpreted Bible readings. They showed the same expectations of the readings as of a sermon, evaluating them as to whether they constituted "a lively contribution to worship."

The Communication Situations

The village churches mostly have homogeneously Manjaku congregations. However, since their beginnings in the 1950s, if the leader/preacher is not a Manjaku, the services have been bilingual, with the entire event interpreted in quasi-simultaneous short-segment mode. The interpreter stands level

---

41. Davies, "Communities of Practice."
42. Soukup, "Understanding Audience Understanding," 91.
43. Manjakus number about 325,000: about 185,000 in Guinea-Bissau, 95,000 in Senegal, 30,000 in France, and 20,000 in The Gambia.
44. Of Bar-Ilan University; in correspondence.

with the leader or reader, about one to two meters away. Since the preachers tend to arrive just in time, or late, for services, the texts usually come to the interpreters with little opportunity for advance preparation. The segments in the Bible-reading phase are particularly short, because the interpreters recognize the inherent difficulty of rendering from a read-aloud ST and ask the readers, as a rule of thumb, to pause at every comma and full-stop.[45] In monolingual services, the preferred mode for rendering the Scriptures is similarly short-segment consecutive if there is another English speaker present to share the task; if not, the leader/preacher renders it into Manjaku by sight-interpreting. In neighborhood Bible studies, the leaders generally render the Scripture readings by sight-interpreting.

In the town church, Manjakus make up about half the regular congregation of thirty to forty adults plus teenagers and children. When non-English-speaking Manjakus started attending in greater numbers, in 1989 the church began bilingual services to meet their needs, using the short-segment mode which was already well-established in the village churches.

Interpreting practice in these churches exemplifies Toury's view that "cultures resort to translating precisely as a major way of filling in gaps, whenever and wherever such gaps manifest themselves either as such, or (very often) from a comparative perspective, that is, in view of a corresponding non-gap in another culture."[46] In each phase of the events, an important element of the communicative purpose of the translational act—its *skopos*[47]—is to fulfill the same ritual purpose as the English source text.

The Interpreters

The anthropologist Finnegan notes the presence in multilingual oral societies of "experienced interpreters who reflect self-consciously on language and translation."[48] The Manjaku interpreters in the Gambian study showed a high level of language awareness in focus groups and workshops, and

---

45. This generally produces meaningful segmentation but sometimes raises oddities in the ST, for instance, if the reader separates the "he said," "she said," or the like from the quotation. Wherever possible, to avoid such problems, interpreters follow the readings in their own Bibles; but not all find themselves able to listen, follow the written text, and process the TT simultaneously.
46. Toury, *Descriptive Translation Studies*, 27.
47. Nord, *Translating as a Purposeful Activity*, 27.
48. Finnegan, *Oral Traditions and the Verbal Arts*, 193.

articulately discussed their reasons for certain translational choices in think-aloud protocols immediately following interpreted events (always with reference to issues of audience comprehension). They consciously aim to achieve successful communication. In this sense, although unpaid and untrained, they exhibit an attitude expected of "language professionals,"[49] which indeed is what other participants expect of them, epitomized in a Guinea-Bissau pastor's description of the interpreter as his "co-preacher."

Furthermore, they show an awareness that interpreting involves an acceptance that "no interpretation is ever perfect,"[50] a point that appears to escape most critics, especially those who are involved in producing written translations. Rather than perfection, the interpreters aim at adequacy in terms of meeting the needs and expectations of the end-users, while also being mindful of the expectations of other participants.[51]

Accuracy

As well as good public communication skills, end-users interestingly also expect fidelity to the ST. They hear the more commonly used biblical passages relayed on multiple occasions, though never with exactly the same text-product since it is always a new live performance. Sometimes an end-user will critique an interpreter if the TT seems to them to carry a different meaning from what they have come to expect from trusted interpreters such as Bible study leaders. This echoes Pöchhacker's view that communities recognize those best fitted for the role: people with "special knowledge (of the culture involved or of the subject matter) and skills . . . as well as other qualifications such as moral integrity and reliability."[52]

Because the ST's are in English, the interpreters are necessarily educated people, since others would not have sufficient knowledge of the source language. Even so, miscues—defined broadly as difference in inferential value (whether propositional or emotive)[53]—can most often be traced to a

---

49. Llewellyn-Jones, lectures; Llewellyn-Jones and Lee, forthcoming.

50. Nida, *Contexts in Translating*, 9. Nida refers here to professional interpreting practice. He does not mention interpreter-mediation in churches.

51. See e.g., Pöchhacker, "Quality Assessment," 419, for discussion of differing user expectations and evaluation of "quality (adequacy) for whom."

52. Pöchhacker, *Introducing Interpreting Studies*, 23.

53. Based on Cokely's definition of miscue as "a lack of concordance between the information in an interpretation and the information in the S(source)L(language) message

faulty understanding or mishearing of the source language. Sometimes this occurs simply because of poor reading aloud; as Roschke has commented, some readers "slaughter" the text.[54]

Given the cultural distance and complexity of the biblical ST's, even an excellent command of English is insufficient for correct inferencing without some knowledge of the biblical sociocultural backgrounds and text-types and of the purpose of the ST for the original hearers. All the regular interpreters grew up in church congregations and some were attending evening Bible school classes or local training for preachers, but it was still not always easy for them to grasp ST implicatures so rapidly. Nevertheless, their error level—at an average of from two to four errors in a thousand words of target text (of which about half could be considered serious)—was lower than I had expected to find.

Based on criteria for the evaluation of accuracy in interpreting from the MA course in the University of Leeds, an item was counted as error if it distorted, added to, or omitted elements of inferential meaning, or failed to steer hearers away from wrong assumptions, unless the point was recovered within the same Bible reading. It was counted as serious error if it affected the overall meaning of the passage, or led to the loss of a significant intertextual metaphor. For instance, the omission of "first" in "firstborn lamb" in Abel's sacrifice in Genesis 4:4 was counted as serious error for this reason; similarly "cut up the bread" as a translation of "broke the bread" in Luke 24:35, because of the intrusion of an unwelcome image into the intertextual metaphor.[55] Both these metaphors may be regarded as "critical points" on which the inferential meaning (or one of the meanings) of the discourse as a whole turns.[56]

It may be unfair to judge such a simple domestication of bread distribution as error, when it would by all ordinary standards be considered appropriate if just the immediate textual environment were under

---

it is supposed to convey," *Interpretation: A Sociolinguistic Model*, 74. Compare Sim's definition of "loss of quality" in translation as "lack of identity of interpretive resemblance," in "Modelling the Translation Task," 123.

54. Roschke, "Postlude," 343.

55 The interpreter herself has since informed me that the Manjaku expression is also used in her semi-rural community in the sense of breaking up bread with your fingers, e.g. for children. It may therefore be considered translationally adequate for her audience, although some Manjaku informants reacted strongly against it, perceiving it only in the meaning of "cut up".

56. Munday, "Evaluation and Intervention in Translation," 91.

consideration. However, for the purpose of assessing the adequacy of the interpreted rendering in the context of church use, applying the criteria in this strict manner enabled me to identify where an interpreter had missed intertextual metaphors that a Bible translation consultant would expect a translator to pick up on, with exegetical helps and time to reflect.

On the other hand, explicitations were accepted as normal features of interpreted text, unless they introduced some distortion of inferential meaning; similarly in the case of ostensive, inclusive, and purely phatic features. If we accept interpreted discourse as a format of Scripture, we need to accept these as characteristic of the format. They are also appropriate in the oral culture, which, as Ong notes, "encourages volubility."[57]

Performative Features in the Text Product

It has been suggested that some features of performance are universal, such as fronting for emphasis, lexical repetition, parallelism, formulaic expressions and variations of pace, pitch, and volume,[58] all of which can be found in the interpreted TT's with raised frequency compared with the natural speech corpus. These and other features relevant to performance are noted in examples that follow. It is possible that some of these may be functioning as markers to clue the audience to perceive the text as performance. But in any case, given the communication situation and the formulaic framing, "Our reading is taken from . . ." and, "Here ends the [first] reading," the congregation processes the biblical TT discourse according to their shared traditions for this regular activity, reinforced by the preaching and teaching that accompany it.

The interpreters' performances generally occur in the presence of other English speakers, including other interpreters, who sometimes act as self-appointed "referees,"[59] overtly commenting afterwards on translational choices made. Although the interpreters recognize that they are not going to get everything "right," the presence of these referees functions to make them self-critical. Bible translators sometimes critique an interpreted TT on the basis of other ST versions that reflect different or amplified inter-

---

57. Ong, *Orality and Literacy*, 40.
58. Maxey, citations, *From Orality*, 156.
59. Mason, "Audience Design in Translating," 6. Mason defines the referee group as "any third-party group (or discourse community) whose attributes, including their speech/writing style, are valued by either the addresser or the addressee or both."

pretations of the underlying Greek or Hebrew text. They do so, however, without regard for the fact that interpreters have no opportunity to consult other versions; an interpreter renders the ST input provided. However, the interpreters do occasionally bring in explicitations from their general knowledge of Scripture, from other versions, and/or from other passages.

The fact that end-users also sometimes critique an interpreter reinforces a tendency to render the passage conservatively, within established traditions. Ong points out that among oral communicators, the need to invest considerable effort in remembering establishes a highly conservative mindset.[60] The interpreters know that the audiences will notice any deviation from the social memory. Talmudic sources indicate that the interpreter in ancient times was expected to accommodate to audience needs, while rendering the sense according to local rabbinical exegesis.[61] The same is true of the church interpreters in relation to the style of exegesis in general use by the preachers.

Features of Presentation

All the regular interpreters meet audience expectations as to presentation by their communicative stance, gesture, eye contact, expressive voice modulation, and inclusive and emphatic texture. According to Shiner,[62] schools of the art of rhetoric in the ancient world taught that rate of speech and modulation of voice should convey sharpness, kindness, sadness, gaiety as appropriate, the tone of voice fitting each character, and reflecting their feeling; there is evidence of this in the interpreted texts.

VOCAL FEATURES—CLARITY, VOLUME, PACE, AND MODULATION/INTONATION

Three trainers of Interpreting Studies students at MA level in the University of Leeds rated the use of voice in the recordings as reaching standards expected of professional interpreters. All have very clear diction.

60. Ong, *Orality and Literacy*, 41.
61. Kaufmann, "Contribution à l'histoire de l'interprétation consécutive," 977, 980ff. Kaufmann considers that it was only later that the practice changed to recitation of a more-or-less fixed oral version, and eventually of a written translation.
62. Shiner, "Oral Performance in the New Testament World," 55, quoting Quintillian, 11.1.39–42.

Translating Scripture for Sound and Performance

Gesture and Eye Contact

During the sermon phase, the interpreters echo the gestures of an animated preacher. Otherwise, they use normal conversational gestures to mark prosodic punctuation and emphasis, although they may be holding a Bible in one hand. They sometimes make eye contact during the production of the TT, even when following the ST in their own Bibles. This contrasts with the lack of gesture or eye contact and sometimes inappropriate intonation from the readers, even those who make a special effort to be "lively."

Evocation of Emotion

The interpreters' facial expressions mark emotions as appropriate, with accompanying modulations of voice and gesture. Sight-interpreting Psalm 139, "even there, your hand will guide me," the interpreter used great tenderness of voice, evoking the Psalmist's emotion in a way that a read-aloud delivery would be highly unlikely to match. Shiner notes that verbal art is judged by the way it affects the emotions of the audience.[63]

Characterization

I regret not having recorded the TT's in video, because some performances particularly evoked characterization. A twenty-eight-year-old school secretary, Esther, when sight-interpreting Hannah's conversation with Eli in I Samuel 1, reflected the emotion of each character in turn, both vocally and by facial expression: Hannah's intensity of commitment in her prayer; Eli's indignation at her apparently drunken state and his sternness in rebuking her; her distress as she pleads with Eli not to misjudge her and as she explains her longing for a child, "I have been pouring out my trouble to the Lord"; and finally Eli's kindly, reassuring tone and benign expression as he pronounces God's blessing on her.

Textural Features

The Manjaku interpreters constantly recycle and resituate referents by means of a variety of particles. This creates tight textural cohesion that

---

63. Shiner, "Proclaiming the Gospel," 57.

maintains coherence in the TT even though the ST input is delivered in very short segments. For instance, if the segmentation by the reader leaves a verb with its subject unspecified, or if the ST separates the subject far from the verb, the interpreters reintroduce it by means of a pronoun. By contrast, in written translations separation of subject and verb sometimes trips up the readers. In Luke 24:2, "they found the stone rolled away from the entrance to the tomb," a written translation has, "they found the-stone which shut-with the-tomb had-been-taken-away," in which I observed that even fairly fluent readers could not make sense of the verb "*had-been taken-away*," separated from its subject. A seventeen-year-old schoolgirl interpreting the same passage for a household Bible study rendered it, "they found the-*stone big, which* you know, shut-with the-mouth [of] the-entrance [to] the-tomb, *it* had-been-taken-away from-there, *it* was at the-side," where the italicized relative and subject pronouns and the adjective "big" are all marked for nominal concord with "stone."

This accords with Hatim and Mason's finding that texture, which they define as "making a sequence of sentences operational (i.e. both cohesive and coherent)," is the priority focus of the interpreter in SI, given that the rhetorical structure and the context is only accessible through the texture and whatever prior experience the interpreter has of the subject.[64]

To facilitate the following comparisons of textural features in the interpreted discourse and the natural speech corpus, I analyzed usage and frequency of occurrence in four hours of the recordings of monolingual sermons and teaching by Bible study leaders.

Emphasis, Fronting and Viewpoint

Quantitative analysis reveals a 20–50 percent higher frequency in the interpreted discourse of particles that express emphasis, fronting, and location, compared with the natural speech corpus. These particles are mostly marked for nominal concord and often also for given/new and temporal/spatial distance.

---

64. Hatim and Mason, *Discourse and the Translator*, 36.

Translating Scripture for Sound and Performance

Given/new

Manjaku clauses carry pairs of markers, at beginning and end. Both are marked for nominal concord (or manner/reason, or location); the end marker is also marked optionally for given/new and spatial/temporal distance. When I edited out the English ST segments, end-users found the interpreters' renderings on the whole very natural due at least in part to the interweaving of clauses by which they maintained coherence. Respondents even preferred them in some cases to the same passages delivered in storytelling mode but by speakers with less clear diction, saying that they "understood better."

In both the interpreted discourse and the natural speech of the Bible studies and sermons, there is a frequently occurring emphatic pronoun + noun (PN+N) structure used to mark a significant given, which does not occur frequently in everyday speech. Sight-interpreting the story of Ananias and Sapphira in Acts 5, Daniel, a forty-two-year-old secondary-school science teacher, uses two occurrences of PN+N in v. 6, "*a ba tsëpand puum, pul puum nul Ananias*" (and they carried out the corpse, that corpse [of] him Ananias). A (written) translator heavily criticized this TT for the "unnecessary addition," there being no other corpse in question. However, as a performative use of language, it made a big impression on the hearers, accompanied by a meaningful glance and nod, somber tone, and raised finger.

The same structure sometimes occurs to mark a significant given outside the immediate linguistic environment, but assumed known to the audience intertextually, as in Acts 1:4, "he, John the Baptist." The structure may also be used to make explicit a referent which has not been named in the ST, or which may otherwise remain ambiguous.

Nuancing of tense and mood

Sometimes two or even three auxiliary verbs (each with a subject pronoun) are used with a main verb to translate a single verb in English, as in Text 1, lines 12 and 15.

INCLUSION

The interpreters all make up to 50 percent more frequent use of "which you know" or "which you remember" in their TT's than in the natural speech corpus. These clauses act as pragmatic fillers while the TT is processed, but do it in a structurally integrated way that fronts the noun or pronoun they grammatically depend on and marks it as a given. Marked for nominal concord and often spatial/temporal distance, they contribute to both cohesion and viewpoint. They may be regarded as a feature of the persuasive/performative speech register, being used also in direct quotations in this register in written Scriptures, as in Luke 4:23, "There isn't a prophet of God, you know, who is honored in his own country."

OSTENSION

The interpreters use ostensive gestures and glances to draw attention to points of significance, sometimes adding ostensive linguistic items. Lamin, an eighteen-year-old high school student interpreting Matt 5:15 (Text 3, line 9) in short-segment consecutive mode, introduces a rhetorical question, "But what will he do?" to express the ST "instead." In vv. 13–14 (Text 3, lines 1 and 6), he uses an emphatic pronoun "you" preceding the regular pronoun, "You, you are like . . ." Its repetition produces patterning, as also with an ostensive feature in Esther's rendering of Isa. 58:6–9 (Text 2, lines 9, 11, 16, 18), "You will see—eh?"

LEXICAL PATTERNING, PARALLELISM, AND POETICS

In Manjaku, most lexical roots can function as either nouns or verbs. Interpreters commonly exploit this potential for parallelism. In Acts 2:2, Abulai, a twenty-four-year old university student rendered, "Suddenly there was a noise from the sky like a strong wind blowing . . ." as, "and suddenly they heard a *noise* which was *sound*ing-here from the heavens/skies, and it resembled a great *wind* which was *blow*ing greatly." "Noise" and "sounding" have the same lexical root, and similarly "wind" and "blowing," the relative pronouns carrying nominal concord with "noise" and "wind" respectively.

Wendland sets out the wide range of "verbal artistry" in biblical discourse and the complex translational issues involved if "literary functional equivalence" is to be achieved,⁶⁵ starting at the most immediately accessible level with "rhythmic, balanced, euphonious target-language renderings." The interpreters relate to the presence of verbal art in the ST at this level and maintain something of its force in their TT's. In 1 Corinthians 13 (Text 1), Daniel quickly establishes the imagery by personifying "love." He resorts to generalization in line 2 with some loss of propositional accuracy; nevertheless, the emotive force of lexical and textural patterning is maintained. However, this is relatively straightforward patterning and familiar imagery.

Interpreting a less familiar passage from Isa 58:6–9 (Text 2), Esther struggled with the images of "yoke of injustice" and "gesture of contempt" in lines 3 and 20, resorting to generalization. She said after the event that she could not think quickly how to combine "yoke" with "injustice" in Manjaku in a way which would convey what she had (correctly) inferred as the figurative meaning; so she chose not to mislead, but to use instead the weak alternative "*wrongdoing.*" Does this loss of completeness cause us to evaluate Text 2 as "outrageously bad"? Or is the inferential meaning of a rather difficult passage conveyed adequately overall? And could it be that textural and prosodic features—which combine to produce a strongly performative TT—offset, to some extent, the loss of propositional completeness?

Naturalness of Texture

The interpreters' use of a wide range of structures does not mirror the distribution of those structures in natural speech; but there is rarely anything in their TT's which end-users feel is "translationese." The interpreters use particles borrowed from Kiriol and French, but these are well-established borrowings and the interpreters themselves are generally not aware of their origin. They are always aware of Wolof borrowings, which are more recent and more local, but justify them on the basis that congregation members use them.⁶⁶

Explicitation

The risk with explicitation, which is a feature of interpreted text, is of introducing some addition to inferential meaning; however, this is rare in

---

65. Wendland, "A Literary Approach to Bible Translation," 192, 229.
66. Wolof borrowings are not familiar in Guinea-Bissau, except to travelers, and so would not be suitable for a translation for wider distribution.

the data. The explicitations are usually simple clarifications, such as the example from Luke 24:2 above, or John 14:13: "and I will do whatever you ask in my name," rendered as: "indeed I will do what you ask God in my name." The difficult-to-translate extended samples contain few explicitations, possibly because explicitation depends, to a large extent, on confidence with the material.[67]

Change of Pronouns

In their effort to emphasize the personal relevance of the TT's, "you plural" may be changed to "we inclusive," as in 1 Peter 1:17, where "So then, spend the rest of your lives in . . ." was rendered as, "Now let us-inclusive set our-inclusive lives to . . ." This may be assumed not to represent a change of inferential meaning, since Peter would have applied the same to himself. However, such changes of pronoun are sometimes applied in passages where it is inappropriate to apply the ST purpose to a new TT audience.[68]

Extended Discourse Examples

In the extended text examples that follow, ST and TT are provided for each segment, together with a back-translation that preserves the TT texture as far as possible, and a more natural English gloss; notes guide the reader to features of particular interest. The use of . . . signifies hesitation, which is usually indicative of the interpreter's search for an appropriate lexical item, often at a "critical point."[69] This may be where the ST refers to a key biblical concept, such as "favor" in Text 2, line 9, or "wrongs" in Text 1, line 9; or, for instance, in the presence of verbal art requiring evaluative interpretation, which may also be a critical point for the discourse as a whole. In Text 1, line 7, in poetic discourse on the nature of love, the interpreter's momentary hesitation (as revealed in think-aloud protocols after the event) is whether to use normal nominal concord with the abstract noun "love" (b-/bul), or to personify "love" (n-/nul/-ul), having used both strategies previously in lines 1, 2, 3, and 6. He opts for neither and uses the neutral pronouns

---

67. Other examples of explicitation are included in Karlik, "Interpreter-Mediated Scriptures."

68. For instance, in 1 Cor 5:7, described in Karlik, "Interpreter-Mediated Scriptures," 180.

69. Munday, "Evaluation and Intervention in Translation," 91.

(u/wul), which he maintains in lines 9, 14 and 15. (Native-speaker reviewers felt that this maintained the imagery successfully, whereas frequent repeated use of nominal concord with "love" could overwork the point.)

TEXT 1

	1 Cor 13: 4–7	Interpreter: Daniel. Mode: Short-segment + text. ST: NIV
1	v 4 ST Manjaku Back-tr'n Gloss	Love is patient, Bëŋal, bëko[1] ci ñaan[2] nan[2] welani beenul[2,3], Love, it is person who lowers head-his[idiom: humbles him/herself], Love, it is a person who humbles himself/herself,
		[1] Emphatic pronoun repeating the subject, carrying nominal concord with "love." [2] Personification of "love," reinforced by human-class pronouns "nan" and "-ul". [3] Patterning: 3 other idioms based on "head" follow, in lines 4, 5 and 7.
2		love is kind. te[1] bëŋal a ba[2] kaka[3] aci kawara[4]. indeed love and it again it-is goodness. indeed, again, love is goodness.
		[1] Connective borrowed from Kiriol. [2] Subject pronoun, concord with bëŋal" (love). [3] Auxiliary verb. [4] Loss of accuracy: "kawara uwaas" (goodness of soul) would convey the meaning of "kindness" better. Counted as error, but not serious.
3		It does not envy, Bëko[1] cits ko wi m les wi[2] atsiji kari-ko, It is-not, thing you remember, has envy, It is not, you know, envious,
		[1] Emphatic pronoun, concord with "bëŋal" (love). [2] Inclusion; and filler
4		it does not boast, te ri ka riang been[1], indeed (it) will not lift-high head [idiom: boast], indeed, it does not boast,
		[1] Idiom with "head." See lines 1, 5, and 7.
5		it is not proud. te ri ka piban been[1]. indeed, [it] will not show head [idiom: show itself off]. indeed, it is not proud.
		[1] Idiom with "head." See lines 1, 4 and 7.

6	v 5	It is not rude, Te cits ko wi m les wi[1] atsiji ko u waraatsa[2] wi di mtumul[3] *Indeed [it] is-not, you remember, has bad thing in mouth-his,* Indeed, it is not, you know, [one who] utters wrong with his mouth, [1] Inclusion; and filler. [2] May have confused two meanings of "rude"—impolite, improper; but not likely to mislead. [3] Human possessive pronoun.
7		it is not self-seeking, te cits pëjaka ne ka tsasar been[1] ... wul[2] kor wul, *indeed is-not to-be-said-to habitually seek head ... its [seek its own benefit],only it,* Indeed, it is not known for seeking ... its own benefit, for itself, [1] Idiom with "head." See lines 1, 4, and 5. [2] Hesitates on possessive pronoun—selects neutral "wul."
8		it is not easily angered, te di ka car përiabatsën, *indeed [it] will not be-quick to-get-angry,* indeed, it does not quickly get angry,
9		it keeps no record of wrongs. te di ka júkan ... ngëko ngan waraatsa[1] ngi, ngan do ngi ro wul[2]. *indeed [it] will not store... things which are-wrong, which had been-done [to] it.* indeed, it does not store up ... wrongs which have been done to it. [1] Avoids traditional word for "sin" denoting very serious offences against the ancestors. [2] Neutral pronoun.
10	v 6	Love does not take delight in evil, Te bëŋal di ka púúriir pëyandaar[1] ni ko u waraatsa wi, *Indeed love will not be-able to-walk with wrongdoing,* Indeed, love cannot walk in wrongdoing, [1] Loss of accuracy. Could have used "lílan" as in segment 11.
11		but rejoices with the truth. maa ka lílan tsi ucär. *but [it] habitually rejoices in truth.* but habitually rejoices in the truth.

Translating Scripture for Sound and Performance

12	v 7	It always protects, Aja[1] u² roon[1] u² ci[1] pëgaariir, *It-whenever it habitually it is protecting,* At any moment, always, it protects,
		[1] String of auxiliary verbs, nuancing the tense; see patterning in line 15. [2] Neutral subject pronouns.
13		always trusts, te aka ufiansa, *indeed it-has trust,* indeed, it has trust,
14		always hopes, te u[1] ka uwats, *indeed it has hope,* indeed, it has hope,
		[1] Neutral subject pronoun.
15		always perseveres. te u[1] ja² u[1] roon² u[1] kontaniir pëci. *indeed it whenever it habitually it continues to-be.* indeed, at any moment, always, it continues to exist.
		[1] Neutral subject pronouns. [2] String of auxiliary verbs, nuancing the tense; patterning from line 12.
16		This is the word of the Lord. Pi[1] ci pun përim Nasien-Batsi². *This is indeed word [of] God [lit. "King of Heaven"].* This is indeed the Word of God.
		[1] Formulaic. ² Explicitation: usual term for "God" in the general community, adopted by all religious groups; a supreme being who is generally benign though distant. "Ajug" (master) is used to translate "the Lord" referring to Jesus in the NT, but is generally thought insufficient to render "Lord" meaning "God."

Text 2

	Isa 58: 6–9	**Interpreter**: Esther. **Mode**: short-segment + text. <u>ST</u>: GNT. Because of space limitations, the first half of this reading is omitted.
1	v 6 ST Manjaku Back- tr'n Gloss	The kind of fasting I want is this: Kabër mlik ki n ŋal ki ci kun¹ ink: *Fasting which I want is indeed like-this:* This is the fasting which I want, like this: 1 Fronting "the fasting which I want."

2		Remove the chains of oppression
		nda pënani . . . nda jejan ngëko unoor
		wunk¹
		   *take-out (imp-pl) . . . take away (imp-pl) things of hardship
		   that-given*
		Remove . . . do away with those things which thus cause hardship
		
		1 Given-emphatic: anaphoric reference to v. 3.

3		and the yoke of injustice, ni ko wi m me wi¹, ne uko ci kawaaratsa, *and that which, you know, that it is wrongdoing,* and that which is, you know, wrongful, 1 Inclusion: also functioning as a filler.
4		and let the oppressed go free. ndë¹ tsu biki m me bukunk² nda tsu ri pëluek, ba tsëp ri pëfac, *and-may-you cause (fut-imp) those-who, you know, thus you put in bondage, may-they go in peace.* and those people who, you know, you put them in bondage like that, let them go in peace. 1 Syntactic patterning: simple imperative in line 2, nda, followed by purposive future imperative in line 4, ndë; repeated in lines 5 and 6. 2 Inclusion: a structurally integrated given, fronting "oppressed."
5	v 7	Share your food with the hungry Nda¹ faari bariala ind ni ban bonats biki *Share (imp-pl) food your(pl) with those-who are-hungry* Share your food with the hungry 1 Syntactic patterning; see line 4.

6		and open your homes to the homeless poor.
		ndë¹ aants ilëman kato ind pur ban kaats biki ito,
		and-may-you(pl) open doors (of) house your(pl.) for those-who have-not houses.
		and open the doors of your houses for those who have no houses.
		1 Syntactic patterning; see line 4.
7		Give clothes to those who have nothing to wear,
		Nda wëlan iɲi bëtiem bañaan ban kaats bukunk¹ ko wi bu tiema² wi,
		Give [of duty](imp-pl) clothing [to] people who have-not thus something to wear,
		Give [as a duty] clothes to those who have nothing to clothe themselves in,
		1 Given-emphatic: fronting "people." 2 Same lexical root as "clothes."
8		and do not refuse to help your own relatives.
		te nda cats pok pëjuraar bayëts ind.
		indeed do-not refuse to-help relatives your(pl).
		and do not, indeed, refuse to help your relatives.
9	v 8	Then my favor will shine on you
		Kë win-e¹, kabalíir inji ... bëtsënk inji ka ci tsi ind
		You(sg)-will see- eh?, worth my ... help my will be with you(pl)
		You will see—eh? My worth ... my help will be with you
		1 Ostension + patterning, see lines 11, 16, and 18.
10		like the morning sun,
		kom unu bi u kur bi bëfä.
		like the sun when it starts out [in the]morning.
		like the sun when it rises in the morning.
11		and your wounds will be quickly healed.
		Kë win-e¹, ko wi kan de wi di uliaf ind ka yës unpankaar umënts.
		You(sg)-will see-eh?, thing which hurts in body your(pl) will be-well, moment that.
		You will see – eh? The painful place in your body will be well immediately.
		1 Patterning of ostension; see line 9.

12		I will always be with you
		Mán ci ni ind uleer un ci wi[1]
		I-shall be with you (pl), time whatever
		I shall always be with you
		1 Structural adjustment: very natural Manjaku; pattern repeated in line 14.
13		to save you;
		pur pëbueran ind;
		to save you(pl);
		to save you;
14		my presence will protect you on every side.
		uforsa inji ka gaaríiri ind uburu un ci wi[1].
		power my will protect you(pl) (on) side whatever.
		my power will protect you on every side.
		1 See line 12.
15	v 9	When you pray,
		Uci nda ñaan,
		If you(pl) pray,
		If you pray,
16		I will answer you.
		kë win-e[1], mán jankma ind.
		you(sg)-will see-eh?, I-will reply-to you(pl).
		you will see – eh? I will reply to you.
		1 Patterning of ostension; see line 9.
17		When you call to me,
		Uci nda ruin,
		If you call-to-me,
		If you call out to me,
18		I will respond,
		kë win-e[1], mán jankma ind,
		you(sg)-will see-eh? I-will reply-to you(pl),
		you will see – eh? I will reply to you,
		1 Patterning of ostension; see line 9.
19		if you put an end to oppression,
		uci nda wëtan ngëko ngi m me ngi[1], nda tsu bañaan ri unoor
		if you(pl) leave the-things which you(sg) know, you(pl) put people in hardship,
		if you stop doing that by which, you know, you put people under hardship,
		1 Inclusion; and filler.

Translating Scripture for Sound and Performance

20	to every gesture of contempt[1],
	tsi ko wi m me wi[2] ne, uko waraats,
	in the-thing which, you know indeed, it is-bad,
	in what, you know, is wrong[1],
	1 Loss of accuracy. 2Inclusion; and filler.
21	and to every evil word.
	ni ngëko kabalíirëts . . . ni ngëko kawaraats ngi ndu ñakan ngi.
	and things (of) worthlessness . . . and things (of) wrongdoing which you-are saying.
	and the worthless things . . . wrongful things you say.

Text 3

	Matt 5: 13–16	<u>Interpreter</u>: Lamin. <u>Mode</u>: short-segment without-text. <u>ST</u>: GNT.
1	v 13 ST Manjaku Back tr'n Gloss	You are like salt for all mankind. Ind[1], nda ci kom pënam pa bañaan bajin bëlieng tu. *You(pl), you(pl) are like salt for people human everyone all.* You, you are like salt for all mankind, everyone.
		1 Emphatic pronoun: ostension.
2		But if salt loses its saltiness, Maa pënam pëmëntsa pi katse ka utapar pul, *But (if) salt that it-no-longer has strong-taste its,* But if that salt no longer has its strong taste
3		there is no way to make it salty again. kaats bëga bëlon kak bi kë tsu bi pul kak a pë tap. *there-isn't way any again how you-will make it again and it taste-strong.* there is no way by which you can make it taste strong again.
4		It has become worthless, Aci pi m les pi[1] katse ka balur. *It-is, as you remember, it-no-longer has value.* It, as you know, no longer has any value.
		1 Inclusion, structurally integrated to agree with "salt."
5		so it is thrown out and people trample on it. Tsi u ci tsink, ka gutsa, bañaan ka pos-na pul. *It being so, it-will be-thrown-out, people will trample-on it.* This being so, it will be thrown out and people will trample on it.

6	v 14	You are like a light for the whole world. Ind¹, nda ci kom ufac kom tsi umúndu bëlieng. *You(pl), you are like light, like in world all.* You, you are like a light, as it were, in the whole world.
		1 Emphatic pronoun: ostension.
7		A city built on a hill cannot be hidden. Përaasa pi m les pi¹ aniewa di ruets untúnda di ka ci pi kan beka pi. *Town, which you remember, is-built on top (of) hill, will not be one-which is-hidden.* A town which, you know, is built on top of a hill will not be a hidden one.
		1 Inclusion, structurally integrated to agree with "town."
8	v 15	Noone lights a lamp and puts it under a bowl; Kaats ñaan, ni m lesi¹, ka taban ulamp në jej wul ka tsu di utsia ubol. *There-isn't person, who you remember, will light lamp to take it, will put (it) under bowl.* There is no-one who, you know, lights a lamp to take it and put it under a bowl.
		1 Inclusion, structurally integrated to agree with "person."
9		instead he puts it on the lampstand, Maa nul ka ro um?¹ Ka jej wul në tsu di pëko pënatsanaani ulamp, *But he will do how? He-will take it in-order-to put (it) on lamp-stand,* But what will he do? He will take it to put it on a lampstand.
		1 Rhetorical question: Ostension.
10		where it gives light for everyone in the house. bi m les bi¹, ka wël ufac bëlieng tsi kara ñaan nan cii di kato. *as you remember, it-will give light all-over, to each person who is in house.* As you know, it will give light everywhere, to each person who is in the house.
		1 Inclusion.
11	v 16	In the same way Tsi bëga bëloole bëmënts bi *In way one this-one* In this very way

Translating Scripture for Sound and Performance

12	your light must shine before people,
	ufac ind(pl) ka pëfiets tsi bañaan,
	light your(pl) has to-shine on people,
	your light must shine on people,
13	so that they will see the good things you do and praise your Father[1] in heaven.
	bu ka ci bañaan biki m les biki bu ka win ngëko ngëwar ngi m do ngi, bu ka rëmban Ajúg di batsi.
	so-that-they will be people, who you remember, they will see things good which you(sg) do, they will praise the-Lord in heaven.
	so that they will be people who, you know, they will see the good things which you do, and they will praise the Lord[1] in heaven.

1 Partial loss of accuracy: "Father," translated as "Lord"

Training Indicators

The analysis finds that these experienced but untrained interpreters have considerable skills in interlingual communication and public performance and seek to communicate Scripture faithfully, which the congregations expect of them. However, they often lack adequate ST frames of reference. Church leaders and seminary trainers have generally overlooked interpreters' needs. Teaching on ST sociocultural backgrounds, purpose, text-types, allusions, and figurative language—especially intertextual metaphors—could readily be offered to interpreters by including them in programs which are offered to preachers, Sunday school teachers, and other leaders, in any accessible language.[70] Most preachers select from a rather restricted range of readings, which could be studied over a period. This could help the interpreters avoid translational errors arising from faulty comprehension of these elements in the ST. And access to language classes could help avoid errors arising at the level of SL syntax, such as failure to recognize a double negative or distinguish between -s for plural and -'s for possession.

Issues of target-culture equivalence could be addressed with the help of Bible translation agencies working together with preachers, interpreters, and other community leaders, whether or not a translation program is in view. However, to develop the specific skills of interpreting, the interpreters for the moment would have to rely on reflective practice and peer review,

---

70. Some training suggestions arising from my study have been incorporated in Hill and Hill, *Translating the Bible into Action*, though only in relation to the interpreting of sermons.

because neither churches nor Bible translation agencies have expertise in interpreter training. Peer review can raise interpreters' awareness of interpreting habits, such as regular fallback on particular phrases as fillers or generalizations, or particular patterns of voice modulation, and can widen their range of TT resources in terms of both structures and lexicon.

Experimental Workshops

To open up dialogue, share experience, and raise levels of awareness, we ran a series of workshops (nine half-days followed by a long weekend) for interpreters and leaders of all categories. Some end-users were always present, to ensure naturalness of the communication-situations. The interpreters gained most benefit from practice in communicating Scripture narratives in story-telling mode. They did not make confident "tellers" of the narratives in spite of their skills in performance, because of being nervous about accidentally omitting something. But learning the narratives and discussing their themes provided them with additional resources in terms of ST frames of reference and a wider repertoire of available TT expressions. Interestingly, their particular contribution to the workshops was to the design of the oral narratives.

Some of the preachers started linking doctrinal passages to narratives; this made the sermon easier for the interpreters to translate and suited the learning mode of the Manjaku end-users (as well as improving communication for end-users in English). With raised awareness, the preachers were also able to appreciate the interpreters' need for contextual framing of the Bible reading in terms of characters and setting, and practised preparing brief introductions to the passages.

Conclusion

This chapter suggests that in the interplay of media in modern churches in Africa, the interpreters who mediate biblical discourse should not be overlooked, since they have an important role in communicating Scripture—whether interpreting sermons or Bible readings—thus consciously or subconsciously influencing the development of vernacular theologies. Viewing the interpreted TT's as a nonbook format of Scripture, analysis of presentational and textural features in them suggests that their acceptability to congregations arises largely from performance factors, which are an essential part of the interpreters' armory of skills. However, they themselves express a need for help.

During my quest for opinions, a Guinea-Bissau pastor commented: "I think there should be oral solutions for oral cultures." For all its limitations, the use of interpreter-mediated Scriptures is an indigenous oral solution, and the only one available for certain communication situations. Since the continued use of interpreter-mediated Scripture in churches can be foreseen for some time to come, readers are invited to consider, in light of strengths and weakness identified in the interpreted product, whether investment in training for interpreters would be worthwhile, given the local significance of their role. If so, more resources of interdisciplinary scholarship will need to be applied in order to gain a deeper understanding of the social and cognitive processes involved.

Bibliography

Bandia, Paul. "African Tradition." In *Routledge Encyclopedia of Translation Studies*, edited by Mona Baker and Gabriela Saldanha, 313–20. 2nd ed. London: Routledge, 2009.

Bartholomew, Adam, with David Rhoads. "Preface." In *The Bible in Ancient and Modern Media: Story and Performance*, edited by Holly E. Hearon and Philip Ruge-Jones, i–xviii. Biblical Performance Criticism Series 1. Eugene, OR Cascade Books, 2009.

Cokely, Dennis. *Interpretation: A Sociolinguistic Model*. Sign Language Dissertation Series. Burtonsville, MD: Linstok, 1992.

Davies, Bethan. "Communities of Practice: Legitimacy and Choice." *Journal of Sociolinguistics* 9 (2005) 557–81.

Dewey, Joanna. "Women on the Way." In *The Bible in Ancient and Modern Media: Story and Performance*, edited by Holly E. Hearon and Philip Ruge-Jones, 36–49. Biblical Performance Criticism Series 1. Eugene, OR: Cascade Books, 2009.

Finnegan, Ruth. *Oral Traditions and the Verbal Arts*. ASA Research Methods in Social Anthropology. London: Routledge, 1992.

Fowler, Robert. "Why Everything We Know about the Bible Is Wrong." In *The Bible in Ancient and Modern Media: Story and Performance*, edited by Holly E. Hearon and Philip Ruge-Jones, 1–18. Biblical Performance Criticism Series 1. Eugene, OR: Cascade Books, 2009.

Fry, Euan McG. "Faithfulness: a Wider Perspective." 1987. Reprinted in *Fidelity and Translation: Communicating the Bible in New Media*, edited by Paul Soukup and Robert Hodgson, 7–29. Franklin, WI: Sheed & Ward, 1999.

Gutt, Ernst-August. *Translation and Relevance: Cognition and Context*. Oxford: Blackwell, 1991.

Halliday, M. A. K. *Spoken and Written Language*. Language Education. Oxford: Oxford University Press, 1989.

Hatim, Basil, and Ian Mason. *Discourse and the Translator*. London: Longman, 1990.

Hermann, Alfred. "Interpreting in Antiquity." 1956. In *The Interpreting Studies Reader*, edited by Franz Pöchhacker and Miriam Shlesinger, 15–22. London: Routledge, 2002.
Hill, Harriet, and Margaret Hill. *Translating the Bible into Action*. Carlisle, UK: Piquant, 2008.
Hill, Margaret. "The Challenge of Acceptability of the Translation by the Target Language Community." Paper presented at the Bible in Africa Conference, University of KwaZulu-Natal, September 2005.
Karlik, Jan. *A Manjaku Grammar*. PhD diss., School of Oriental and African Studies, University of London, 1972.
Karlik, Jill. "Interpreter-Mediated Scriptures: Expectation and Performance." *Interpreting* 12/2 (2010) 60–185.
Kaufmann, Francine. "Interpreters in Early Judaism." *Jerome Quarterly* 9/3 (1994) 2.
———. "Contribution à l'histoire de l'interprétation consécutive: le *metourguemane* dans les synagogues de l'Antiquité." *Meta* 50 (2005) 972–86.
Klem, Herbert. *Oral Communication of the Scripture: Insights from African Oral Art*. Pasadena, CA: William Carey Library, 1972. Revised edition. St. Paul, MN: Bethel Theological Seminary, 1995.
———. "Dependence on Literacy Strategy: Taking a Hard Second Look." *International Journal of Frontier Missiology* 12/2 (1995) 59–64.
Koops, Robert. "From Moses to Dilbert: Similarity and Difference in Print, Audio and Comic-Strip versions." In *Similarity and Difference in Translation*, edited by Stefano Arduini and Robert Hodgson, 169–99. Rimini, Italy: Guaraldi, 2004.
Llewellyn-Jones, Peter. Lectures 2008–2012. MODL 5001. Centre for Translation Studies. University of Leeds.
———. *Three Interpretations* (video and booklet). Coleford: Forest Books, 2002.
Llewellyn-Jones, Peter, and Robert G. Lee. Forthcoming.
Mason, Ian. "Audience Design in Translating." *The Translator* 6/1 (2000) 1–22.
Maxey, James A. *From Orality to Orality: A New Paradigm for Contextual Translation of the Bible*. Biblical Performance Criticism Series 2. Eugene, OR: Cascade Books, 2010.
Metzger, Bruce. *The Early Versions of the New Testament*. Oxford: Clarendon, 1977.
Mikkelson, Holly. "Relay Interpreting and Languages of Limited Diffusion." *The Translator* 5/2 (1999) 360–374.
Munday, Jeremy. "Evaluation and Intervention in Translation." In *Text and Context: Essays on Translation & Interpreting in Honour of Ian Mason*, edited by Mona Baker et al., 77–94. Manchester, UK: St Jerome, 2010.
Nida, Eugene. *Contexts in Translating*. Benjamins Translation Library 41. Amsterdam: Benjamins, 2000.
Nord, Christiane. *Translating as a Purposeful Activity: Functionalist Approaches Explained*. Translation Theories Explained 1. Manchester, UK: St Jerome, 1997.
Ong, Walter. *Orality and Literacy: The Technologizing of the Word*. 1982. New Accents. London: Routledge, 2002.
Pöchhacker, Franz. *Introducing Interpreting Studies*. London: Routledge, 2004.
———. "Quality Assessment in Conference and Community Interpreting." *Meta* 46 (2001) 410–25.
Pobee, John. "Oral Theology and Christian Oral Tradition: Challenge to Our Traditional Archival Concept." *Mission Studies* 6 (1989) 87–93.

Rhoads, David. "What Is Performance Criticism?" In *The Bible in Ancient and Modern Media: Story and Performance*, edited by Holly E. Hearon and Philip Ruge-Jones, 83–100. Biblical Performance Criticism Series 1. Eugene, OR: Cascade Books, 2009.

Roschke, Ronald W. "Postlude." In *From One Medium to Another: Basic Issues for Communicating the Scriptures in New Media*, edited by Robert Hodgson and Paul Soukup, 337–344. Kansas City: Sheed & Ward, 1997.

Schank, Roger C. *Dynamic Memory Revisited.* 2nd ed. Cambridge: Cambridge University Press. 1999.

Sim, Ronald J. "Modelling the Translation Task." In *Similarity and Difference in Translation*, edited by Stefano Arduini and Robert Hodgson, 103–123. Rimini, Italy: Guaraldi, 2004.

Shiner, Whitney. "Oral Performance in the New Testament World." In *The Bible in Ancient and Modern Media*, edited by Holly E. Hearon and Philip Ruge-Jones, 49–64. Biblical Performance Criticism Series 1. Eugene OR: Cascade Books, 2009.

———. *Proclaiming the Gospel: First-Century Performance in Mark.* Harrisburg PA: Trinity, 2003.

Soukup, Paul. "Understanding Audience Understanding." In *From One Medium to Another: Basic Issues for Communicating the Scriptures in New Media*, edited by Paul Soukup and Robert Hodgson, 91–107, Kansas City: Sheed & Ward, 1997.

Sterk, Jan, and Margaret Muthwii. "The Publishing of Christian Scriptures in Africa: Sociolinguistic Challenges." In *Biblical Texts and African Audiences*, edited by Ernst Wendland and J.-C. Loba-Mkole, 150–79. Bible Translation in Africa. Nairobi: Acton, 2004.

Toury, Gideon. *Descriptive Translation Studies and Beyond.* Benjamins Translation Library 4. Amsterdam: Benjamins, 1995.

Wadensjö, Cecilia. *Interpreting as Interaction.* Language in Social Life Series. London: Longman, 1998.

Wendland, Ernst. "A Literary Approach to Biblical Text Analysis and Translation." In *Bible Translation: Frames of Reference*, edited by Timothy Wilt, 179–226. Manchester, UK: St Jerome, 2003.

West, Gerald. "On the Eve of an African Bible Studies: Trajectories and Trends." *Journal of Theology for Southern Africa* 99 (1997) 99–115.

Wire, Antionette Clark. *The Case for Mark Composed in Performance.* Biblical Performance Criticism Series 3. Eugene, OR: Cascade Books, 2011.

Wilt, Timothy. "Translation and Communication." In *Bible Translation: Frames of Reference*, 27–80. Manchester, UK: St Jerome, 2003.

www.ingramcontent.com/pod-product-compliance
Lightning Source LLC
Chambersburg PA
CBHW031356230426
43670CB00006B/559